Taking Your iPhone 4 to the Max

Steve Sande

Erica Sadun

Apress®

Taking Your iPhone 4 to the Max

ISBN-13 (pbk): 978-1-4302-3255-1

ISBN-13 (electronic): 978-1-4302-3256-8

Printed and bound in the United States of America 9 8 7 6 5 4 3 2 1

President and Publisher: Paul Manning
Lead Editor: Clay Andres
Development Editor: Tom Welsh
Technical Reviewer: Erica Sadun
Editorial Board: Clay Andres, Steve Anglin, Mark Beckner, Ewan Buckingham, Gary
    Cornell, Jonathan Gennick, Jonathan Hassell, Michelle Lowman, Matthew Moodie,
    Duncan Parkes, Jeffrey Pepper, Frank Pohlmann, Douglas Pundick, Ben Renow-Clarke,
    Dominic Shakeshaft, Matt Wade, Tom Welsh
Coordinating Editor: Kelly Moritz
Copy Editor: Kim Wimpsett
Compositor: MacPS, LLC
Indexer: Toma Mulligan
Artist: April Milne
Cover Designer: Anna Ishchenko

Distributed to the book trade worldwide by Springer Science+Business Media, LLC., 233 Spring Street, 6th Floor, New York, NY 10013. Phone 1-800-SPRINGER, fax (201) 348-4505, e-mail orders-ny@springer-sbm.com, or visit www.springeronline.com.

For information on translations, please e-mail rights@apress.com, or visit www.apress.com.

Apress and friends of ED books may be purchased in bulk for academic, corporate, or promotional use. eBook versions and licenses are also available for most titles. For more information, reference our Special Bulk Sales–eBook Licensing web page at www.apress.com/info/bulksales.

To my wife, Barb, for being by my side as I realize my dreams.

Contents at a Glance

Contents

About the Authors

 **Steve Sande** has been a loyal fan of Apple technology since buying his first Mac in 1984. Originally trained as a civil engineer, Steve's career as an IT professional blossomed in the 1990s. A longtime blogger, Steve is an editor at The Unofficial Apple Weblog (TUAW.com), the author of three books about Apple's iWeb application, and a collaborator on the recent Apress title *Taking Your iPad to the Max*. Steve is certified as an Apple Certified Technical Consultant and is the founder and owner of Raven Solutions, LLC, a company specializing in support and system consulting for Apple devices. He lives with his wife of 31 years and an aging (but feisty) cat in Highlands Ranch, Colorado.

About the Technical Reviewer

Erica Sadun has a PhD in computer science from the Georgia Institute of Technology. She has written, cowritten, and contributed to almost three dozen books about technology, particularly in the areas of programming, digital video, and digital photography. An unrepentant geek, Sadun has never met a gadget she didn't need. Her checkered past includes run-ins with NeXT, Newton, and a vast myriad of both successful and unsuccessful technologies. When not writing, she and her geek husband parent three adorable geeks-in-training, who regard their parents with restrained bemusement. *Eight Ways to Get the Most Out of Your Zune*, the O'Reilly short cut, and *Modding Mac OS X*, also with O'Reilly, are her latest books. She also wrote the first edition of *Taking Your iPhone to the Max*.

Acknowledgments

Steve Sande wishes to thank technical editor and first-edition author Erica Sadun, the tireless and hard-working team at Apress, and his colleagues at The Unofficial Apple Weblog.

Introduction

Before the iPhone, every smartphone on the market had a little screen, a tiny thumb keyboard, and a user interface that confused even the experts. Then, in June of 2007, everything changed.

In the three years since the introduction of the first iPhone, we've seen a tremendous change in the way that people work with smartphones and computing devices in general. Most smartphones have emulated the touch screen and gesture-based user interface of the iPhone in an attempt to cash in on the success of the device. It's estimated that Apple has sold more than 100 million iOS devices (which includes the iPhone, the iPod touch, and the iPad), making the platform a roaring success.

But the iPhone has continued to evolve in those three years. In 2008, the iPhone 3G was released, linking the iPhone to a much faster data network and providing true geolocation through the addition of a built-in Global Positioning System receiver. In that same year, developers were given the tools with which to create new applications to run on the device, and the App Store opened to rave reviews. Suddenly, purchasing games, utilities, and other apps became as easy as browsing an electronic store and pushing a Buy button.

The App Store has become the gold rush of the 21st century, with developers creating well over 225,000 apps in a little over two years. Some developers have made millions with innovative and useful products, further fueling the fire to push the technological edge with unique applications that take advantage of the iPhone's powerful hardware. The year 2009 saw the introduction of the iPhone 3GS, a phone that provided video capture for the first time. The 3GS also added an electronic compass that made augmented reality apps possible.

But it was the iPhone 4 and its next-generation operating system—iOS 4—that made a huge impact in 2010. The phone has been a huge success despite early issues concerning dropped calls, and once again Apple has set the bar so high that it will be difficult for the competition to catch up. The Retina display of the iPhone 4 makes everything on the screen look photorealistic, for the first time creating a smartphone display that actually has better resolution than the human eye can discern. An Apple-designed processor, the A4, drives the device at amazing speeds. The built-in camera jumped in resolution to 5 megapixels, and there's now a front-facing camera that enables another groundbreaking app: FaceTime. The iPhone 4 now has the distinction of being the first device to make video calling easy.

It's often said that Apple has provided developers with the infinite tool, something that turns into whatever you want it to be when equipped with the proper app. With so many possibilities for the iPhone, it can sometimes be daunting to new users. *Taking your iPhone 4 to the Max* introduces you to the iPhone 4. Starting with assistance on how to choose the iPhone that's right for you, we walk you through purchasing your phone and setting it up for the first time. You'll learn the gesture-based, Multi-Touch vocabulary that allows you to manipulate the iPhone and its hundreds of thousands of apps.

We'll show you how to connect to the Internet over cellular and Wi-Fi connections, browse the Web, touch your music and videos, and find and download apps from the App Store. You'll discover how to purchase and navigate books using Apple's revolutionary iBooks app, view and organize photos, send e-mail and use other messaging services, create notes and update calendars, and even take high-definition video with your iPhone 4.

This book is written for anyone with an iPhone or anyone who is thinking of getting one. It doesn't matter if you're a Windows or Mac user or, in fact, even if you've never used a computer at all. This book's thorough coverage and step-by-step discussions allow all iPhone owners to learn about their device and come away with both the skills and the knowledge that they need to use it to its fullest.

How you read the book is up to you. If you are totally new to the iPhone or sometimes feel overwhelmed by technology, we suggest you read the book cover to cover. You can also feel free to jump around from chapter to chapter, trying different things out as the mood strikes you. Above all, we want you to have fun while you're learning everything that the iPhone can do. We honestly love our iPhones and love getting people excited about this technological wonder. Thanks for letting us show it to you.

Steve Sande
Highlands Ranch, Colorado, USA

Erica Sadun
Denver, Colorado, USA

Chapter 1

Selecting, Buying, and Activating Your iPhone

Now that Apple's iPhone has been out for a number of years, you may have seen horror stories in the press about how an iPhone is going to cost you thousands of dollars over its lifetime. You have to buy the iPhone, pay for activation, and fork out money for expensive monthly service voice, data, and text plans (not to mention taxes and other fees). If you decide to back out any time during the standard two-year mobile phone contract, you're going to hand over even more money in early termination fees.

Well, there's more than a grain of truth to what you read. Since you're going to be spending a couple thousand dollars over the next few years, you need to know what you're doing when you buy that iPhone. If you're weighing the choice of whether to purchase an iPhone and trying to figure out exactly how much you're going to be paying, this chapter is for you. You'll also discover the down-and-dirty secrets of iPhone activation, plan selection, and even return policies. This chapter contains all the basic facts you need to select, buy, and activate your iPhone.

Selecting Your iOS4 iPhone

At any given time, there are relatively few models of iPhones available. As of the publication of this book, all of them come with iOS 4, representing a new generation of the operating system software that powers the features of the iPhone. Usually you'll see an entry-level iPhone that is less powerful and has less memory, as well as the current model with state-of-the-art features and much more memory.

How do you choose the model that's right for you? It all comes down to two factors: cameras and memory. The first generation of the iPhone 4 has two cameras: a 5-megapixel camera with an LED flash that's capable of taking high-definition video and a front-facing camera that is perfect for shooting self-portraits and making video calls. As for memory, you need to make a decision about whether you want to double the purchase price of your phone for a few more gigabytes of memory. We recommend getting as much memory as you can. If you load a lot of movies and videos onto your device, you can run out of space on a top-of-the-line iPhone very quickly.

Here are some questions to ask yourself while selecting the model of iPhone to purchase:

- *How big is your music library?* If your library is small, a unit with less memory might be fine. If it's large, the extra space on some iPhone models helps to store additional music and podcasts.

- *How many videos do you want to carry around?* A single two-hour movie may occupy more than a gigabyte of storage. If you travel a lot, especially on airplanes, you may want to pay more to store additional movies and TV shows with those extra gigabytes.

- *Do you plan on using your iPhone as your primary camera and camcorder?* If you do, then look at the more sophisticated models with higher resolution, flash, and high-definition (HD) video capabilities. If you already carry a digital camera or camcorder with you on a regular basis or don't frequently shoot photos or video with your existing phone, then the base iPhone model may be for you.

- *Is the thought of making video calls exciting to you?* For some people, just answering a regular cell phone call is a challenge. But if you love to have regular face-to-face conversations with friends and relatives, then you may want to consider the model with the built-in FaceTime video calling feature.

- *Do you need to carry lots of data?* Many iPhone apps use iTunes data storage and can synchronize files with your computer. Whether that data consists of presentation slide shows, project management files, or some other information that you need at your fingertips, the size of the data being stored can add up quickly. If you think you might need to do this, maybe the extra gigabytes on a more expensive iPhone model could be put to good use.

- *How long do you intend to keep this iPhone?* If you're an early adopter who likes to trade up at the earliest possible opportunity whenever Apple offers a new model of iPhone, you may want to "buy in cheap" each time the new models are released and sell your old iPhone on the aftermarket. If you'd rather get the most use out of the iPhone over the longest period of time, then paying more up front means you won't outgrow the iPhone quite as fast.

Considering System Requirements

iPhones are unlike most other cell phones. Like the iPod, you'll need a computer to connect your phone to. iPhones need to connect to computers regularly to synchronize music, videos, photos, e-mail, contacts, calendars, and more. You also won't be able to activate your phone on the AT&T network until you successfully connect your iPhone to Apple's iTunes program. For the iPhones in production at the time of publication, the computer system requirements are as follows:

- A Mac computer running OS X 10.5.8 or newer with a USB 2.0 port, or a Windows computer with a USB 2.0 port and Windows 7, Vista, or XP Home or Professional with Service Pack 3 or newer. Note that the system requirements are constantly changing as both iPhone and computer features evolve. We recommend viewing the most recent system requirements before you make any purchase decision (http://www.apple.com/iphone/specs.html).

- iTunes 9.2 or newer.

- iTunes Store account.

- Internet access.

Before you purchase an iPhone, make sure that you have a computer on hand that is up to the task.

> **NOTE:** If you haven't installed iTunes on your computer, download a free copy from http://www.apple.com/itunes. Versions are available for both Mac OS X and Windows systems, and they're easy and quick to install.

Buying Your iPhone

Once you've decided what iPhone model to buy (Figure 1-1), you're probably ready to pull out your credit card and buy that phone as quickly as possible. So, where you should buy it? At an AT&T store or at an Apple Store? Or should you purchase it online? You might be surprised to learn that your choice does matter.

Figure 1-1. *The Apple iPhone 4 (left) and iPhone 3GS are typical of the models of iPhones available at any particular point in time.*

Although it's possible to purchase an iPhone from any number of online stores, we recommend buying your iPhone in person at a store. You can ask questions. You can make human connections. You can have your iPhone activated and ready for calling when you leave the store. If something goes wrong with your purchase, you have a person who's there to help you work through it.

The sad fact of the matter is that a significant, although small, percentage of iPhone purchases go awry. Some people end up with a screen flaw, such as dead screen pixels. It's not an uncommon problem, and if found soon after purchase, it may involve a trade-in for a new unit. Others may have problems with their antennas or with activating their service. The chances of resolving these issues may be better if you have a real person to help.

As for the question of Apple or a carrier, we lean slightly toward buying at an Apple Store. It's an Apple product you're buying, and the Apple staff members are more knowledgeable about their products.

This rule of thumb does not apply to iPhones with defects. Apple Stores will happily replace defective iPhones regardless of their point of purchase, and if you have problems with your phone service, you can go to any of the carrier's store locations whether you purchased your phone there or not; it's the service you're dealing with, not the physical iPhone unit.

Returns and Exchange Policies

The return policy for iPhones has improved since the release of the phone. If you're not happy with your iPhone purchase, you can return the undamaged phone to an Apple Store or the Apple Online Store within 30 days of purchase for a full refund. You must return the phone in the original packaging, including all the accessories, manuals, and documentation, and you won't be charged a restocking fee.

If your iPhone is returned to Apple within 30 days from the date of purchase (or shipment in the case of a purchase from the Apple Online Store), your wireless service is canceled automatically, and you are not charged an early termination fee (ETF). However, you will be charged for all usage fees; prorated access charges, taxes, and surcharges; and any other fees your carrier may charge.

If you purchased your iPhone at a cellular carrier store, things aren't as rosy. A restocking fee will generally be applied to the return, unless you purchased it without service and the phone box was never opened.

In the United States, where AT&T is the only carrier available for iPhone owners at the time this book was going to press, getting out of a standard two-year postpaid contract (meaning that you are billed at the end of each month of use) can be expensive. You can cancel the service within 30 days of activation without being charged for an ETF. After 30 days, the ETF is $325 minus $10 for each full month of your service commitment that you complete. For example, if you cancel your AT&T contract after 12 months, the ETF is $325 − (12 x $10) = $205. Canceling 23 months into a contract, you'd still be charged a $95 ETF. Once you've fulfilled the two-year agreement, your service switches to a month-to-month automatic renewal.

If you opt for a nonstandard, no-contract, month-by-month plan, you pay only for the months you use, and there are no early termination fees. Your credit card is charged in advance for each month of use, and you must contact AT&T before the monthly charge date when you want to cancel. Otherwise, you will have paid for an extra month of service that you will not use. Learn more about the available plans and their trade-offs later in this chapter.

Bringing Home Your iPhone

Once you buy your iPhone, it's time to take it home, unpack it, and set it up. iPhone packaging (see Figure 1-2) is a small work of art. The iPhone ships in a box containing the phone itself, a USB connector cable, a USB power adapter, those famous white earbuds, and a packet of documentation. Each of these items is important and will help you in your day-to-day use.

Figure 1-2. *The content of that nice iPhone box usually consists of a USB to Dock Connector Cable (bottom), a USB power adapter (center), and a stereo headset (top). You can find your complimentary Apple sticker in the packet at right.*

■ *Cable*: The USB cable attaches your iPhone to either your computer or the USB power adapter. If you've purchased an optional dock, the cable plugs into it, and the iPhone is then placed into the dock for charging or syncing.

■ *USB power adapter*: The power adapter included with your iPhone plugs directly into the wall and allows you to charge your iPhone (or any USB device, for that matter). It offers a single USB port. To use it, just connect your iPhone to the adapter using the USB cable. The adapter supplies the 5 volts required for powering USB devices.

■ *Stereo headset (earbuds)*: The earbuds included with the iPhone differ slightly from those included with normal iPods. This stereo headset contains a built-in microphone and switch. The microphone allows you to take calls on your iPhone without holding the phone up to your ear, and the switch allows you to end calls as well as control music playback. The switch is also used to initiate Voice Control of your iPhone.

NOTE The features of older or newer models of the iPhone may vary from what you see in the following feature overview.

iPhone 4 Feature Overview

The iPhone 4 is similar to the iPhone 3GS in terms of external features. The top of the iPhone houses a jack into which you can plug your earbuds, a Subscriber Identity Module (SIM) tray (where your phone's SIM card is stored), and a Sleep/Wake button that is used to power on and off certain features. The bottom of your iPhone has a built-in speaker and microphone and an indented slot for connecting to your dock. The iPhone's front has a receiver (earpiece) on top, which you use to listen to phone calls, a large touchscreen, and a single Home button. You will not see the interactive screen shown in Figure 1-3 until you have activated your iPhone through iTunes.

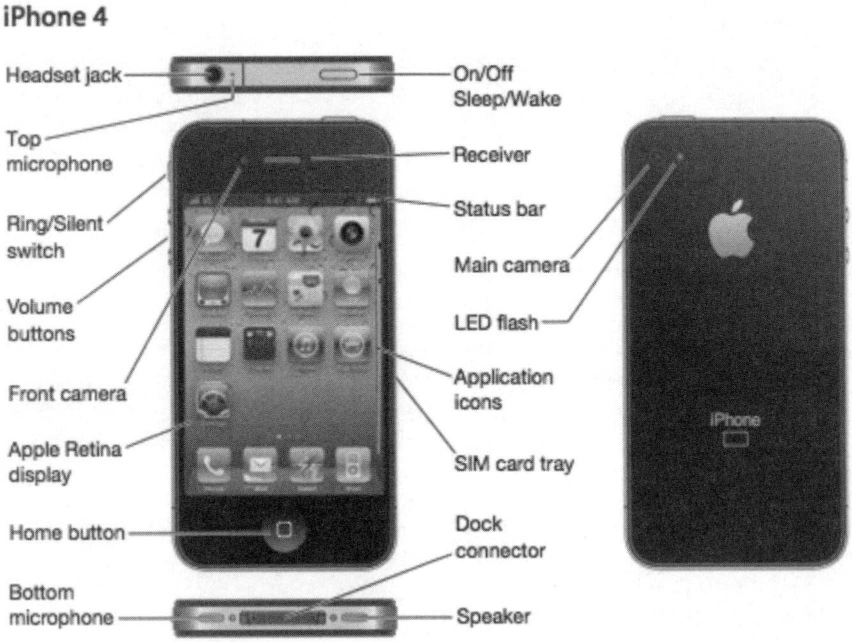

Figure 1-3. *iPhone 4 feature overview*

Activation at the Store

If you purchase an iPhone at an Apple or cellular service provider store in the Apple Stores in the United States and many other countries, you'll find that the activation process is taken care of in the store at the time you pay for the phone.

After you've made your choice as to the model of iPhone you want to purchase and have picked out accessories (cases, cables, and other goodies) to go with it, it's time to pay for the goods. When the Apple Store associate scans the iPhone box with an iOS-based point-of-sale device, the device immediately starts asking questions that you'll need to answer. Among those questions are the following:

- Are you a current customer of a particular mobile phone company that features the iPhone? If so, what is your telephone number?

- Are you coming over from another cell phone company? If so, what company, and what is your telephone number?

- What voice, data, and text plan would you like to sign up for?

- If you are not eligible for a phone upgrade on your existing plan, are you willing to pay the extra cost to buy the unsubsidized phone? (Many carriers subsidize the cost of the phone, knowing that you'll more than pay them back in your monthly subscription fees.)

In the case of an existing iPhone owner upgrading to a newer iPhone, the point-of-sale device will check your existing phone number and will immediately let the Apple Store associate know whether you're eligible for an upgrade. There's usually a nominal fee associated with the upgrade, and you will be asked if you want to accept that fee. The associate will then display your existing voice, data, and text plans, and you'll be asked if you want to stay with those plans or change to a different plan. Of course, you'll also need to swipe the credit card that you'll use to pay for the phone and the plan, and your signature is required on the point-of-sale device.

Upon agreement to the terms and conditions of the carrier's plan and the use of Apple's hardware and software, your new iPhone is activated. Note that if you have an existing phone, the service to it will be cut off immediately.

Activating your iPhone at an Apple or a carrier store has another benefit. Most of the stores have a set of cables and special software that are used to transfer all your settings, data, addresses, photos, and more from your existing phone to the iPhone. This is especially important if you are getting your first iPhone and coming over from another phone platform.

Regardless of whether you choose to pick up your new iPhone in person at an Apple or cellular service provider's store or if you have it shipped to you from Apple or Amazon, you still won't be able to use the phone (except to make emergency phone calls) until you connect it to your computer. That's the second part of activation.

Preparing for Activation

You have unpacked your iPhone but haven't yet connected it to iTunes. Now is a good time to review data on your computer. When your iPhone is activated for the first time, it synchronizes with iTunes and, depending on your computer, to your e-mail accounts, your calendars, and so forth. Before you begin, here are some items you may want to review and clean up so your iPhone begins life with the freshest possible data:

- *Contacts*: The iPhone can sync with Microsoft Outlook 2003, 2007, or 2010 on Windows, Address Book or Entourage on a Macintosh, and Yahoo! Address Book on the Internet. To prepare for your first sync, review your existing contacts, and make sure they're up-to-date with current phone numbers and e-mail addresses. If you use another program to manage contacts, consider migrating your contacts to one of these solutions. If you'd rather not, that's OK too. You can add contact information directly to your iPhone, although it's not as convenient as having the information automatically loaded for you.

- *Calendar*: Your iPhone can synchronize with computer-based calendars just like it does with contacts. iPhone supports iCal and Entourage calendars on the Mac and Outlook 2003, 2007, and 2010 calendars on Windows. Get your calendars into shape before your first synchronization, and you'll be ready to immediately manage your schedule both from your computer and from your iPhone.

- *E-mail*: Your iPhone works with most e-mail providers including Yahoo! Mail, Google Gmail, AOL, and of course Apple's MobileMe. If your e-mail provider uses the industry-standard POP3 and IMAP services, your service will work with iPhone. You may want to establish new accounts with these providers before you activate your iPhone. That way, they'll load onto your unit the first time you synchronize. You can always add new e-mail accounts later, but it's nice to have them all set up and available for use right away.

NOTE: iPhone owners who use Microsoft Exchange as an e-mail, contacts, and calendar server will be happy to hear that their phone can tie into an Exchange server with no problems.

■ *Media*: Current iPhone models offer relatively small storage space when compared to, for example, iPod Classic's generous 160GB hard drive. To make the most of this limited space, set up playlists for your favorite songs and podcasts, and consider removing TV shows and movies from your device once you've watched them. You can store your electronic books "in the cloud" on the Internet and download them when you want to read them, so why load all of them onto your iPhone at once? Since, in all likelihood, you won't be able to synchronize your entire media library to your new iPhone, invest time now in organizing your media to find those items you most want to have on hand.

■ *Software and OS*: You should update to iTunes 9.2 or newer before you attempt to activate your iPhone. And, if you're using a Macintosh, make sure you've updated your OS to at least OS X 10.5.8. You can download the latest version of iTunes from Apple at `http://www.apple.com/itunes/download`. Remember that the system requirements may change at any time, so be sure to check the web page we mentioned earlier: `http://www.apple.com/iphone/specs.html`.

■ *iTunes account*: Apple requires a current iTunes account to activate your iPhone. If you do not already have one, you must sign up for a U.S. account with the iTunes store. This requires a U.S. address and credit card. Here are the steps you'll need to follow in order to create that new iTunes account:

1. Launch the iTunes application, and wait for it to load.

2. Locate iTunes Store in the sidebar on the left side of the iTunes window. Click iTunes Store, and wait for the store window to load. Your Windows computer or Mac must be connected to the Internet for this to happen, since all storefront information is stored on Apple's servers.

3. Find and click the Sign In button in the top-right corner of the screen. iTunes displays the sign-in screen shown in Figure 1-4. If you currently have an iTunes account, enter your Apple ID and password, and then click the Sign In button to sign into iTunes. No iTunes account? Click the Create New Account button, and follow the remaining steps to create your iTunes account.

Figure 1-4. *Use the iTunes Sign In window to access iTunes with your existing account or begin the process of creating a new account.*

4. Click Create New Account. The screen clears and displays a message welcoming you to the iTunes store. Click Continue to start the process of creating your account.

5. Review the terms of service, check the box that says "I have read and agree to the iTunes Terms and Conditions and Apple's Privacy Policy," and then click Continue. A new window appears prompting you to create your account.

6. Enter your e-mail address and a password. You must enter the password twice to verify that it was typed correctly. You also need to enter a security question—something only you would know the answer to, such as "What was the name of my third-grade teacher? or "What color was my first car?" Supply the answer to that question in the next space, and then enter your date of birth. Finally, review the questions about opting into e-mail notifications, and then click Continue.

7. A payment information screen now appears. You'll need to enter a valid form of payment, either a credit card or a PayPal account. For a credit card, you must enter the card number, CVV number, and billing information. Those must match in order to complete account creation. If you choose to use PayPal, your web browser launches, and you're asked to log into the PayPal account to verify that you're a valid member. Finally, you can also choose to use an iTunes gift card or certificate as a form of payment by entering the redemption code on the card. Once the payment information has been entered, click the Continue button.

After following these steps, iTunes displays a screen congratulating you on creating the new account, and you'll also receive a confirmation e-mail at the address you specified during sign-up. The e-mail welcomes you to the iTunes Store and thoughtfully provides the customer service web address. In case you ever need it, that address is http://www.apple.com/support/itunes/.

Connecting Your iPhone to Your Computer

Once you have an active iTunes account, it's time to unpack your iPhone and connect it to your computer. Follow along as we connect to your computer in preparation for service activation:

1. Remove the iPhone from its box, take off the plastic factory wrapping, and remove the Dock Connector to USB cable.

2. Locate the two ends of the Dock Connector to USB cable. One is thin and marked with a standard three-pronged USB symbol, while the other is wide and marked with a rectangle with a line inside of it.

3. Connect the thin end of the cable to a spare USB 2.0 port on your computer.

4. Orient your phone with the screen facing you and the Home button pointing toward you (see Figure 1-5).

Figure 1-5. *Plug the Dock Connector to USB cable into the iPhone with the rectangle mark facing you.*

5. Locate the universal dock connector on the bottom of your iPhone. It's that rectangular hole about an inch wide that is located under the Home button. Gently yet firmly push the cable into the dock connector without twisting or forcing the connection. iTunes launches, and your iPhone should automatically power on.

If your iPhone doesn't automatically power on and display either a white Apple logo or a Connect to iTunes message, press and hold the Sleep/Wake button on the top of the iPhone—it's the button on the top right of the iPhone. After a few seconds, the iPhone should wake up and display the white Apple logo as it powers on. If the iPhone doesn't respond with some sort of message on the display, contact the store where you purchased the phone.

Activating Your iPhone (Nonstore Version)

Until you activate your iPhone, you won't be able to use it for anything except calls to emergency services. All you'll see initially is a prompt directing you to connect to iTunes. Activating the iPhone involves nothing more than selecting a service plan and registering your phone with your cellular carrier. In theory, this process is simple, and it works properly for the vast majority of new iPhone owners. However, if you're porting a number from another carrier or selecting a less popular plan, it can take a while to get your iPhone "on the air."

TIP If you run into significant delays during iPhone activation, call your carrier's customer service team. They'll usually refund the activation charge as a courtesy.

Selecting a Plan

Before you can send and receive calls, check your e-mail, or send text messages to your friends from your new iPhone, it needs to be set up with a plan, that is, a monthly rate plan that provides a certain number of minutes of voice calling as well as text or multimedia messages and data transfer.

At the time of publication, the iPhone voice, data, and messaging plans provided by AT&T for U.S. customers are relatively simple. You select a voice plan, add a data plan, and then add a messaging plan if you want. These plans change frequently, so you should *always* check the Apple (http://www.apple.com/iphone) or AT&T (http://www.att.com/wireless/iphone/) iPhone pages for the latest pricing information. In all cases, a two-year commitment is required on your part. Let's look at the voice, data, and text messaging options.

Voice Plans

Voice plans are for those times when you're not playing with your iPhone but instead having a conversation with others using the Phone app on your device. As an example, AT&T customers in the United States have a choice of several plans in place ranging from a low-cost minimum number of minutes per month (450) up to an unlimited calling plan. The difference in price between 450 minutes of talk time and unlimited was, at the time of publication, only $30. If you do a lot of talking, an unlimited voice plan may be perfect for you.

Cellular carriers often provide other features with the voice plans. Visual Voicemail, which is Apple's proprietary way of implementing a voice mail inbox on the iPhone that you can see and interact with, is included. Carriers may also provide rollover minutes, which means that unused plan minutes can be used in future months, as well as provide "free" night and weekend minutes in excess of the plan minutes.

If you're having difficulty making your mind up about a voice plan, consider how much total time you currently spend per month talking on your existing mobile or landline phone. Most cellular providers will provide you with exact usage statistics. Also consider if you're going to be replacing a landline with your new iPhone. Many people are doing this, and it can increase your monthly usage.

Regardless of the plan you select, know that most cellular carriers allow you to adjust your plans for more or less minutes while you're in a contract. They understand that your needs can change and are usually more than willing to provide you with a more or less expensive plan in order to keep you as a customer.

Data Plans

Data plans charge you for every little bit of information that you send or receive from your iPhone. Data is what you're consuming when you access the Internet, surf the Web, or check e-mail. Many cellular service providers sell "packages" containing a specific amount of data—say 200MB or 2GB—to be used during a month. If you use more, you're charged an extra amount for the extra usage. If you don't use all your data, you won't be able to carry over those extra megabytes.

How much data will you use in a month? That's dependent totally on what you use your iPhone for. For many users, 2GB of data transfer per month will be more than enough, especially if you're using your iPhone in an environment where you can use a Wi-Fi connection for most of your data needs. As with voice plans, many carriers offer a way to change your requirements up or down depending on your actual usage. Once you've used your iPhone for a few months, you'll be able to see your usage patterns and adjust accordingly.

There's one other feature that is offered by most carriers—tethering. Tethering allows you to share the 3G data connection on your iPhone with your Windows laptop or MacBook and connect to the Internet. While your iPhone is tethered, you can still send and receive data and make phone calls. Depending on the carrier, tethering may be included as part of your data plan, or it may be an additional cost per month.

Messaging Plans

If you're planning to use text or multimedia messages to contact your friends, you'll also need to add a messaging plan. These plans vary; in some cases, you will pay a set charge per text (SMS) or multimedia (MMS) message. Multimedia messages are used for sending pictures or video through the iPhone Messages app.

Some carriers sell "buckets" of messages. You pay a set fee for a certain number of messages per month, and if you send or receive more messages than that number, you a charged per additional message. Most carriers also offer unlimited messaging packages for those customers who are addicted to text or multimedia messages.

Note that the monthly fees are usually for national or regional messaging only. If you plan on doing any international messaging, contact your carrier for details.

The Activation Process

Now, you've selected a plan, made sure you have the latest version of iTunes installed on your computer, have your iPhone connected to your computer, and you're anxious to get it all working. Let's activate the phone on your carrier's network. Since the process varies from carrier to carrier and is frequently changed, we'll give you a general idea of what to expect. The process is quite easy to follow and simply requires that you register your iPhone with Apple, agree to terms and conditions of usage for both Apple and your carrier, and notify the carrier if you're coming over from another phone on their network, activating a new account, or transferring a number from another carrier.

If at any time you feel uncertain or confused about a step in the activation process, grab another phone and call your carrier. They'll be more than happy to step you through the process.

When the activation of your iPhone is nearing completion, a Completing Activation screen appears exclaiming, "Congratulations, AT&T is activating your iPhone" (assuming you're an AT&T customer, of course). If you're an existing AT&T customer and upgrading your phone, this screen displays the number that is being transferred to your phone. If it's a new number or you're having a number transferred from another cell phone provider, you'll see that number on this screen.

Insuring and Repairing Your iPhone

AT&T does not, at the time of this writing, offer an insurance plan for the iPhone. Instead, you'll need to call your renter's or home insurance carrier to see how much you'll have to pay for an iPhone *rider* (a rider is placed on top of an existing policy, adding coverage for a specific item not covered under the standard plan). Allstate, Geico, and State Farm quote $5–$20 per year on top of an existing policy.

Your iPhone is covered under Apple's Limited Warranty for one year. You can add one extra year of iPhone AppleCare for $69. This extends your hardware repair coverage to two years in total. If interested, you can purchase this option online at the Apple Store (http://store.apple.com). Once the warranty has expired, your best bet is to have any repairs done at an authorized Apple repair center.

If you can, be sure to back up your iPhone by syncing it to iTunes *before* bringing it in for service. Apple usually restores your iPhone to factory condition, which means you'll lose any data stored on the iPhone during the repair and service process. We recommend doing a backup and full erase of your iPhone before bringing it in for service so that the private information stored on the phone remains private. You can perform a full erase by selecting Settings ä General ä Reset ä Erase All Content and Settings.

Whether you buy an AppleCare protection plan or not, be aware that AT&T customers in the United States are entitled to two years of complimentary telephone support (1-800-MY-IPHONE) during the term of their AT&T wireless contract. You can find a complete list of ways to contact Apple Support at http://apple.com/support/contact.

Accessorizing Your iPhone

The iPhone accessory business is a huge and thriving economy. A visit to the iPhone accessories pages on the Apple online store shows a fraction of the iPhone cases, cables, docks, and other accessories that have been developed.

If you purchase your iPhone in an Apple Store, your Apple sales associate will show you many accessories that are available for it. These accessories are from Apple and third-party sources, and they provide your iPhone with protection and added functionality.

Let's talk about some of the accessories that can make your iPhone experience more pleasant and fun.

iPhone Bumpers and Cases

One of the most popular categories of products for the iPhone consists of cases or, in the case of the iPhone 4, bumpers. A case is exactly what it sounds like—something that encases the iPhone in fabric, plastic, carbon fiber, or metal to protect the phone from scratches or accidental damage because of a drop.

The phone-surrounding metal antenna of the iPhone 4 caused a stir when initial buyers of the phone complained of issues with signal strength. Apple responded shortly with an acknowledgment that most cell phones exhibit the same loss of signal when held a certain way by offering initial buyers a free iPhone 4 Bumper (Figure 1-6). The Bumper ($29) is an attractive two-tone band that wraps the external stainless steel antenna in hard plastic.

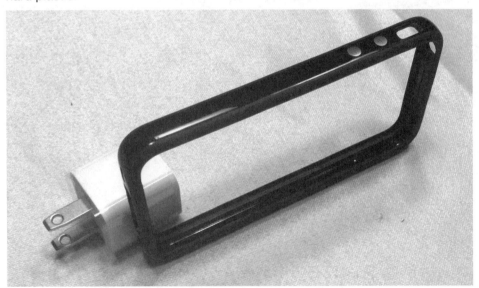

Figure 1-6. *The Apple Bumper fits around the perimeter of the iPhone 4, providing protection to the stainless steel antenna on the edges of the phone. That's the Apple USB Power Adapter at left, providing support to the iPhone 4 Bumper.*

The iPhone 4 Bumper does not protect the screen or back of the iPhone 4. It's made of a hard aluminum-doped glass that is almost metallic in strength. The material can withstand impacts, can withstand drops, and is virtually scratch-proof, but that doesn't keep iPhone owners from wanting to protect their devices.

There are hundreds, if not thousands, of cases made for the entire family of iPhones. Some popular models are made by OtterBox (http://www.otterbox.com), Case-Mate (http://www.case-mate.com), Incipio (http://www.myincipio.com), Griffin (http://www.griffintechnology.com), and Marware (http://www.marware.com).

iPhone Skins

Skins are another popular form of protective gear for the iPhone. Instead of a thick shell of some other material encasing the device, skins literally stick to the iPhone like a second skin. Some are brightly decorated, while others are completely transparent.

GelaSkins (`http://www.gelaskins.com`) makes colorful designs from a number of artists, and you can also create your own designs from photos or original artwork. The skins are inexpensive, provide protection against scratches, and turn your iPhone into a movable feast of art (Figure 1-7).

Figure 1-7. *GelaSkins are one of several skins made for iPhone. These skins feature dynamic custom artwork designed for the company, but you can supply your own photos or art. Image courtesy GelaSkins and artist Joe Ledbetter.*

Two other manufacturers make very popular skins for iPhone. Zagg (`http://www.zagg.com`), makers of Invisible Shields, can send you a kit to install your own iPhone skin, or you can have one installed at thousands of retail locations. We're also fond of StealthArmor (`http://www.fusionofideas.com/stealtharmor-iphone4.html`), which comes in both transparent and patterned materials.

Power Adapters

Even though newer iPhones tend to get better battery life than the older models did, you still need to keep your battery charged. Apple sells the $29 USB Power Adapter (see Figure 1-6), which is exactly what comes with your new iPhone. Why would you want another one? It's always nice to have an extra to keep in your office for away-from-home charging or to take with you when you travel.

Speaking of travel, you'll want to keep your iPhone charged when you're in the car, so why not consider a car charger? Several models are popular, including the Griffin PowerJolt ($24.95, Figure 1-8) and the Belkin Micro Auto Charger ($24.95).

Figure 1-8. *The Griffin PowerJolt is one of a number of car chargers available for iPhone. Image courtesy of Griffin Technology.*

Your computer can also charge your iPhone through the regular Dock Connector to USB cable that comes with the device. However, some people prefer the vertical orientation and ease of plug-in that comes with a dock.

Docks

Docks come in a variety of sizes, shapes, and capabilities. The most bare-bones dock that you'll find is the $29 Apple iPhone Dock, which allows you to place an iPhone onto the dock connector for charging and syncing while putting the device into a portrait orientation for easy viewing.

From there, your imagination and wallet are the limit. Higher-end models are equipped with speakers to turn your sleek little iPhone into a loud "clock radio" or boom box. The latter category is well represented by the $300 Harmon Kardon Go + Play Micro Portable Loudspeaker Dock for iPod and iPhone, while the former category is described by the iHome iP42 Dual Alarm FM Clock Radio for iPhone and iPod (http://ihomeaudio.com; Figure 1-9; $100).

Figure 1-9. *Looking for something that can wake you up and charge your iPhone at the same time? This iHome iP42 Dual Dock is functional and looks good enough to sit on your nightstand.*

Cables

Although the only cable you may ever need for your iPhone is the included Dock Connector to USB cable, there are other cables that can provide video-out functionality—perfect for watching photo slide shows or video stored on your iPhone on a big-screen TV.

Apple makes the Component AV Cable ($49) and Composite AV Cable ($49) for connecting an iPhone to either Component (Y, Pb, and Pr video and red/white analog audio ports) or Composite (composite video, red/white analog audio cables) television inputs.

The $29 Apple iPad Dock Connector to VGA Adapter also works with the iPhone 4 and newer models to provide a VGA attachment to a television, projector, or VGA display.

CAUTION: Not all applications support these connection cables, so be sure to contact app developers for assurance that their app will drive your TV, projector, or display prior to purchase.

Summary

In this chapter, you've learned how to select and purchase your iPhone. You've discovered what's involved in activating your iPhone and become aware of the various service plans that you'll need to choose from. To wind things up, here is a quick overview of some key points from this chapter:

- Only a handful of iPhone models are available at any time. Whatever model you select, buying it at the Apple Store (retail or online) provides you with the best opportunities for returns and repairs if necessary.

- Make sure your computer is compatible with iPhone before you buy by comparing it to the system requirements listed in this chapter.

- When activating, know in advance what kind of plans are available and which ones you want to use. Deciding in advance can save you many activation headaches.

- iPhones are not cheap. Protect your investment by insuring your phone. Also consider adding AppleCare for an additional year's coverage against hardware repairs.

- iPhone technical support is free for two years. Take advantage of it at 1-800-MY-IPHONE (1-800-694-7466).

Chapter **2**

Interacting with Your New iPhone

If your previous mobile phones have not been iPhones, then you're in for a treat. Your iPhone introduces a revolutionary new way to interact. It responds to the language of your touch. The vocabulary of touch includes taps, drags, pinches, and flicks. With these motions, you control your iPhone as easily as using a mouse with your personal computer.

There's more to those touch gestures than just single-finger interactions; the iPhone offers Multi-Touch technology. That means the iPhone can recognize and respond to more than one touch at a time. In this chapter, you're about to discover all of the different ways that you can interact with your iPhone—zooming in and out of maps and photos, using the iPhone's built-in touch keyboard, and playing with its sensors. You'll learn how all these features work and how to take advantage of some secret ways of interacting with your iPhone.

Interaction Basics

Whether you're a Windows user, a friend of the Linux penguin, or a Mac fan, you know that a mouse or trackpad is the way to interact with a computer. On the iPhone and iPad, your fingers are the tools for interacting with the device. The iPhone requires real finger contact. It doesn't sense pressure; it detects the small electrical charge transferred from your skin. You can use your iPhone with your fingers, your knuckles, your toes, or, if you're feeling up to it, your nose, but you can't use a pencil eraser, Q-tip, or one of those old PDA styluses. The electrical charges in your touch make it possible for the iPhone to detect and respond to one or more contacts at a time, otherwise known as Multi-Touch technology.

The iPhone Language

The ways in which you touch your iPhone screen are the words in your communication vocabulary. Here's a quick rundown of the many ways you can speak to your iPhone:

- *Pressing the Home button*: The iPhone's Home button lives below the touchscreen and is marked with a white or gray square. Press the Home button at any time to return to your Home screen with its list of applications. Double-pressing the Home button displays icons in a row at the bottom of the screen for all apps that are currently running and, with a flick to the right, displays a set of controls for operating the iPod app.

- *Tapping*: Tap your iPhone by touching your finger to the screen and removing it quickly. Tapping selects web links, activates buttons on the screen, and launches iPhone apps. When typing text on the iPhone's virtual keyboard, you may want to tap with your forefinger or, if it's more comfortable, your thumb.

- *Double-tapping*: Double-tapping means tapping your iPhone's screen twice in quick succession. Double-clicking may be important on your personal computer, but double-tapping isn't used all that much on the iPhone. In Safari, you can zoom into columns of text or pictures on a web page by double-tapping them, and then you can zoom back out by double-tapping again. In the Photos app, double-tapping is used to zoom into and out from pictures.

- *Two-fingered tap*: The iPhone's Multi-Touch technology means you can tap the screen with more than one finger at a time. To do this, tap the iPhone display with your forefinger and middle finger at the same time. In Maps, double-tapping zooms into the map, while a two-fingered tap zooms out.

- *Holding*: This gesture consists of putting your finger on the screen and leaving it there until something happens. Holding brings up the magnifying glass while you're typing. You can also move app icons around on your iPhone by holding an icon until the app icons begin to "wiggle." They can then be moved around the display and between Home screens to organize your apps, and they can be fixed in place by pressing the Home button. For apps that you've installed on your iPhone, holding an app icon also displays a small circle with an *X* in it in the upper-left corner of the icon. Tap that icon to delete the app from your iPhone.

- *Dragging*: Drag your finger by pressing it to the screen and moving it in any direction before lifting it. Use dragging to position the view in Maps or to scroll up or down a list of messages in Mail. Some apps offer an alphabetical index on the right side, such as the one shown in Figure 2–1. To use this index, drag your finger along it until the item you want becomes visible.

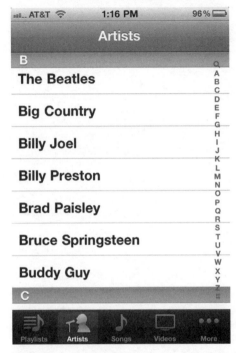

Figure 2–1. *Use dragging to move quickly through an index. In the iPod app artist screen shown here, dragging on the index allows you to jump through the alphabet to find the artist you're searching for. You can also tap a letter to jump to it.*

- *Flicking:* When you're dealing with long lists, you can give the list a quick flick. Place your finger onto the screen, and then move it rapidly in one direction—up, down, left, or right. The display responds by scrolling quickly in the direction you've indicated. Use flicking to move the names in your Contacts app quickly.

- *Stopping*: During a scroll, press and hold your finger to the screen to stop the scroll. Apple's legal text provides a great place to practice flicking, dragging, and stopping. To get there, select **Settings** ➤ **General** ➤ **About** ➤ **Legal**. Have fun with its endless content of legalese that you can flick, drag, and stop to your heart's content. If you don't want to stop a scroll, just wait. The scroll will slow and stop by itself.

■ *Swiping*: To swipe your iPhone, drag a finger from the left side of the screen toward the right. Swiping is used to unlock your phone and to indicate you want to delete list items, such as an e-mail item or contact (see Figure 2–2).

Figure 2–2. *To swipe, drag your finger from left to right across an item you want to delete. After, the Delete button (shown here) appears for the item you swiped. To delete, tap Delete. Otherwise, tap anywhere else to hide the Delete button again.*

TIP: Flicking and dragging will not select or activate items on the iPhone's display. You can try this yourself by dragging and flicking on the Home screen.

■ *Pinching*: On the iPhone, you pinch by placing your thumb and forefinger onto the screen with a space between them. Then, with the fingers touching the screen, move the two fingers together as if you're pinching the screen. Pinching allows you to zoom out in many iPhone programs, including the photo viewer, Safari, and Maps.

■ *Unpinching*: To unpinch, you perform the pinch in reverse. Start with your thumb and forefinger placed together on your screen and, with the fingers touching the screen, spread them apart. Unpinching allows you to zoom into those same iPhone applications that pinching zooms out of.

About the iPhone Home Screen

The iPhone's Home screen allows you to launch any application with a single tap. The Home screen, unofficially called SpringBoard, provides app-launching abilities. Tap the Home button to return to the Home screen at any time.

A Back button appears on many iPhone screens in the upper-left corner. Tap this button to return to the previous screen in the application. This is different from pressing Home. A Back button moves you between screens within an application. The Home button leaves an application and returns you to the Home screen.

iOS 4, the fourth generation of the operating system software used on iPhones, is somewhat different from earlier versions in that returning to the Home screen from an app does not necessarily quit the app. Later in this chapter, we'll tell you how to properly quit apps that are running.

The iPhone Sensors

In addition to the touchscreen, your iPhone contains either five or seven important sensors depending on the model. Both the iPhone 3GS and iPhone 4 contain a proximity sensor, an ambient light sensor, a tilt sensor (also known as an *accelerometer*), a digital compass, and a Global Positioning System (GPS) receiver. The iPhone 4 also adds a built-in three-axis gyroscope and a noise-cancellation microphone to the array of sensors. These sensors give your iPhone some science-fiction-grade features that set it apart from the crowd.

Proximity Sensor

The proximity sensor is located on your iPhone right near the earpiece. Its job is to blank the screen when the iPhone is held up to your ear. This means your ear and chin won't accidentally hang up your calls with their stray touches, and it means you'll save some power during those phone calls.

You can see the proximity sensor in action by going to **Phone ➤ Voicemail**. Set Speaker to off (on is a brighter blue; off a dimmer blue), and then play a voicemail message by tapping the name or phone number of the person who left it. With the speaker off, place a finger just above the earpiece. The iPhone display goes dark. Remove the finger, and the screen returns.

Test the sensor range by placing your iPhone on a flat surface and holding your finger in the air about an inch above the earpiece. Move the finger up and down slightly, and you'll discover exactly where the sensor gets triggered.

The proximity sensor works by shooting out an infrared (IR) beam, which is reflected back and picked up by the iPhone's light sensor. If the range is short enough, the iPhone switches off the screen.

You can also *see* the IR source for the proximity sensor by using a digital camera. The IR beam is visible to the camera's CCD detector. To take the picture shown in Figure 2–3, we switched off a camera's flash, enabled its Macro settings (because we needed the camera to be pretty close to the iPhone), and waited for the source to flash red. You can't see it with your eyes, but you can with your camera's IR-sensitive detectors.

Figure 2–3. *You can "see" the iPhone's IR light from its proximity sensor if you own a digital camera. Its IR beam is visible to the camera's detector. Make sure to cover the iPhone's screen when you take the photograph, because it's bright and the IR light is dim.*

Tilt Sensor

The iPhone uses an accelerometer (what we're going to call the *tilt sensor*) to detect when your iPhone tilts. Many apps, including Safari, update their displays when you turn the iPhone on its side. This allows you to use your iPhone in both portrait and landscape modes.

If you feel like playing with the tilt sensor, try this: go into Photos, and select a favorite picture. Hold the iPhone up normally in portrait orientation, press one finger onto the screen, and then tilt the phone into landscape orientation. The picture will not change. Now, lift the finger off the screen. Presto—the iPhone finally rotates the display.

Many iPhone games use the accelerometer for user interaction. For example, with the very popular Flick Fishing game, you "cast" a line out to catch fish by moving your hand and arm in the motion of casting. Many driving games let you use your iPhone as a steering wheel as your drive along a virtual course.

Ambient Light Sensor

The ambient light sensor detects whether you're in bright or dark lighting conditions and then adjusts the overall brightness of your iPhone display to match. For example, if it's extremely bright outside and you pull out your iPhone to make a call, the light sensor will judge the surrounding brightness when you unlock the phone and let the iPhone know that it needs to compensate by making the display brighter so you can read it. Going the other way, the screen will dim when you're in a dark room to protect your eyes from the glare of a bright screen as well as save some battery power.

Want to have fun with this sensor? When you cover the sensor (found just above the ear speaker on the top front of the phone) with a finger and then unlock the phone, you'll find that the screen brightness is quite dim. On the other hand, if you shine a bright light at the sensor when you unlock the iPhone, you'll see the screen at a very bright setting.

You can toggle the autobrightness feature off and on in **Settings ➤ Brightness**. This setting also offers direct control over the brightness of the iPhone's screen, which is handy when you need immediate results instead of playing with bright lights, fingers, and unlocking your iPhone.

Digital Compass

The digital compass (also known as a *magnetometer*; see Figure 2–4) built into the iPhone 3GS and iPhone 4 is similar to a magnetic compass. In other words, if you happen to be near a strong magnetic field such as the magnets contained in the iPhone earbuds, the compass needle may not be pointing toward true or magnetic north. On occasion, the digital compass may need recalibrating.

Figure 2–4. *The iPhone's digital compass can get you pointed in the right direction, but be sure to recalibrate it when it asks you to do so.*

The iPhone Compass app will inform you of those rare occasions by displaying a message that says "Re-calibrate compass. Wave in a figure 8 motion." That's your cue to hold the iPhone out in front of you and draw a big figure eight, with the eight lying on its side. Keep moving the iPhone until the calibration message disappears. Yes, you will look like a total geek while doing this, but it's better than getting lost, right?

If you're in a car and driving around, you don't need to wave the iPhone at the windshield. Just make a few turns, and the compass will recalibrate itself. That's much safer for everyone in and outside of your car.

GPS Receiver

Not only is your iPhone 3GS or iPhone 4 an amazing, powerful pocket computer and a very capable phone, but it's also a state-of-the-art navigation tool. Built inside the latest iPhones is a GPS receiver that is capable of pinpointing your exact location on the globe within about 30 feet (10 meters).

> **NOTE:** The Global Positioning System consists of a constellation of 24 to 32 satellites in precisely known orbits about 12,550 miles above the earth's surface, all equipped with extremely accurate clocks and powerful radio transmitters. GPS receivers determine their location by timing the reception of signals from four or more satellites and then performing a series of complex calculations.

In fact, your iPhone has an advantage that many dedicated GPS receivers do not. Since it is constantly in touch with cell phone towers with precisely known locations, it can determine your approximate location within several seconds of being turned on. Once the iPhone has locked onto several GPS satellites, it pinpoints the location with even more accuracy. This capability of blending the GPS satellite signals and known cell tower locations is known as Assisted GPS (A-GPS).

The GPS receiver is used in most iPhone apps that contain some sort of geolocation feature. Some examples of these apps include Maps, the Navigon, Tom Tom, and AT&T navigation apps, and the official Geocaching (`www.geocaching.com`) app.

Three-Axis Gyroscope

The iPhone 4 is the first mobile phone to contain a miniaturized three-axis gyroscope to determine the precise orientation of the phone at every moment. This is handy in gaming apps that may need to track the motion of the phone more accurately than the tilt sensors can and also in apps such as You Gotta See This! (`www.boinx.com/seethis`). The latter is an iPhone 4–specific app that creates photo collages simply by waving the phone around in front of you. The iPhone shoots photos as it is moving, and since the app knows the orientation of the iPhone's camera as each photo is being taken, it can easily stitch them into an attractive collage in seconds.

The gyroscope can be used by iPhone developers to capture movement that isn't sensed by the accelerometer. Although the accelerometer does a good job of detecting whether the iPhone has been tilted one way or another, the gyroscope allows the device to be moved left or right, up and down, or forward and back, and that motion can be understood by apps. These additional movements provide another layer of precise control to the gestures that the iPhone understands.

Noise Cancellation Microphone

A glance at the top of an iPhone 4 will show a tiny hole next to the headset jack. This hole is actually a microphone, given the name *top microphone* by Apple. What's it used for? It's for improving the quality of your voice phone calls.

The Noise Cancellation microphone samples the ambient noise level around you. It then subtracts much of that ambient noise from the signal being sent to the person on the receiving end of your phone call. The result is much more clarity when you're making phone calls in noisy conditions.

iPhone Power Tricks

There are many ways to switch your iPhone on and off. The following are the most important methods that every iPhone owner should know.

Unlocking Your iPhone

When your iPhone has been idle for a while, it automatically locks, and the screen goes dark. When this happens, press Home. The locked iPhone screen shown in Figure 2–5 appears. To unlock your phone, swipe the slider from the left to the right. The lock screen clears, and the Home screen springs into place.

Screen locking is a form of power saving. If your iPhone never turned off its bright display, it would go through a battery charge much faster. Shutting down the screen and going into lock mode extends your battery life and optionally allows you to protect your iPhone by requiring a passcode to use the device after it has been locked.

If it seems like your iPhone is locking too frequently, you can adjust how long it should wait before locking. Tap your way to **Settings ➤ General ➤ Auto-Lock**, and select how many minutes you want your iPhone to wait before going dark. Sometimes you may want to just power the iPhone off by yourself and disable autolocking. There's a choice for that in the autolock settings, when you set the duration to Never. Make sure you have a good power source available at all times if you disable autolocking, since autolocking is a power-saving feature. Disabling it means your iPhone will use up battery power more rapidly.

Figure 2–5. *This is the lock screen from an iPhone 4 with its default "rain on the window" wallpaper. To unlock your phone, swipe the slider from left to right. If the default wallpaper is too boring for your tastes, you can change it in the Photos app.*

Putting Your iPhone to Sleep

For iPhones, sleep mode offers a power-saving way to use your device. Press the Sleep/Wake button once. The screen turns off, and your iPhone locks and enters its low-power mode. You can still listen to music and receive phone calls. The volume control buttons on the left side of your iPhone work, and the switch on your iPhone headset continues to control music playback and allows you to answer calls.

Under iOS 4.0 on devices newer than the iPhone 3G, some apps can continue to run in the background even when the device is asleep. As an example, some location-aware apps continuously update the location of the iPhone although it is asleep.

To wake up your iPhone again, press Home, and swipe to unlock.

Securing Your iPhone with a Passcode Lock

For security, you can assign a passcode lock for your iPhone. There are two types of passcodes: a simple passcode, which consists of four easily remembered and typed numbers, and a regular passcode, which can include text. When locked, your iPhone cannot be used except for emergency calls. Go to **Settings** ➤ **General**, and tap Passcode Lock to establish a new passcode. As you can see in Figure 2–6, there's a button that turns on the passcode lock feature. If a four-digit simple passcode is all you'd like to enter, make sure that the Simple Passcode switch is set to the default value of on. If you'd rather enter a text passcode, flip that switch to the off position.

Figure 2–6. *Securing your iPhone with a passcode lock is a good idea so that personal information isn't compromised in case of loss or theft of your phone.*

Once you've decided what kind of passcode you want, tap Turn Passcode On to enter it. If you have chosen simple passcode, you're prompted to enter four digits twice— once to enter the numbers and again to verify that you entered it correctly the first time (see Figure 2–7, left). For regular passcodes, you're prompted to enter your passcode with text, symbols, and numbers (Figure 2–7, right). Once again, you'll have to enter the passcode twice to make sure that it has been entered properly.

As soon as you've set a passcode, you can change some other settings that are related to the passcode lock. Tap the Require Passcode button to set the time interval before your iPhone requests the passcode. Shorter times are more secure, although you'll need to enter your passcode more frequently as a result.

If you like to use Voice Control and your iPhone or Bluetooth headset to do voice dialing or control the iPod app, slide the Voice Dial switch to on to make sure that Voice Control is always enabled, even when the phone is locked. This makes it handy for you to use a Bluetooth headset to dial and control your phone, even when it's sitting in your pocket or in a briefcase or purse.

Figure 2–7. *On the left is the standard keypad for entering a simple passcode, while the full iPhone keyboard appears for typing a regular passcode.*

The final button on the Passcode Lock screen ensures absolute security in case your iPhone is lost or stolen. Sliding the Erase Data button to on will erase the contents of the iPhone if someone incorrectly enters the passcode ten times. Before you engage this setting, be sure that you know your password.

How can you test your passcode? Press the Sleep/Wake button once to put your iPhone to sleep, wait for the time interval to pass, and then wake the iPhone by either pressing the Sleep/Wake button again or pressing the Home button. A passcode challenge screen appears (Figure 2–8 shows the challenge screen for a simple passcode). Enter your passcode correctly, and your iPhone unlocks.

To remove the passcode from your iPhone, go back to the Passcode Lock screen. Tap the Turn Passcode Off button, and then reenter the passcode one more time to confirm that the rightful owner of the iPhone is making the request.

What can you do if you forget your passcode or a mean-spirited colleague adds one to your iPhone without telling you? Unfortunately, you will have to connect the iPhone to your computer and use iTunes to restore the iPhone to factory defaults. Why? Well, for security reasons, there's absolutely no way to reset the passcode since that would defeat the purpose of the passcode.

Figure 2–8. *With passcode lock enabled, you'll be prompted to enter the passcode before you can use your iPhone to do anything other than make an emergency phone call. This figure shows the passcode keypad for a simple passcode.*

Multitasking and Quitting Applications

Prior to iOS 4, iPhones could not perform more than one task at a time. Well, they *could* play music from the iPod app while performing some other tasks, but that was about it.

iOS now acts more like a modern multitasking operating system by allowing multiple apps to run simultaneously. One example that many people pointed at as proof of the need for iOS multitasking was being able to play tunes using the popular Pandora music-streaming app while performing other tasks, such as reading e-mail, at the same time.

When you're using an app, pressing the Home button returns you to the Home screen, but the app is either suspended or may actually be running. In fact, if the app has been written to take advantage of backgrounding, it will continue to run when you're viewing the Home screen or running other apps. In other words, don't assume that when an app is out of sight, it's shut down.

To see what's currently running on your iPhone under iOS 4, double-click the Home button. The current Home screen becomes transparent, and a side-scrolling list of active apps appears at the bottom of the screen.

Flicking the active apps to the right, you'll eventually get to a control panel for whatever music app happens to be active at the time. This control panel is equipped with play, pause, fast-forward, and fast-reverse buttons, as well as a screen orientation lock button. The far-right icon on the control panel shows which music app you're currently controlling.

On an iPhone 3G or 3GS running iOS4, having multiple apps still running in background can increase usage of the processor to the point that your iPhone heats up, the device uses much more power, and the response of the phone becomes sluggish. Even with the iPhone 4's powerful and fast Apple A4 processor, too many apps running simultaneously can slow things down dramatically. Idle applications occupy your iPhone's memory, which may eventually cause it to balk when you try to open another app.

So, how do you quit apps? Double-click the Home button, and at the bottom of the iPhone display you'll see a side-scrolling list of all the apps that are currently running (Figure 2–9). To turn off an app, tap and hold an app icon in the list until it begins to jiggle. A small minus sign in a red circle appears at the top-left corner of the icon. Tap the minus sign to quit the application.

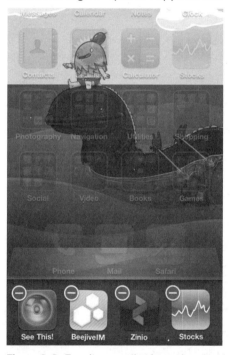

Figure 2–9. *To quit an app that is running, double-click the Home button to display all the currently active apps, and then tap and hold one of the apps. When the small minus sign in the red circle appears, tap it to quit the app.*

Powering Your iPhone Off and On

To power off your iPhone, press and hold the Sleep/Wake button for about five seconds. A slider appears prompting you to slide the red button that appears to the right in order to power off. To cancel, either tap Cancel or just wait about ten seconds. The iPhone automatically returns you to the Home screen if you don't power down within that time.

When your iPhone is powered off, it ceases to function. You cannot listen to music. You cannot receive phone calls. You must power your iPhone back on for it to do these things.

To power on your iPhone, press and hold Sleep/Wake for two to three seconds. Release the button when you see the white Apple icon. The iPhone starts up and returns you automatically to the unlock screen.

Rebooting Your iPhone

At times, you may need to reboot your iPhone. The most common reason for doing this is that you have installed a new app that recommends a reboot after installation. Although you can reboot just by powering down and then powering back up, Apple provides a much easier way do this. Press and hold both the Home and Sleep/Wake buttons for eight to ten seconds. Ignore the "slide to power off" message, and keep holding both buttons until the white Apple logo appears. Once it shows up, release both buttons, and let the iPhone finish its reboot. You will return automatically to the unlock screen.

Placing Your iPhone into Recovery Mode

On occasion, you might encounter one of these odd symptoms:

- Your iPhone continually restarts but never displays the Home screen.

- An update or restore did not complete, and the device is no longer recognized in iTunes.

- The iPhone stops responding, displaying the Apple logo with no progress bar or a stopped progress bar for more than ten minutes.

If this happens to you, you can place the iPhone into recovery mode and attempt to restore it. Here's how to put your iPhone into recovery mode:

1. Disconnect the USB cable from your iPhone, but leave the other end connected to the USB port on your computer.

2. Turn off your iPhone. Press and hold the Sleep/Wake button until the red slider appears, and then slide it to the right. Wait for the iPhone to turn off. If you can't turn off the iPhone using the slider, press and hold the Sleep/Wake and Home buttons at the same time. When the iPhone finally turns off, release the buttons.

3. While pressing and holding the Home button, reconnect the USB cable to your iPhone. When you reconnect the USB cable, the device should power on. If a depleted battery icon appears on the iPhone screen, let your iPhone charge for at least ten minutes and then start over again at step 2.

4. Hold the Home button down until you see the Connect to iTunes screen. It displays an iTunes icon (a music CD with musical notes in front of it) and a USB cable.

5. At this point, if iTunes isn't running on your computer, launch it. You should see a "recovery mode" prompt in iTunes that says, "iTunes has detected an iPhone in recovery mode. You must restore this iPhone before it can be used with iTunes." Click the OK button to begin using iTunes to restore the iPhone.

Changing iPhone Wallpapers

An iPhone comes out of its box with a default picture installed as "wallpaper." Wallpapers are the pictures that are used as a background on your iPhone's Home and Lock screens. On the iPhone 4, the standard wallpaper looks like glass with raindrops on it. Although it does a great job of showing just how good the iPhone 4's Retina Display is, since it looks like real water on your screen, it's not unique to you.

Changing the wallpapers is an easy way to customize your iPhone:

1. If you have a favorite artwork or photo that you want as wallpaper on your iPhone, make sure it's in the Photo Library first. You can move photos and artwork to your iPhone by e-mailing them to your phone's e-mail address and then tapping and holding the photo. A Save Image button appears; tap that, and the photo is saved into your iPhone's Photo Library.

2. Select Settings ➤ Wallpaper. A screen appears showing the current Lock screen and Home screen wallpapers.

3. Tap the image of the current wallpapers. Two buttons appear; one is marked Wallpaper and contains a number of built-in textures and photos that can be used as wallpapers, while the other is marked Camera Roll and includes the photos that are in your Photo Library.

4. Tap either one of the buttons to preview the pictures that can be used as wallpaper. If you select a photo from your Photo Library, you'll be asked to move and scale the photo before you tap Set to assign it to a wallpaper (Figure 2–10).

Figure 2–10. *When you assign one of the images in your Photo Library to be a wallpaper, you'll be asked to move and scale the image so that it looks its best. Once that's done, tap the Set button.*

5. If you choose one of the built-in wallpapers or have moved and scaled your photo, you're now asked whether you want to make the picture your wallpaper for your Home or Lock screen, or for both. Tap the appropriate button, and the image appears as wallpaper.

Organizing Apps with Folders

iOS 4 brought a smile to the face of many longtime iPhone users with the addition of folders. Previously, app icons could not be organized except by locating them all on the same page. Each page could contain up to 16 apps, so if you had a lot of apps, you were often flipping through ten or more screens of apps to find the one you needed.

Now, iOS 4 provides folders. Each folder can hold up to 12 apps, and each Home screen can have up to 12 folders—that's 144 apps per screen, not including those in the Home row at the bottom of the iPhone display.

Here are some tips on creating and using folders:

■ To organize similar apps into folders, tap and hold one app until it begins to wiggle, and then drag and drop it on another app of the same type. For example, to create a game folder, you can tap and hold the Angry Birds app icon until it wiggles and then drag it over to the Chopper 2 icon and drop it. Since both apps are in the Games category of the iTunes App Store, the iPhone automatically selects Games as the name of the folder.

■ Once a folder is created, you can add any other app (up to a total of 12) to it by repeating the process of dragging and dropping icons.

■ To rename a folder, tap and hold the folder icon until it wiggles. Tap the folder icon, and the folder opens with an editable title at the top. When you're done renaming the folder, press the Home button to save the new name.

■ You can also organize your apps and folders in iTunes. With your iPhone connected to your computer, click its name under Devices in the iTunes sidebar, and then click the Apps tab. In the image on the right side of the iTunes screen (Figure 2–11), drag and drop app icons to organize them the way that you want them.

Figure 2–11. *That simulation of your iPhone display on the right side of the iTunes screen is a fast way to organize your apps into folders or pages.*

Using the iPhone Keyboard

Let's start talking about the iPhone keyboard by quoting verbatim from an early iPhone e-mail written by one of the authors:

> *I would like to sat that the iPhone has turned me into a tupong expert, but that would ne far far far from the truth. The fact is that I type on the iPhone like a cow, working with the iPhone keyboard is norm hard and frustrating. Foe all this Rhine is supposed to be smart and press five, I find that in actual use it is slow and mistake-prone. Will my accuracy improve as I get more experience? Probably. Will my fingers become smaller and less oqlike?almost certainly nor.*

That e-mail was written within the first 24 hours of ownership, causing a lot of consternation about the whole iPhone keyboard thing. Within a week, however, iPhone typing progressed from horrible to readable, and within another week, from readable to pretty darn good. The entire paragraph in Figure 2–12 was written on an iPhone and transferred to this manuscript (see Figure 2–12).

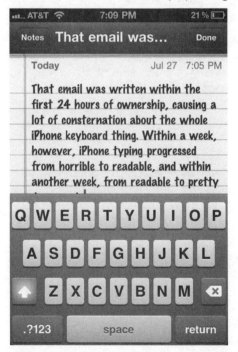

Figure 2–12. *The iPhone keyboard grows easier to use with more experience. Within a couple of weeks, you'll master its quirks. Notice the Shift key (arrow pointing up) to the left of the Z key and the Backspace/Delete key (pentagon pointing left with an X in it) to the right of the letter M. The .?123 button switches the keyboard to a number and symbols layout, and the Return button lets you add carriage returns to your text.*

The secret to success is that the iPhone keyboard is smart—so smart, in fact, that it corrects a lot of typos and compensates for misaligned fingers. It automatically capitalizes the beginning of sentences. It suggests corrections for misspelled words and uses something called *predictive zones* to make it easier to hit the right keys. Here are some of the key technologies that make the iPhone keyboard work:

- *Dictionary*: The iPhone has an onboard dictionary that learns frequently used words as you type. It also picks up names and spellings from your address book. This means it gets better at guessing your intention as it builds its data.

- *Automatic correction*: As you type, the iPhone looks for words similar to what you're typing and guesses them, placing the guess just below the word you're typing. To accept the word, tap the spacebar. (You don't have to finish typing the word. The iPhone puts it in there for you.) To decline the correction, tap the word itself. The iPhone will not make a substitution, even when you press the spacebar.

- *Predictive mapping*: The iPhone uses its dictionary to predict which word you're about to type. It then readjusts the keyboard response zones to make it easier for you to hit the right letters. Likely letters get bigger tap zones; unlikely letters smaller ones.

- *Offset correction*: The iPhone understands that people sometimes misalign fingers. So if you mean to type *pizza* but you press O instead of P and U instead of I (that is, *ouzza*), the iPhone is smart enough to know that the typing pattern you used matches a known word in its dictionary.

Getting Started

When you're new to the iPhone, start by typing slowly. Pay attention to those confirmation pop-ups that appear every time you tap a key. We find it easiest to use our fingertips to type. Others prefer to use their thumbs. Whatever method you use, make sure to go at a pace that allows you to keep track of what you're typing and make corrections on the go.

- *Automatic corrections*: The iPhone displays suggested corrections just below the word you're typing (see Figure 2–13). To accept the suggestion, tap the spacebar. To disable correction for the current word, tap the word itself in the text area, and iPhone will leave the word exactly as you have entered it. You can also turn off autocorrection by opening **Settings ➤ General ➤ Keyboard** and sliding the autocorrection switch to off.

Figure 2–13. *iPhone suggestions appear just below the word you type. Tap the spacebar to accept the suggestion, or tap the word you're typing to disable autocorrection for that word.*

- *Using the magnifying glass (loupe):* While you're typing, you can adjust the cursor by using the iPhone's built-in magnifying glass feature, also known as the *loupe* (see Figure 2–14). Hold your finger somewhere in the text area until the loupe appears, and then use the magnified view to drag the cursor exactly where you need it.

- *Summoning the keyboard:* To make the keyboard appear, tap in any editable text area on the iPhone screen.

- *Dismissing the keyboard:* There's no standard way to dismiss the keyboard, but many programs offer a Done button indicating that you're done typing. In Safari, tap Go instead of Done.

- *Select/Select All:* You can select either a single word or all text in an editable area on the iPhone by using Select or Select All. In a text area, tap and hold your finger until the loupe appears. When you remove your finger, a small pop-up menu appears (Figure 2–15), allowing you to select either a single word or all the text on the page. If any text has been copied or cut, you may also see the Paste command in the menu (see next item).

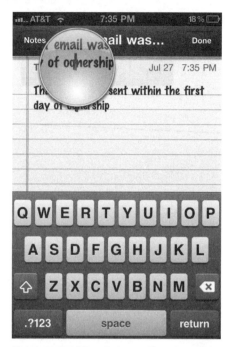

Figure 2–14. *iPhone's loupe offers a magnified view that makes it easy to position the cursor exactly where you need it to be.*

Figure 2–15. *If you need to select a word or phrase to copy, double-tap a word to bring up this pop-up menu. Select either the word you tapped or all of the text on the page.*

- *Cut/Copy/Paste/Replace:* Like a computer, there are functions within the iPhone that allow you to cut, copy, and paste text. To enable these, double-tap a word in a text area. The word is selected, with small "handles" on either side that can be moved left or right to expand the area that is selected. In addition, a pop-up menu appears with the commands Cut, Copy, Paste, and Replace to select from (Figure 2–16).

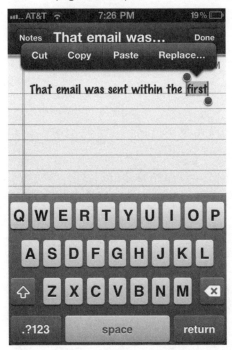

Figure 2–16. *Just like in a word processing application on a computer, the iPhone can cut, copy, and paste text. It can also replace the highlighted text with similarly spelled words.*

Cut removes the selected text and keeps it stored in the iPhone's clipboard until you paste it somewhere else. Copy saves a copy of the selected text in the clipboard but does not remove it from the existing text file. Paste takes whatever text is currently in the clipboard and pastes it at the cursor point in any text field. Replace (Figure 2–17) displays a list of words that are spelled similarly to the selected word so that accidentally misspelled words can be replaced with the correct word with a tap of a finger.

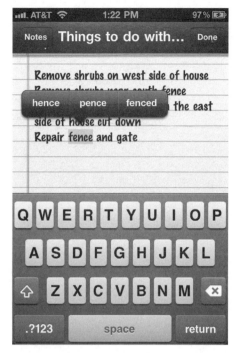

Figure 2–17. *If the app you're typing in has replaced your word with something that is spelled similarly, use the Replace command to display a list of words that you can insert with a tap of a finger.*

iPhone Typing Tricks

Once you're comfortable with the keyboard, there are further ways to make typing easier. Here are a few more iPhone typing tricks you can use to make your keyboard entry faster and easier.

Contractions

When you want to type a contraction like *can't* or *shouldn't,* don't bother putting in the apostrophe. The iPhone is smart enough to guess that *cant* is *can't*. Of course, if you're referring to a slope or tilt, be sure to tap the word itself to decline the change from the noun to the contraction.

If you're typing a word like *we'll*, where the uncontracted word *well* is a common word, just add an extra *l*. The iPhone corrects *welll* to *we'll* and *shelll* to *she'll*.

> **TIP:** Other contraction tricks include *itsa*, which gets corrected to *its*, and *weree*, which gets corrected to *we're*.

Punctuation Dragging

If you plan to use only one item of punctuation at a time, such as a comma or period, save time by dragging. Drag from the .?123 button to the item you want to include. By starting the drag at .?123, the iPhone switches momentarily to the numbers and punctuation view. After selecting your item, the keyboard automatically bounces back to the alphabet.

> **TIP:** Another punctuation trick for the end of sentences is to tap .?123, the punctuation item you want to use, and then the spacebar. The iPhone is smart enough to recognize the end of a sentence and put you back in alphabet mode. You can also double-tap the spacebar to add a period followed by a space.

Accents

Tap and hold any keyboard letter to view accented versions of that letter. For example, tapping and holding N presents you with the option of adding n, ´n, or ñ. This shortcut makes it much easier to type foreign words.

If you need to do a lot of typing in a foreign language, you can add new keyboards to your iPhone by going to **Settings ➤ General ➤ Keyboard**, tapping International Keyboards, and then adding the keyboards you need from a palette of 51 that are available. To use the keyboards to enter text, open a keyboard, and then tap the small globe to the left of the spacebar, which will display a list of the international keyboards you have installed. Yes, you too can write in Russian on any iPhone (Figure 2–18).

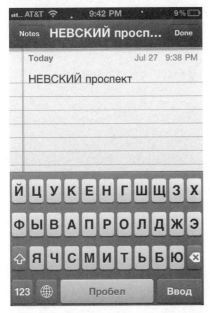

Figure 2–18. *The Russian keyboard has been enabled in Notes, and the keyboard is full of Cyrillic characters. Tap the globe to the left of the spacebar to choose another keyboard or return to your default keyboard.*

Caps Lock

To enable Caps Lock, go to **Settings ➤ General ➤ Keyboard Preferences**. When that's enabled, you can double-tap the Caps button to toggle the lock on and off.

Deleting Multiple Words at a Time

When you press and hold the Delete key, it starts off by deleting one letter and then the next. But if you hold it for longer than about a line of text, it switches to word deletion and starts removing entire words at a time, making it easier to clear text quickly.

Autocapitalization

Autocapitalization means the iPhone automatically capitalizes the start of sentences. So, you can type *the day has begun*, and the iPhone is smart enough to capitalize *the*: "The day has begun." This means you don't have to worry about pressing the Shift key at the beginning of every sentence or even when you type *i* because *i went to the park* becomes *I went to the park*.

> **TIP:** Enable or disable autocapitalization in **Settings ➤ General ➤ Keyboard Preferences**.

iPhone Typing Test

You may be curious just how fast you can type on your iPhone keyboard. There are several apps in the App Store that can test your typing speed. Search the App Store for *typing test* to find those apps.

Using a Bluetooth Keyboard with Your iPhone

That little iPhone virtual keyboard can be annoying for typing in large amounts of text. Can you imagine writing a book on an iPhone, tapping away with one finger or two thumbs?

Thankfully, iPhones running iOS 4 can use with Bluetooth keyboards. Apple's Wireless Keyboard is a perfect example of a compact, battery-powered keyboard that links to the iPhone and works well for typing e-mails or writing books. Here are some instructions on setting up your Bluetooth keyboard with your iPhone:

- *Make sure that your Bluetooth keyboard is not paired with another device*: Pairing is the act of making the two devices (a computer and a keyboard) aware of each other. If you've been using your Apple Wireless Keyboard with a Mac, for example, you'll want to unpair the two before pairing the iPhone and the keyboard. To do that, open **System Preferences ➤ Bluetooth** on your Mac, find the listing for your Bluetooth keyboard, and then click the gear icon at the bottom of the Settings pane (Figure 2–19). Click Disconnect to break the connection between the keyboard and Mac, and then click the minus sign to delete the keyboard from the Bluetooth settings.

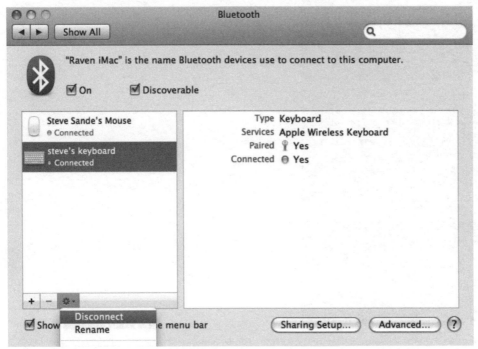

Figure 2–19. *To unpair your Bluetooth keyboard from a Mac, disconnect it first, and then click the minus sign to delete the keyboard from the list of Bluetooth devices.*

- *Make your Bluetooth keyboard discoverable*: When a Bluetooth device is discoverable, it can be discovered by other devices like your iPhone and paired to them. Continuing the previous example with the Apple Wireless Keyboard, you make the keyboard discoverable simply by pressing the power button on the right side of the keyboard. The tiny green LED on the keyboard begins to blink, signaling that the keyboard is now discoverable.

- *Pair your iPhone and the Bluetooth keyboard*: Once more using the Apple Wireless Keyboard example, go to **Settings ➤ General ➤ Bluetooth**, slide Bluetooth to on if it's currently turned off, and then tap the name of the keyboard in the list of discoverable devices. When the two devices begin to talk, the iPhone displays a four-digit number that you need to type on the keyboard (Figure 2–20). Once the number has been entered, the two devices are paired, and you can use the Bluetooth keyboard anywhere on the iPhone that you'd normally use the on-screen virtual keyboard.

Figure 2–20. *To pair your iPhone to a Bluetooth keyboard, make the keyboard discoverable, find it in the iPhone's Bluetooth settings, and then tap the keyboard name. To consummate the pairing, you'll need to type in a random passkey created by the iPhone.*

The standard Apple Wireless Keyboard works much like it does on a Mac when it's being used on an iPhone. The brightness keys (F1 and F2) brighten and dim the iPhone screen, the play/pause/fast-forward/rewind keys F7 through F9 work with the iPod app, and the volume keys (F10 through F12) adjust the volume of sounds playing on the iPhone. If at any point you need to use the iPhone's virtual keyboard, just tap the Eject button (top-right corner of the keyboard), and it appears. Tap it again to make the virtual keyboard disappear.

Used with an app like My Writing Nook (www.mywritingnook.com) or Documents To Go (www.dataviz.com/products/documentstogo/iphone/), a Bluetooth keyboard makes writing large documents on an iPhone a reality.

Using the iPhone Stereo Headset

If you look carefully at the headset packaged with your iPhone, you'll discover a small, thin cylinder about 6 inches below one of the two earpieces. This cylinder contains both a microphone and a switch. Go ahead and squeeze it, and you can feel the switch react. This switch has several functions:

- *Music*: When listening to music, squeeze once to pause the music; squeeze again to resume playback. Double-squeeze (two quick squeezes in a row) to skip to the next song.

Tip You can also pause your music by pulling out the headset plug from the iPhone jack.

- *Phone calls*: When an incoming call rings on your iPhone, squeeze once to answer the call. Squeeze again to hang up. In theory, you can double-squeeze to send the call to voicemail, but I find that *really* difficult to do. It's much easier in my opinion to use the Sleep/Wake button. Press the Sleep/Wake button once to silence an incoming call and twice to send the incoming call to voicemail.

- *Voice Control:* Did you know that it's possible to control your iPhone by talking to it? If you squeeze the headset switch until you hear a double-tone in the earbuds, you can command the iPhone to either make a phone call or play music using the iPod app. If you are looking at the iPhone screen when it goes into Voice Control mode, the various voice commands are visible floating across a blue background (Figure 2– 21).

  For example, squeezing the switch until you hear the prompt and then saying "Call Joe Smith at Home" causes the phone to call Joe at his home phone number, provided that his name and home number are in your Contacts list.

  If you simply say "Call Joe Smith" and Joe has more than one phone number, you'll be asked which number to call—"Home, Work, or iPhone?" The iPhone prefers for you to tell it which number to call, and voice recognition is improved drastically. Use the short form of this voice command only in those situations where you aren't sure that there are multiple numbers for a contact.

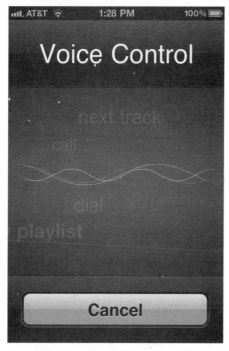

Figure 2–21. *The iPhone's Voice Control capability is a futuristic and useful way to call people or listen to music.*

Voice Control can be very useful when you are walking or running. Rather than stopping to pick a song in the iPod app, just squeeze the headset switch, and tell your iPhone what you want to hear. The following is a list of the voice commands that your iPhone understands:

- "Call [contact name]"

- "Dial [name or phone number]"

- "Shuffle"

- "Pause music"

- "Play more music like this"

- "Play playlist"

- "Next song"

- "Play songs by"

- "Next track"/"previous track"

- "What group is this song by?"

- "What is this song?"

Summary

This chapter has explored many of the ways you can interact with your iPhone from taps to buttons to switches. You've read about the touchscreen and how you can communicate with it as well as about other sensors built into the phone. You've discovered how to put your phone to sleep, how to lock it, and how to power it off completely. After finishing this chapter, you will have been introduced to all the basic ways you and your iPhone can communicate with each other. Here are a few key lessons for you to carry away with you:

- Build up your working iPhone interaction vocabulary. You'd be surprised how often one of the lesser-known gestures, such as the two-fingered tap, will prove useful.

- Understand how the iPhone sensors are supposed to work so you won't be surprised when they're doing their job. Are you wondering why the iPhone is so dim when you wake it up in a dark room? Knowing about the light sensor will put you on the path to adjusting the phone to the brightness you need.

- Know the difference between powering your iPhone down and putting it to sleep. When it's powered off, you can't receive any calls, but you'll conserve battery power. When it's asleep, you can still listen to music and take calls.

- Folders make it possible to group similar apps together. This is a new feature of iOS 4.

- If you forget your iPhone's passcode, you'll need to restore the iPhone at your computer.

- Do you need to do a lot of text entry on an iPhone? Consider using a Bluetooth keyboard with the iPhone to make fast and more accurate typing a breeze.

- Voice Control can do the job of dialing a number or playing music when your hands are too busy to keep them on the iPhone. Just remember that Voice Control's ability to recognize your voice isn't perfect and that your iPhone may not necessarily do what you intend it to do.

Chapter 3

Placing Calls with iPhone

iPhones are versatile devices. They can surf the Web, check the latest stock prices, request a weather report, play thousands of games, and map out directions. But at its core, the iPhone remains a cell phone, which means that making phone calls is its primary function. In this chapter, you'll learn the essential things you need to know to place and receive iPhone calls with ease. You'll discover ways you can get up to speed and make the most of your iPhone as a cell phone.

Checking the Cell Network Indicator

The bars at the top-left corner of your iPhone screen indicate how strong a signal you're receiving from the local cellular network. Five bars indicate the strongest signal. No bars or the words "No Service" indicate a complete lack of signal strength: no bars means no calls.

Reception problems can stem from many causes: distance to the nearest cell tower, hills and trees blocking reception, or even wiring or ducts inside your building. When you're not receiving a good signal, you'll need to move. Go to a place where the signal is stronger. This can mean many things, such as moving around a room, getting closer to a window, stepping outside your building, or driving toward a tower. Can they hear you now?

> **NOTE:** The iPhone 4 has a well-publicized design issue in which holding a bare phone a certain way causes a dramatic drop in signal quality. As a result, Apple recommends the use of an iPhone 4 case or the Apple Bumper to reduce the issue's effect on your calls.

Finding good reception can be an art, but most mobile phone carriers try to help by making coverage maps on their web sites that show where you should be able to receive service. In the United States, AT&T offers a coverage map at www.wireless.att.com/coverageviewer/. In the United Kingdom, it's all up to the carrier. Here's a list of coverage maps for various carriers:

- O2:
  www.webmap.o2.co.uk

- Orange UK:
  search.orange.co.uk/ouk/portal/coveragechecker.html

- T-Mobile UK: www.t-mobile.co.uk/services/coverage/street-check/

- Vodafone UK:
  online.vodafone.co.uk/mobile_services/mobile_network_cover
  age/ Coverage_map_signal_strength_tester

A network provider that offers excellent coverage in one region might provide only spotty reception in another. Since AT&T is the exclusive iPhone provider in the United States and the iPhone is locked to the AT&T network, Americans are pretty much stuck with whatever coverage AT&T provides in their area.

> **TIP:** When attempting to place calls, make sure you haven't enabled Airplane Mode, which turns off all the radios on your iPhone—the cell phone radio, Wi-Fi, and Bluetooth. If you can't make a call, first check to see whether there's a little orange airplane icon at the top-left corner of your iPhone screen. That means Airplane Mode is turned on, blocking all of your radios. To place calls, go to Settings and set Airplane Mode to off.

iPhone Basics

As with all Apple products, there's never just one way to do anything. In this section, you'll find many ways to perform the most basic iPhone tasks, including answering calls, sending calls to voicemail, and even hanging up. You may be surprised to discover just how many options Apple has built into your iPhone to get the job done.

Launching the Phone App

By default, the green phone icon appears in the lower-left corner of your iPhone's Home screen. It's the app that you use to place and receive phone calls, check your voicemail, review recent calls, and more. There's a shortcut bar at the bottom of the Phone app screen with the following features:

- *Favorites* allows you to create a list of the most frequently called contacts for instant dialing.

- *Recents* lists all your recent incoming, outgoing, and missed calls. To call back, tap any phone number in the list.

- *Contacts* provides your complete address book. You can sync it to your Windows computer or Mac and also to Apple's MobileMe and other online services.

- *Keypad* is used to manually call phone numbers.

- *Voicemail* is the gateway to Visual Voicemail, where you can listen to voice messages people have left when you miss their phone calls.

To leave the Phone app, press the Home button.

Placing Calls

Tap Keypad to enter the iPhone dialing screen shown in Figure 3–1. From here, you can place a call by tapping in a number to dial.

Figure 3–1. *The iPhone keypad, from which you can dial numbers and make phone calls.*

Here is an overview of the many ways the Phone app can be used to place calls:

- *Dial directly*: To place a call manually, tap the Keypad icon at the bottom of the Phone app. Use the keypad to enter the phone number, and then tap Call to place the call. If you make a mistake while typing, tap the Backspace key. It's just to the right of the Call button and looks like a sideways-pointing pentagon with an *X* in it.

■ *Add contacts*: The Add Contact button, just to the left of the Call button, provides a fast way to create a new contact using the number you just entered. Enter a phone number, press the Add Contact button, and a details screen opens (Figure 3–2). On the details screen, enter the details for the new contact, such as name, address, and company. If you need to add the number to an existing contact rather than create a new contact, choose Add to Existing Contact instead.

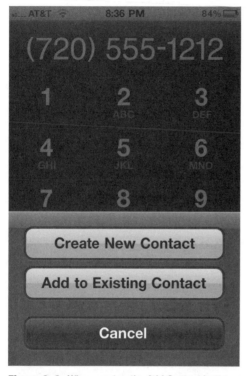

Figure 3–2. *When you tap the Add Contact button, you're given the choice of creating a new contact with the phone number you just entered or adding that phone number to an existing contact. Add to Existing Contact is very useful when someone you know calls from a new phone number.*

■ *Select a contact*: To call someone in your address book, tap Contacts. The scrolling Contacts screen opens. Search down the list of names until you find the person you want to call. To speed this along, you can drag through the alphabet at the right side of the screen. Tap a name to display its address book entry, and then tap a phone number to place your call.

■ *Call favorites*: The Favorites screen lets you add your most frequently called contacts to a quick-call list. To call, just tap any name in the list. Since the Favorites screen stores a preferred number for your contacts, you don't have to select a specific phone number (for example, home or work) each time the way you do with the Contacts screen.

- *Reply to recent calls*: Tap the Recents icon to open a list of your most recent incoming, outgoing, and missed calls. Missed calls appear in red, while incoming and outgoing calls are listed in black. Tap any number to instantly place a call to that number.

NOTE: Buttons at the top of the Recents screen let you view all calls, let you view only the missed calls, and let you clear the list entirely.

- *Call via e-mail, calendar, note, and web links*: The iPhone knows what a phone number looks like, and it will automatically add links to your e-mails, calendar events, notes, and web links. Telephone links show up as blue underlined text in e-mails, calendar events, and on web pages. In notes, they show up in brown underlined text. To call an embedded phone number, just tap it.

- *Place international calls*: Mobile phone carrier policies range widely in terms of placing international calls and using the iPhone while roaming. Be sure to call your carrier before leaving on a foreign trip or placing international calls. Avoid the horror stories of thousand-dollar phone bills by checking your facts before you use your iPhone in unconventional ways and locations. As a rule, you can usually add international calling to your iPhone plan and will need to shop the current deals to find the best rates for your package.

Using your iPhone for international calls adds a few more features and rules that you should be aware of. Here are a few tips to keep in mind regarding international calling:

- Use the plus (+) symbol to prefix international calls, for example +44 800 555 1212. To add + to a phone number, press and hold the 0 button on the iPhone keypad for about two seconds (note the + symbol under 0 in Figure 3–1). A tone sounds as you hold the button. Just ignore it. After a second or two, the 0 turns to a +, and you're ready to continue entering the number.

- When traveling outside the United States, add +1 to your numbers to call back to America, for example, +1 (212) 555 1212. If you do foreign travel regularly, use this style for all your contacts. Calls placed with +1 work both inside and outside the United States. Calls without +1 work only inside the United States. Your iPhone is smart enough to know when you're dialing from the United States, and you won't be charged extra for using +1.

- Check with your carrier for international calling rates. Rates change all the time. At the time of writing, the rates for international calls for AT&T customers were as follows: for calls from the United States to other countries, AT&T offers the WorldConnect plan for $3.99 per month, plus a per-minute rate varying from $0.09 to $9.99 depending on the country you're calling. If you're traveling abroad and want to use your AT&T iPhone to call home, the World Traveler package costs $5.99 per month plus a per-minute roaming charge ranging from $0.59 to $4.99, dependent on the country you're calling from. Be sure to read the "VoIP Calling" section of this chapter to get details about a much less expensive option for international calls.

- If you're a fan of SMS text or MMS multimedia (picture and video) messaging, you may want to text friends abroad. Once again, rates depend on the carrier. For AT&T customers texting to friends overseas, the International Long Distance Messaging 100 plan lets you send 100 texts (SMS or MMS) per month for only $10. If you're an AT&T customer sending MMS photo messages to your friends back home in America, the Global Messaging 50 plan lets you send 50 messages for $10 per month. If you're not going to use SMS regularly, you can opt out of a plan and just pay $0.25 per message.

- When you're using your using your iPhone in a foreign country, be aware of data roaming costs. These can easily add up without you really knowing what's happening, because the iPhone often sends and receives data behind the scenes. If you don't want to get accidentally charged for data roaming, you can disable it by selecting **Settings** ➤ **General** ➤ **Network** and sliding Data Roaming to off.

- If, on the other hand, you do want to use data services while abroad, consider using Wi-Fi only. Many hotels, restaurants, and bars offer free Wi-Fi to visitors, or you can pay a nominal fee for access. If you must use a 3G or EDGE network in a foreign country, check with your carrier for a discounted rate plan. AT&T offers four different packages offering anywhere from 20 MB ($24.99) to 200 MB ($199.99) of data transfer per month in more than 100 countries. Visit `att.com/dataconnectglobal` for details.

- Find out whether cell phone carriers abroad provide short-term pay-as-you-go plans or iPhone rentals. This can reduce your cost significantly because the iPhone you're using is tied to the local carrier in the country you're visiting.

Placing Calls with Voice Control

As we mentioned in Chapter 2, the iPhone includes a method of interaction called Voice Control. Not only is Voice Control fun to use, but it can also be very useful for making phone calls with or without the iPhone stereo headset. To enable voice control, press and hold the Home button for two seconds or squeeze the stereo headset button for two seconds. The Voice Control screen appears, and you can begin speaking to your iPhone to dial a number.

To place a call to someone who is in your Contacts list, simply say the following:

- *Call Bob Smith Work/Home/iPhone/Mobile*: Here you're telling the iPhone which number to call. This works much better than the second and third choices in this list, so much so that we recommend using this format for calling someone even if there is only one number listed for a person.

- *Call Bob Smith*: If there's more than one number for Bob, the iPhone will prompt you for the proper phone.

- *Dial Bob Smith*: This works identically to saying "Call Bob Smith."

- *Dial 1-720-555-1212*: If dialing internationally, you can preface the first number with "plus." This dials the number you read to the phone.

Voice Control dialing also works with many Bluetooth headsets. Read the user manual for your specific Bluetooth headset for instructions on how to initiate Voice Control. With many headsets, pressing the Answer/Hangup button for two seconds displays the Voice Control screen.

Answering Calls

When your iPhone receive calls, it rings, playing back whatever ringtone you have selected and, if you've set it up that way, vibrates. The screen updates and tells you (to the best of its ability) who is calling by showing you a contact name and picture. If you're using the iPhone when a call comes in, the screen offers you the option of answering or declining the call (see Figure 3–3, left).

When your iPhone is in sleep mode, you'll see a different screen when there's an incoming call (Figure 3–3, right). To answer the phone when it wakes from sleep and is ringing, slide the green arrow button to the right.

Figure 3–3. *When you receive a call, your iPhone identifies the caller with a name (if possible), contact photo, and the phone (work, home, iPhone, and so on) from which the call was placed. Tap Answer (or slide the green arrow button to the right) to accept the call and talk, or tap Decline to send the call directly to voicemail. When two or more contacts share the same number (as shown here), your iPhone lists each possible caller.*

Here are the ways you can answer and manage your calls:

- *Answering calls*: Tap the green Answer button to accept the call. The iPhone connects you to the caller, and you proceed with your call. You can also answer calls by squeezing the iPhone headset control once.

- *Sending calls to voicemail*: To decline a call, sending that call to voicemail, tap Decline. Alternatively, press and hold the headset control for about two seconds, or press the Sleep/Wake button. AT&T's automated answering service prompts your caller to leave a message, which you can check later at your convenience.

- *Silencing the ringer*: Sometimes you forget to power off your phone before meetings. If this happens to you, silence the ringer by pressing one of the volume buttons. The iPhone stops ringing immediately. You can still answer the call for the normal period of time until it gets sent to voicemail.

The iPhone's Ring/Silent switch is located just above the volume controls on the top-left side of the phone. Toggle your iPhone between ring mode (all black) and silent mode (red dot) by flipping the switch. You can set whether the iPhone vibrates upon receiving a call in Settings ➤ Sounds, where you'll find two vibrate settings: one for silent mode and another to make the phone vibrate when it's in ring mode.

Managing Calls

During conversations, your iPhone provides several ways to handle calls from muting your caller to handling call waiting (see Figure 3–4).

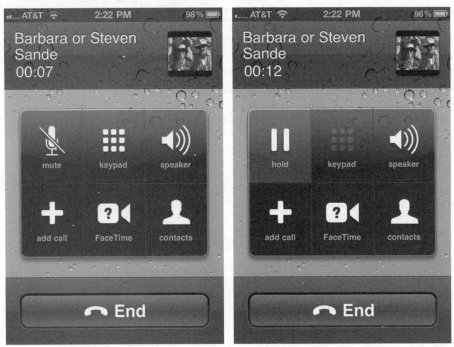

Figure 3–4. *The iPhone options available while you're on a call allow you to mute the microphone, place a call on speaker, establish a conference call, and more.*

When you need control your conversation, here are the options available to you:

- *Mute the microphone*: Tap Mute to temporarily disable your microphone. You can still hear your caller, but your caller will not be able to hear you until you tap Mute a second time. When enabled, the Mute button turns blue.

- *Use the keypad*: Tap the Keypad icon to open the iPhone keypad during a call. The keypad lets you navigate through automated voice systems (e.g., "Press 1 for English") or enter a PIN. Tap Hide Keypad to return to the options shown in Figure 3–4.

- *Use the speakerphone*: Tap the Speaker icon once to switch sound output from the earpiece to the built-in iPhone speaker. Like Mute, the Speaker icon turns blue when enabled. Tap a second time to return sound to the earpiece.

NOTE: As described in Chapter 2, your iPhone uses its proximity sensor to determine when the phone is held up to your ear. This blanks the screen but has no effect on the speaker. If you've enabled the speakerphone and hold the iPhone up to your ear, it remains on speakerphone but with a black screen.

- *Placing a call on hold*: To place a call on hold, tap and hold the Mute button for two seconds. It will turn blue and display the hold icon shown in Figure 3–4, right. To take a caller off of hold, tap the Hold button again.

- *Conference calling*: To add another party to your call, tap the Add Call button. This places your current call on hold and allows you to place a new call. After establishing the new call, tap Merge Calls to add the new call to the on-hold call. If needed, repeat these hold, call, and merge actions to bring additional parties into the conference call.

- *Begin a FaceTime video chat (iPhone 4 only)*: FaceTime is Apple's unique videophone application that works only with the iPhone 4 and newer iPhones. We'll talk more about FaceTime in Chapter 4, but for the time being remember that you can start a FaceTime chat with another iPhone 4 caller by tapping the FaceTime button.

- *Accessing Contacts*: Tap the Contacts icon to look up another contact during a call. Tapping a contact's phone number is equivalent to tapping Add Call and then selecting that contact.

TIP: You can run normal iPhone applications during your calls. Click the Home button, and select an application to open. To return to the call screen, tap the green bar that appears at the top of each screen during an active call.

- *Handling Call Waiting*: When receiving a new call during a conversation, the iPhone asks whether to switch to that new call.

  - To end your current call and answer the new one, tap the red End Call and Answer buttons.

  - Tap Ignore to continue with your current call. Alternatively, squeeze and hold the headset control for about two seconds and then release. Your iPhone beeps twice to confirm.

- Tap Hold Call and Answer to place your conversation on hold and answer the incoming call. Once answered, you can merge calls into the call on hold.

- Squeeze the headset control once to place the current call on hold and answer the incoming call. Squeeze again to toggle back and forth between the first call and the new one.

TIP: When using headphones, your iPhone rings through both the handset and the attached headset—very convenient when you've put the iPhone down with the headphones still plugged in.

- *Ending a call*: Tap End Call to hang up. You can also end calls by squeezing the iPhone headset control once.

TIP: Living in an age of quick-dial and disposable phone numbers, you might not always remember your iPhone's number. Fortunately, Apple makes it easy to look up. On the iPhone, select **Settings ➤ Phone**. Your number appears at the top of the settings pane: "My Number: 1 (555) 555-1212." You can also check your iPhone's telephone number by docking it to your computer. Select your iPhone from the Sources list (the blue column on the left side of the iTunes screen), and check the number on the Summary page. It appears toward the top of the page, just under the serial number.

There's one more thing you'll need to manage if you're using a Bluetooth headset: how you're communicating with your iPhone. When you make or receive a call while a Bluetooth headset is paired with your iPhone, you must choose whether you're going to speak through the iPhone, through the speakerphone on the iPhone, or through the Bluetooth headset.

Buttons designating each of these choices appear on your iPhone screen (Figure 3–5), and you may need to tap one of them to direct the call to the proper speaker and microphone.

The default device always appears with a small speaker icon next to it on the button, so you know at a glance whether the call is being routed to the proper device. In Figure 3–5, the call is being made through a Plantronics 640 Bluetooth headset and will connect without the caller making a choice. If the caller wants the call to go through the speakerphone instead, she would tap Speaker.

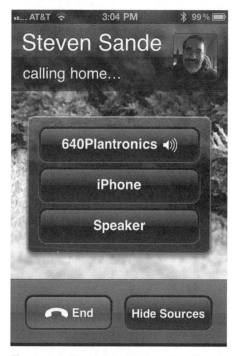

Figure 3–5. *Bluetooth headsets add another step of complexity to answering or making a phone call.*

Managing Favorites

The Favorites screen offers one-touch access to your most often-used phone numbers. It can be a little counterintuitive to manage your favorites, because this one-tap behavior means you can't select a contact and then edit it. When you tap a name, the iPhone immediately calls it. Instead, here are the ways you should use to keep your Favorites list in line:

- *Adding a favorite*: In the Favorites screen, tap the plus (+) button in the top-right corner. Select a contact and then a phone number from that contact. The iPhone adds the number to Favorites and returns you to the Favorites screen.

- *Removing a favorite*: Tap Edit to place Favorites into edit mode (see Figure 3–6). Red circles with minus signs appear next to each contact. To delete a contact, tap the red circle and then confirm by tapping Remove. To cancel without removing the selected favorite, tap anyplace else on the screen. Tap Done to leave edit mode.

- *Reordering favorites*: Tap Edit at the top-left corner of the Favorites screen. In addition to the red circles to the left of each name, notice the gray bars to the right of each name. Drag these handles to move names into new positions. Tap Done when finished.

Tip: Although you can edit contact information on your iPhone—as when you add a new phone number on the go—the best place to manage contacts is on your computer. Your iPhone updates its contact information every time you synchronize. In iTunes, make sure you've chosen to sync your contacts by checking the appropriate option in the iPhone Info tab. You can also sync contact information over the air using Apple's MobileMe service.

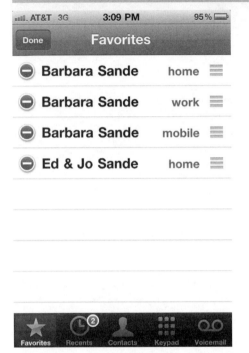

Figure 3–6. *In Edit mode, tap the red buttons to delete contacts, and use the gray drag handles on the right to reorder contacts.*

Using Visual Voicemail

When someone calls and you can't or don't answer, they're transferred to your carrier's voicemail system and prompted to leave a message. Your iPhone's Visual Voicemail allows you to see a list of messages that have been left for you, where you can select which ones you want to hear.

Setting Up Your Voicemail Passcode

The first time you enter the Voicemail screen, your iPhone prompts you to enter a new voicemail passcode (PIN). Select a number you will remember and make a note of it someplace secure and private; in other words, not in your wallet or on a sticky note attached to your computer.

To change your passcode at a later date, go to **Settings** ➤ **Phone**, and tap Change Voicemail Password. The iPhone prompts you for the current passcode. Enter it, and tap Done. Then enter the new passcode, and tap Done. To confirm the new passcode, enter it one more time, and tap Done.

> **Tip** Advanced iPhone users should note that the **Settings** ➤ **Phone** screen also allows you to specify a SIM PIN. This number locks your SIM card, so it can't be used in other phones. When enabled, you must enter the SIM passcode every time you power on your iPhone.

Choosing Your Greeting

To set the message that plays when your mobile carrier transfers a call to voicemail, tap Greeting at the top left of the Voicemail screen. Select Default to use the standard message or tap Custom to record a greeting as follows: tap Record; speak your message; tap Stop. You can review your recording by tapping Play and save it by tapping Save.

Managing Voicemail Messages

The small red number that appears on the green Phone icon on your Home screen indicates the combined number of accumulated missed calls and voicemails. When you tap the icon and enter the Phone application, these numbers break down individually, as shown in Figure 3–1. Tap the Voicemail icon to open the Voicemail screen and see your message list (Figure 3–7).

From the Voicemail screen, you can perform the following functions:

- *Toggling the speaker*: By default, voicemail audio plays back through the iPhone's earpiece. Tap the Speaker button to play back voicemail through the iPhone's built-in speaker system instead. It turns a brighter, lighter blue when enabled. Tap again to redirect audio back to the earpiece.

- *Playing messages*: To listen to voicemail, select a message, and tap the Play button that appears to the left of the contact name or phone number, as shown in Figure 3–7. The button switches to a two-lined Pause indicator, which you can tap again to pause playback. You also can rewind and fast-forward by adjusting the playhead on the scrubber bar that appears just above the Call Back and Delete buttons.

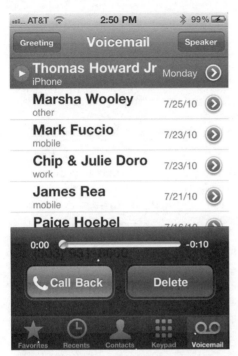

Figure 3–7. *The iPhone's Visual Voicemail lists your messages. To play back a message, select it and tap the Play button to the left of the name or number.*

- *Removing voicemail*: Tap Delete to remove the currently selected message. The iPhone moves that item into its Deleted Messages list. To undelete, select Deleted Messages, tap the item you want to restore, and tap Undelete. Permanently remove deleted voicemails by tapping Clear All in the Deleted Messages list. When the iPhone prompts you, confirm by tapping Clear All again.

- *Reviewing contact information*: The Disclose button at the right of each message links to the informational page for that contact. If you haven't assigned a phone number to a contact, use this page to add the selected number to an existing contact or to create a new contact for the number. Tap the Voicemail button in the upper-left corner to return to the Voicemail screen.

- *Returning a call*: Select any message from the list, and tap Call Back to return the call.

Accessing Voicemail Files

If you have a need to save important voicemail that you've received, you may want to look into a third-party Mac application from Mark/Space called The Missing Sync for iPhone (www.markspace.com/products/iphone). With the application, you can move voicemail messages to your Mac for future reference. eCamm PhoneView (www.ecamm.com/mac/phoneview/) is another excellent choice for archiving voicemail messages and other important iPhone data. There is no similar application for Windows.

Another way you can save those messages on just about any computer is to play the voicemails on the iPhone through the speaker and use a sound recording application to record the voicemail to the Windows computer or Mac. On most Windows machines, you can use the Sound Recorder accessory, found in the list of All Programs under Accessories, to record the voicemail. On the Mac, the GarageBand application (part of iLife) is useful for recording and editing voicemail messages.

Sending Voicemail Indirectly

AT&T customers can uncover their AT&T message center phone number by opening the Phone application. Tap Keypad, enter ***#61#** (i.e., star, pound, 6, 1, pound), and tap Call. The iPhone responds with "Please wait." After a few seconds, the screen updates with overlaid text. One message will read, "Setting interrogation Succeeded. Voice Call Forwarding When Unanswered Forwards to" followed by a number. This number is the AT&T voice-messaging center. When you call this number, AT&T welcomes you and asks you to enter a ten-digit phone number. By entering the phone number for your iPhone, it's as if you'd dialed the iPhone directly. You hear the greeting you've set and can leave a message for your iPhone.

Managing Ringtones and Other iPhone Alerts

The Sounds pane (**Settings** ➤ **Sounds**) allows you to choose how your iPhone responds to incoming calls and other events. Here, you can both set the volume of the ringtone and choose which ringtone to play when calls arrive.

To switch to a new sound, tap Ringtone, and choose any of the sounds listed. The iPhone plays it back for you to hear. When you're satisfied with your selection, tap Sounds to set the ringtone and return to the previous screen.

NOTE: In addition to setting ringtones, the Sounds pane allows you to choose whether to play sounds for new voicemail, new text messages, new mail, sent mail, calendar alerts, locking your iPhone, and keyboard clicks.

The iPhone allows you to assign custom ringtones to individual contacts. This allows you to instantly know which contact is calling: a happy song for your spouse or an alarm for your boss (or vice versa, depending on how much you like your job). Choose **Phone ➤ Contacts**, and select a contact. Scroll down the contact information page, and tap Assign Ringtone. Select a ringtone, and tap Save to select that sound or select Cancel to use the default ringtone for this contact.

Adding Custom Ringtones

The iPhone uses m4a audio files (AAC format) as ringtones. Although almost any sound file can be converted to this format in iTunes, third-party applications such as Ambrosia Software's iToner2 (www.ambrosiasw.com/utilities/itoner/) make this simple.

You can also turn a short segment of a song that you've purchased from the iTunes store into a ringtone. Here's how:

1. Launch iTunes on your Mac or Windows computer.

2. To find songs that you've purchased in iTunes, click the Purchased icon under the Store listing. You will also see a Purchased icon for each device that you've used to buy iTunes content.

3. Click a purchased song in the list, and then select **Store ➤ Create Ringtone**. If it's possible to convert a portion of the song into a ringtone, a small ringtone editor appears at the bottom of the iTunes screen (Figure 3–8). You can drag the highlighted area to any point of the song, make the ringtone longer (up to 30 seconds) or shorter, and choose to loop the ringtone over and over. There's an adjustable time gap between rings as well.

4. When you've edited the ringtone to your satisfaction, click the Buy button to purchase the ringtone for $0.99. It is saved to your Library under a section titled Ringtones.

5. Connect your iPhone to your computer. Under the Ringtones tab for your iPhone, make sure that Sync Ringtones is selected and that you have chosen either "All ringtones" or "Selected ringtones" to sync.

6. Click Apply, and the ringtones are transferred to your iPhone.

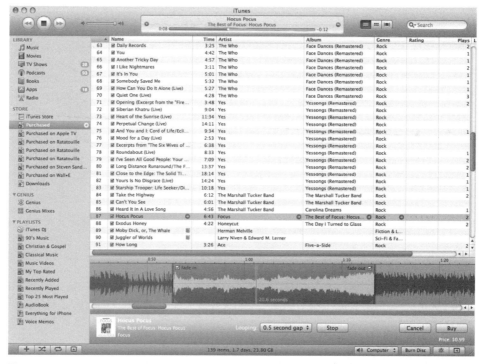

Figure 3–8. *The ringtone editor in iTunes provides a way to turn some purchased songs into iPhone ringtones.*

NOTE: Not all songs in iTunes can be purchased as ringtones. Apple previously put a small icon next to songs in iTunes that could be made into ringtones but has stopped doing that recently. The only way to determine whether a song can be turned into a ringtone is to try it.

Advanced Phone Preferences

The Phone Settings pane (Settings ➤ Phone) allows you to enable and disable several key features including call forwarding, call waiting, and caller ID (that is, showing your caller ID information to other cell phones). Each of these preferences leads to a toggle switch, which selects whether the feature is enabled. In addition, the Call Forwarding setting lets you specify which number to forward calls to when the feature is in use. Choosing to hide your Caller ID means that others will not be able to see either your name or phone number when you call them or answer their calls.

TIP: The Settings ➤ Phone pane allows you enable iPhone use with a Teletype machine. To use a TTY system with your iPhone, you must purchase a separate iPhone TTY adapter cable at the online Apple Store.

iPhone Codes

Every phone has a "secret" vocabulary, codes that you can type into the number pad that provide backdoor access to phone information. To use these codes, open the Phone application, and tap Keypad. Next, enter the codes exactly as stated, including any stars and pound signs. Tap Call after entering the code. The iPhone implements a large subset of the standard GSM service codes as well as a number of carrier-specific ones. Here is a sampling of the codes you can use on your iPhone in the United States on the AT&T network. To learn more, use Google to search for *GSM codes*.

Basic iPhone Information

Use these shortcuts to view information about your iPhone's core functionality:

- *#06#: Displays your iPhone IMEI, the unique identifier for your cell phone hardware. (There's no need to tap Call.) Together with your SIM information, it identifies you to the provider network.

Service Shortcuts

These shortcuts provide quick access to information about your account for AT&T users—the codes will vary for readers in other countries:

- *225#: Current bill balance. (Postpaid service only; the acronym is BAL for balance.)

- *646#: Check remaining minutes. (Postpaid service only; the acronym is MIN for minutes.)

- *3282#: Check your data usage. (Postpaid service only; the acronym is DATA.)

- *729: Make a payment. (The acronym is PAY.)

- 611: Connect to customer service.

FaceTime: Tomorrow's Videophone, Today

One of the more widely touted features of the iPhone 4 was the addition of a video calling function called FaceTime. Like the fictional videophones in *The Jetsons* and *2001: A Space Odyssey*, FaceTime provides a way for two iPhone 4 owners to see each other as they're talking.

Realizing that video calling requires more bandwidth than a simple voice phone call, Apple wisely chose to require a Wi-Fi network connection for FaceTime to work properly. There are ways of working around the Wi-Fi requirement, but before we show you them, we'll demonstrate how to use FaceTime in the Apple-approved way:

1. Before you do anything else, set **Settings ➤ Phone ➤ FaceTime** to on. You must do this or your FaceTime calls will fail.

2. To start setting up a FaceTime call, make sure that the recipient is also using an iPhone 4 (or newer model) and that you're both connected to the Internet via Wi-Fi. We recommend that you check your Internet connection by checking e-mail or visiting a web site—anything that will verify that your connection is working.

3. The first time you try to connect via FaceTime, your iPhone verifies that the recipient of the call is also on a FaceTime-compatible iPhone. Sometimes the initial FaceTime call can be somewhat slow in connecting. Be patient, or if it doesn't connect, have the recipient try to set up a FaceTime chat with you.

4. Once your iPhone "knows" that the other iPhone can accept FaceTime calls, the FaceTime button on the recipient's contact info page will display a small video camera icon. In the future, just tap the FaceTime button to make a video call to that person. No dialing is necessary.

5. When the FaceTime connection has been made, you'll see the person you're talking to on the iPhone screen, or at least what their camera is looking at (Figure 3–9). What the person on the other side of the FaceTime chat sees is what's in the small window in the corner of the display. You can drag that window around the screen if it's blocking an important detail of your chat.

6. Since the iPhone 4 has two cameras, one that faces you and one that faces away, you can tap the Switch Camera button (the small camera icon in the lower-right corner of the FaceTime screen) to switch between the cameras. That also changes what your chat buddy sees on their screen.

7. On occasion, you may need to mute a conversation from your end. To mute, just tap the Mute button (the small microphone icon with a line through it that is on the lower-left corner of the FaceTime screen). To unmute, tap the button again.

8. When you're ready to stop the FaceTime chat, tap the End button in the bottom center of the FaceTime screen.

Figure 3–9. *FaceTime calls can sometimes surprise you. The image in the upper-right corner is what the caller is sending to the rather scary recipient. We're not sure who is the most surprised....*

Although Apple officially supports FaceTime only over Wi-Fi connections, we've tested it on 3G data connections using mobile broadband hotspots such as the Sprint or Verizon MiFi with amazing success. 4G mobile broadband hotspots like the Sierra Wireless Overdrive from Sprint or Clearwire's Clear iSpot are an emerging way to get an iPhone data connection without the need for an AT&T data plan.

VoIP Calling

For anyone who needs to make a lot of international phone calls, Voice over IP (VoIP) is a money-saving boon. VoIP uses the Internet to make the connection between two parties rather than the traditional phone system, and there is always a computer or adapter box on each end of the connection. Vonage (www.vonage.com) is a popular United States–based VoIP provider, using an adapter to connect standard phones to the Internet, while Skype (www.skype.com) is used by many people worldwide to make VoIP calls between computers.

Your iPhone is a powerful computer, and it uses either a 3G or Wi-Fi connection to send data over the Internet. As a result, you can use your iPhone to make VoIP calls. All it takes is the proper software.

Although there are a number of VoIP carriers in the world, Skype has the most account holders, handles the most calls, and has an excellent and free iPhone app. For that reason, it's going to be our example for this book. You'll need to have a Skype account if you want to try Skype VoIP calling. Signing up for an account is free; point a web browser on any computer to go.skype.com/register to get a Skype account.

Once you've signed up, you might want to make a couple of VoIP calls from your computer to become familiar with Skype's features and limitations. Software is available for Windows, Mac OS X, and Linux at www.skype.com/intl/en-us/get-skype.

When you're feeling confident with your ability to make Skype calls on a computer, you can apply your knowledge and make VoIP calls from your iPhone. Search on the keyword *skype* in the App Store, and then install the free app on your iPhone. As soon as the app is installed, launch it and you are greeted with a sign-in screen (Figure 3–10):

Figure 3–10. *Signing into Skype from the Skype app for iPhone*

Enter your Skype user name and password, and once a connection has been made over Wi-Fi or 3G, you'll see a list of all of your Skype contacts (provided that you have entered them at one point or another). Tapping any contact displays a profile for a user, including their current online status, and three buttons—one to call, one to initiate an instant messaging chat session, and one to send an SMS text message to the contact. We'll talk more about instant messaging and SMS in the next chapter of this book.

Tapping the call button creates the VoIP connection between your iPhone and the recipient, and you'll soon be talking with the other person. Be aware, though, that network latency (particularly over 3G connections) can make your call break up and/or disconnect. Your best VoIP calls are made on a fast Wi-Fi network with a strong signal, not over a "barely there" 3G connection on the edge of a mobile phone network.

Even with these limitations, VoIP calls provide another powerful tool for business and home users who need to communicate worldwide without spending a lot of money.

Summary

They don't call it an iPhone for nothing. This chapter has introduced the "phone" part of the iPhone. In it, you have read about placing calls, receiving calls, and managing your iPhone contacts. You've learned about some of the ways to access and control calling features, and you've seen a few added features like adding ringtones and using GSM codes. Before you go away, here are a few key points that you may want to remember about making calls with the iPhone:

- AT&T is the sole U.S. iPhone provider. The iPhone is locked to the AT&T service. If you don't receive good local AT&T reception, you may want to consider other cell phone options. In the United States and other countries, be sure to check with local carriers to determine whether service at your most frequently visited locations is good.

- It takes only a few seconds to get acquainted with many of the advanced iPhone calling features such as multiway conference calling. If you're unsure how to proceed, just look at the menus on the iPhone screen. They are clear, explicit, and indicate what you need to do next.

- Although Apple's official policy is that third-party ringtones aren't allowed, it's easy to purchase an inexpensive application to add those ringtones to your iPhone. You may have to reinstall ringtones after iPhone firmware upgrades.

- If you have a lot of music in your iTunes library that has been purchased from iTunes, you may be able to create, edit, and transfer your own ringtone to your iPhone.

- Many of the iPhone code shortcuts are both safe and convenient to use. Check your balance or your minutes directly from your iPhone without fear.

- FaceTime, available only on the iPhone 4 and newer phones, is a pocketable videophone. You can make video phone calls from any location with Wi-Fi or a mobile broadband hotspot.

- Consider using VoIP to make inexpensive international phone calls. The free Skype app is a perfect way to use your iPhone to talk with friends, relatives, and business associates overseas.

iPhone Messaging and Social Networking

Your iPhone is not only a powerful phone but also a messaging heavyweight. It supports text and multimedia messaging out of the box, can do AIM-style instant messaging and Internet chats with third-party apps, and can even be used for voice and video chats. Social networking services have expanded exponentially over the past few years, and the iPhone has been at the forefront of this explosion. In this chapter, you'll discover a lot of creative ways to talk to the world with your iPhone.

A Variety of Chats

Messaging allows you to communicate instantly with colleagues and friends. It brings people closer together without relying on the immediacy of a phone call. Instant messaging is asynchronous; you send a message, and the recipient can respond to it (or not) at their leisure. That's unlike a phone conversation, which is synchronous, where you and the recipient have an immediate back-and-forth interchange of ideas.

Several big players dominate the messaging world: e-mail, SMS, MMS, IM, IRC, Facebook, and Twitter. If these names already sound familiar to you, feel free to skip ahead. If not, don't let the acronyms dampen your enthusiasm. You are probably already familiar with these technologies. Here's a quick rundown:

- *SMS*: SMS stands for Short Message Service. It's the feature that most people call *text messaging*. With it, you can send short messages from one phone to another. It lets you carry on typed conversations without placing a voice-based call. The iPhone fully supports SMS messaging, and it's the most common way to conduct iPhone chats. SMS operates on the same network as your voice phone calls, so it often works when your data connection is down. SMS messages can arrive any time your phone is turned on, and they don't require a special app to be running on your iPhone.

- *MMS*: MMS is the multimedia version of SMS; it stands for Multimedia Messaging Service. MMS messages can include audio, video, and images, and text can be formatted to include multiple fonts as well as italics and bold. If a picture can tell a thousand words, sending an MMS message with a photo might keep you from doing a lot of unnecessary text messaging. As with SMS, MMS works over the voice network, not the data network.

- *IM*: IM means instant messaging. It's a way to communicate in real time by typing text. If you use AIM, Yahoo! Messenger, or iChat, you're using IM. There are many instant messaging apps for the iPhone, so you'll be able to keep in touch with your friends and co-workers easily. We'll discuss some of the third-party apps later in this chapter.

- IM is different from text and multimedia messaging in five key ways. First, it requires a connection to a data network. Second, the service itself is free—you pay only for the data plan on your iPhone. Next, it can allow typed conversations with more than one person at a time. Fourth, you need to sign into an IM server. The server acts as the gateway for messages to pass between you and others. Finally, it requires that your IM app be up and running for the duration of the chat. If you've quit the app, you're not going to receive messages.

- *IRC*: Internet Relay Chat is a relatively ancient (1988) messaging technology that's still going strong. You can find IRC clients for nearly every operating system on Earth. Third-party developers have created IRC apps for iPhone, so you can continue using IRC into the future. Like IM apps, IRC apps must be constantly connected to a server in order to send and receive messages, and you must sign in to the server before conducting a typed conversation.

- SMS, MMS, IM, and IRC messages also have one thing in common compared to email; the messages are much shorter. Although you might provide a complete business proposal to a client in an email, you'd be much more likely to send a short "I'm on my way home" message to your spouse in an SMS message.

- *Facebook*: As of July 2010, Facebook had more than 500 million users. It's a way for many people to get together and find friends, old and new. With your iPhone, you never need to be out of touch with Facebook. Facebook requires you to log into the Facebook service and use a special Facebook app to send messages, photos, and videos to your friends.

■ *Twitter*: Twitter answers the question "What are you doing right now?" in 140 characters or less and then displays your answer to the world. There are many Twitter apps for iPhone, so you can find one that fits your particular style of tweeting. Tweets are essentially one-way blasts of information to the world, although two-way conversations that are tweeted back and forth are common. Twitter requires a special app and a connection to the Twitter service.

SMS/MMS Costs

SMS and MMS messages are expensive. If you like to chat, either of these methods is probably the most expensive way to do it. The details vary by plan. The standard U.S. AT&T iPhone plans do not include text or multimedia messages; if you plan on doing a lot of messaging, you'll want to purchase one of the plans, which include anywhere from 200 to an unlimited number of messages per month at a cost of $5 to $20. These prices are for the AT&T network—if your iPhone is running on another network, be sure to check with your provider for messaging pricing.

What's more, expect to be charged for both incoming and outgoing messages. You'll be charged against your message balance whether you're sending a friend a quick photo message, receiving an automated SMS alert, or (if you're into reality TV) texting your vote to *American Idol*. It's staggeringly easy to run through those 200 base messages on the most inexpensive plan very, very quickly.

With an AT&T family plan, you can add unlimited messaging for a flat $30 per month, regardless of the number of phones. If you're just not sure how much you're going to use the Messages app to send text and multimedia messages to others, you can also pay as you go at $0.20 per text message or $0.30 per multimedia message. Note that these prices and the prices mentioned elsewhere in this text are representative of the rates in force at the time the book was being written and may very well be different when you read this.

Checking Your Reception

Text and MMS messaging use your local cell network. As a rule, if you can talk, you can text. That holds true even when you have no access to 3G or Wi-Fi network data. Text and MMS messaging use the same technology used to place phone calls.

The other messaging services described in this chapter use cellular data services (GPRS, EDGE, 3G) or Wi-Fi to transmit information. Even if you don't have a cellular signal, you can use IM, IRC, Facebook, and Twitter over a Wi-Fi wireless network.

Check the vertical signal strength bars at the top-left corner of your iPhone. The more bars you see, the better your coverage is. If you see no bars or the words *No Service*, you won't be able to place calls, and you won't be able to send or receive messages. Should this happen, try moving toward a window or stepping outdoors. Hills and trees may also interfere. See Chapter 3 for more information about cell phone connectivity and enhancing your reception.

Keep in mind that you cannot message while Airplane Mode is enabled. If you see a small orange airplane in the location where the signal strength bars should be, then Airplane Mode is enabled, and you'll need to disable it before sending any messages. You can use IM, IRC, Twitter, and Facebook on aircraft that are equipped with Wi-Fi. Just put your iPhone into Airplane Mode, and then turn Wi-Fi on. Just remember to turn Wi-Fi off again when asked to shut off all electronics toward the end of a flight.

Getting Started with the Messages Application

Tap the green Messages icon, which is initially located at the top left of your Home screen (Figure 4–1), to open the Messages app. Sometimes it displays a red circle with a number in it. This number indicates the number of unread text messages you have received.

Figure 4–1. *A red circle is sometimes found on the Messages icon, indicating how many unread messages have been received by your iPhone.*

Tapping the Messages icon opens the application and places you on the Messages screen where you can review existing messages and send new ones (Figure 4–2). When text messages arrive, a small notification window appears letting you know who the message is from and displaying some of the text. If sound is turned on, you'll hear a small "tri-tone" noise (you can change this in **Settings ➤ Sounds ➤ New Text Message**) when a message arrives. When you send an SMS or MMS message, a small "whoop" noise heralds a successful send.

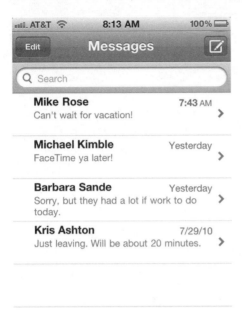

Figure 4–2. *The main Messages screen displays your current and saved conversations in a list. Unread messages are marked with a blue dot on the left side of the message.*

The Messages screen allows you to edit messages (using the Edit button in the top-left corner) and create new messages (using the Compose button in the top-right corner). Blue dots at the left of a message indicate that they have not been read. The number of unread messages also appears in parentheses at the top of the screen.

> **TIP:** SMS text messages are limited to 160 characters each. Your iPhone is smart enough to break up longer messages as needed.

Creating a New Message

To write a new message, tap the Compose message button at the top right of the Text Messages screen. This button looks like a square with a pencil in it (see Figure 4–2). When tapped, a New Message screen appears (Figure 4–3). This screen allows you to address, compose, and send your message.

> **TIP:** You can also start a new text message conversation directly from any contact's Info page. Scroll to the bottom of the screen, and tap Text Message.

Figure 4–3. *The New Message screen is where you address, compose, and send your text and MMS messages.*

Start by tapping in the To field at the top of the message. You can use the keyboard to enter the phone number you want to text (for example, 5055551212), or you can enter a few letters of a contact name. Since messages are specifically tied to phone numbers, the iPhone lists each contact number separately (for example, Jane Doe home, Jane Doe work, Jane Doe mobile). If you haven't yet entered a name or number in the To field, a plus sign appears at the right edge. Tap it to view your contacts list.

After entering the To information, tap in the message field just above the keyboard. Enter the text you want to deliver, and tap Send. A progress indicator appears, tracking as your message gets sent. It may take a few seconds for the message to arrive.

If you want to send a photo or video, tap the camera icon to the left of the message field. Buttons appear allowing you to either shoot a new photo or video with your iPhone's camera or select existing media stored in your photo library on the iPhone. When you add a photo or video, the words *New Message* at the top of the iPhone screen change to *New MMS*. With a multimedia message, you can also type a short message to the recipient and then tap Send.

NOTE: You receive no confirmation when text or MMS messages are either delayed or received. When a recipient's phone is off, messages are stored for later. Messages arrive when the phone powers back on. This may take hours or days to happen, depending on your recipient's phone use habits.

Conversations

The iPhone organizes messages as conversations. All your messages back and forth with Jane Doe or John Appleseed, for example, get sorted into conversation threads. Each thread depends on the contact number used (Figure 4–4). Be aware that although this screen looks a lot like iChat on the Mac, it's not based on iChat at all. FaceTime, which we'll discuss shortly, *is* based on iChat, although it certainly doesn't look like it. iChat offers free peer-to-peer messaging. You pay for every message you send on your iPhone, whether you have a text message plan or not.

Figure 4–4. *The iPhone displays messages as conversation threads, with one thread shown per contact. The sender's side of the conversation is on the right, while the recipient's responses are on the left. This allows you to review past conversations with a given party on one screen at a time. Conversations with other contacts are on separate screens.*

Managing a Conversation

Conversation screens allow you to view each discussion separately. You might carry on one conversation with, for example, John Appleseed, and another with Beth Haystack. Figure 4–4 shows an ongoing conversation with Jane Doe; you can see her name at the top. The iPhone labels each screen with either the name (preferred) or the contact number (when the iPhone can't find a name). This depends on the available address book information.

Use conversation screens to carry on your discussions over time. As you send and receive your messages, the conversation grows. From any conversation screen, you can perform the following actions:

- *Reply to a message*: Enter message text into the field at the bottom of your screen, and tap Send to send it to your correspondent. You need not wait for the other person to reply to you before texting again. Feel free to send several messages in a row.

- *Clear out messages*: Tap Clear in the top-right corner to clear the screen when your conversation gets too long for comfortable viewing and scrolling. Use caution when clearing your history; once you've cleared messages, they're gone for good unless you've backed them up.

- *Call your correspondent*: Tap the Call button in the top-left corner to place a voice call back to your contact. This can be faster (and cheaper) than carrying on extended messaging conversations when you're both available at the same time. Your phone minutes and text messages are billed independently, so it may be cheaper to make a five-minute call than to pay for sending and receiving a series of text messages.

- *View contact information*: Tap Contact Info to view your contact's iPhone information screen. Return to the app by tapping the left-pointing arrow containing the contact's name that appears at the top of the screen.

- *Go back to the Messages screen*: The Messages button returns you to the main Messages screen. That's the screen that lists all ongoing conversations. Tap any contact name to pop back to the current conversation. Figure 4–2 shows the Messages screen with a number of ongoing conversations.

TIP: Want to keep all of those messages for posterity? The Mac applications described in Chapter 3, eCamm PhoneView and The Missing Sync for iPhone, both provide a way to download and save your iPhone messages.

Adding a Contact

You don't have to laboriously enter a phone number each time you start a new conversation. Contact numbers and contact names ease your texting life. Here's a quick review on adding a contact to your address book while on the go:

1. Press Home to return to the Home screen.

2. Tap the Contacts icon (hint: it looks like an address book), or tap the Contacts button at the bottom of the Phone application.

3. Tap the plus (+) button at the top right of the All Contacts screen.

4. Tap the First field, and add a first name.

5. Tap the Last field, and add a last name. Note that this is optional—you can just enter "Mom" for a name if you'd like.

6. Tap the Company field, and type a company name if you so desire. You can create a contact for a company this way.

7. Tap Mobile to add the contact's phone number. The default number type is mobile. To change this, tap Mobile, and select a new type (home, work, iPhone, other, and so on) from the displayed list. Selecting a type automatically returns you to the Edit Phone screen.

8. Note that there are many additional fields you can fill in—email address, home page, street address, and even an untitled field that can be used to add a nickname, a birthday, a job title, or a number of other pieces of valuable information.

9. Tap Done. The iPhone saves your new contact.

10. Tap Home to return to the home page, and tap Messages to return to the Messages app.

> **NOTE:** When you send messages, the person who receives your text or multimedia message must use a phone that can receive them. Most home landline phones are not equipped to receive text messages. Although the ability to send and receive SMS and MMS messages on cell phones is pretty universal these days, you might want to ask first. Since mobile phone customers in the United States pay for both incoming and outgoing texts, it is just courtesy to check in advance. Some people request that their provider disable messaging for various reasons—to avoid text spam, to put a rein on their teen's messaging addiction, or to limit their monthly costs.

Using the Messages Screen

The Messages screen (Figure 4–2) provides an overview of your message threads, allowing you to review and manage ongoing conversations. Those blue dots next to contact names indicate unread messages, and the total number of unread messages appears at the top of the screen in parentheses. Here are a few convenient ways to manage your messages:

■ Tap any name to open that contact's conversation thread. Tap Messages to return to the Text Messages screen.

■ Tap the Compose button to create new conversations. After sending the first message, a new thread appears in your Text Messages list. Tap it to view and track this new discussion thread.

■ The Edit button enters edit mode, allowing you to organize your conversations. After tapping Edit, you can tap the red delete dot next to each name. A red Delete button appears. Tap it to confirm deletion, or tap anywhere else on the screen to cancel and keep the selected message thread. Tap Done to leave Edit mode.

TIP: You don't actually have to enter Edit mode to delete conversations. Simply swipe your finger in either direction across any contact name to make the Delete button appear. Tap Delete to confirm or tap anywhere else to cancel.

Enabling and Disabling SMS Alerts

The Settings ➤ Sounds screen allows you to enable or disable New Text Message alerts. When disabled, you'll still be able to receive messages, but your iPhone will not buzz and ring at their arrival. This can prove to be convenient while carrying on a back-and-forth texting conversation (especially during meetings), keeping you safe from a thousand little annoying sounds.

Three Ways iPhone Messaging Is Better Than What's Available on Other Phones

When it comes to messaging, the iPhone offers several advantages over the rest of the field. First, there's the keyboard. The iPhone keyboard is far easier to use than any other cell phone keyboard. It makes it simple to type and edit messages.

For years, teenagers have been wearing their fingers to a nub texting each other. Texting on standard cell phones is hard work. Because of this, an entire language of texting shorthand has sprung up from "lol" (laughing out loud) to "pos" (parents are watching over my shoulder) to "kthxbai" (OK, thank you, good bye). The idea is to keep everything short and easy to type. Unfortunately, clarity is sacrificed to ease of typing. The iPhone brings simple typing back and allows you to properly say "thank you," instead of "ty" or "thx."

> **NOTE:** If you're new to texting and your text partner is used to cell phone keys, you might want to acquaint yourself with the keypress-saving SMS shorthand. Those abbreviations are more likely to come up with experienced texters. Search the Internet for *text message abbreviations* for assistance.

Second, the iPhone remembers conversations. You can easily see entire text conversations on a single screen. The iPhone organizes messages by sender, not by date or time. This means that messages from one person, even messages that are separated by hours or days, are grouped together into one easy-to-read presentation.

Third, the iPhone makes it easy to do all the stuff connected with messaging that *should* be connected with messaging, such as calling the person back directly or updating your calendar when someone mentions meeting you for dinner. Jump out of the text program (tap Home), pop over to your calendar, and then return exactly where you left off.

Instant Messaging on Your iPhone

Although there is no built-in IM app on the iPhone, third-party apps make connecting with iChat, AIM, MSN/Windows Live Messenger, Yahoo!, GoogleTalk, and other IM services a snap. Instant messaging is different from text or multimedia messaging in that the messages are sent and delivered in real time over the iPhone's data connection, not in a delayed fashion over the phone connection. This can also save you money by using your existing data plan or a Wi-Fi connection instead of requiring a message plan.

With SMS or MMS messages, the message is sent to another cell phone number over what is called the *control channel*. Your iPhone is constantly listening to this control channel, which tells it to ring when somebody calls you. When you send a message to another phone, it flows to a nearby cell tower and then to a special computer server called an SMSC. This server stores the message until it detects the receiving cell phone on the control channel, and then it sends the message to the recipient.

All the services that we'll talk about from here on out use a data connection that relies on the standard Internet Transmission Control Protocol/Internet Protocol (TCP/IP) protocols for sending and receiving data. With IM and IRC, you log into a server and can immediately see your buddies who are also logged in. There's the catch—if they're not logged into the server, you can't chat with them. On the other hand, when they're logged in and visible to you, any IM or IRC message is sent directly between the two of you without being stored and forwarded.

Although several apps provide IM capabilities, a favorite among bloggers at The Unofficial Apple Weblog (TUAW.com) is BeeJive IM with Push (www.beejive.com, $9.99). It connects to just about every IM system on the planet, works with chat rooms as well as individual person-to-person chats, and provides notifications of new chat messages when you're using another app. Your iPhone can even be asleep, and you'll still receive audible notification of incoming messages.

BeeJive IM (Figure 4–5) even lets you carry on multiple chat sessions at once. If you're in one chat and a message appears in another, a small icon appears at the top of the current chat telling you how many unread messages there are. Tapping that icon takes you right into the other chat.

Figure 4–5. *BeeJive IM can handle multiple chat sessions on different IM platforms at the same time. Push notification will alert you to incoming chat messages, even when you're not actively using the app.*

Another popular IM app for iPhone is Meebo (www.meebo.com/iphone/, Figure 4–6). It has one major advantage over BeeJive IM—it's free. It has a huge number of IM networks built in and requires a free Meebo account that can also be used from any web browser to log into an IM chat.

To use any instant messaging app, you'll need an IM account. Fortunately, most of the services are free or low cost. If you're a Mac user, you can use your Apple ID to log into iChat and then use the iChat account with other iChat and AIM users. AIM provides free accounts as well, simply by signing up at http://settings.aim.com. Click the Get a Screen Name link to activate an account in minutes. For Windows users, AIM and the popular Windows Live Messenger accounts are common IM clients. If you don't have a Windows Live account, they're available for free at http://login.live.com. Just click the "Sign up for an account" link, and you'll be chatting with friends in no time.

Figure 4–6. *The selection of IM chat networks available through the free Meebo iPhone app is staggering.*

IRC on iPhone

What AIM is to personal chats, IRC is to community chats. A technology that has been around since the late 1980s and still in wide use, Internet Relay Chat (IRC) allows users to connect to live community forums.

IM accounts usually require that the account be tied to a specific e-mail address for verification purposes. IRC has no such requirement, allowing users to be much more anonymous. Many informal forums, including many frequented by hackers, are available as "channels" on IRC servers.

Several IRC apps are available in the App Store that work on your iPhone. Colloquy (Figure 4–7; http://colloquy.mobi; $1.99) is a popular IRC app, as is LimeChat (http://limechat.net/iphone; $4.99). Two other apps with loyal followings are Rooms (www.roomsapp.mobi/blog/; $1.99) and Linkinus (linkinus.com; $2.99).

IRC may be an ancient (in Internet years) technology, but with apps such as Colloquy and LimeChat for the iPhone, it will live for many years to come.

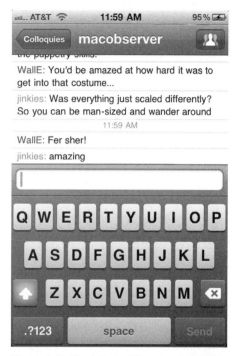

Figure 4–7. *The Colloquy iPhone app is a full-featured IRC client. It supports push notification of incoming messages, secure connections over SSL, and the ability to vibrate your phone when your nickname is mentioned.*

Facebook

At the time of publication of this book, there's probably no more widely used way of keeping in touch with friends, family, and companies than Facebook. With your iPhone and the free Facebook app (www.facebook.com/iphone), you can read updated news and comments from friends, "like" posts that have been made by others, and even post photos and create photo galleries.

If you are not currently a Facebook user, why not join? It's free, and there's no better way to find old friends and make new ones than to join this gigantic community. The iOS Facebook app (Figure 4–8; free from the App Store) provides access to most Facebook functions from your iPhone, including the ability to engage in IM chats with Facebook friends.

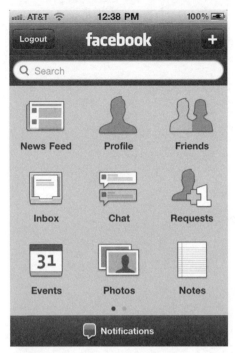

Figure 4–8. *The Facebook app places much of the functionality of the Facebook web site into a compact, iPhone-sized package. What better way to make use of your spare time than keeping up with your friends?*

Twitter

You can think of Twitter as telling the world what you're up to by sending out short bursts (tweets) of information. Most tweets are 140 characters of text or less but can also contain links to photos, video, and web pages. If you like something that someone else has sent, with a tap you can retweet it to friends and followers.

Like Facebook and many of the other messaging tools we've talked about, Twitter is entirely free. To sign up, visit `http://twitter.com`, and then consider one of the many Twitter apps that have made their way into the App Store. Let's talk about a couple of them:

- *Twitter*: This free app is, as the name suggests, the official Twitter app for iPhone. If you don't already have a Twitter account, sign up for one from the app itself.

- *Twittelator* : Twittelator (Figure 4–9) is the personal favorite of one of the authors of this book. With a built-in web browser for viewing links, easy ways to save or e-mail tweets, and a one-tap method of saving information to the popular Instapaper offline reading service (`instapaper.com`), Twittelator is an established and powerful Twitter client.

Figure 4–9. *Twittelator, from Stone Design Corp, is a full-featured Twitter client that surpasses many similar applications on traditional computers.*

- *Echofon/Echofon Pro for Twitter*: This is another nice and popular Twitter app; Echofon is fast and full-featured, and the Pro version of the app also notifies you instantly of direct messages or replies via push notification. That feature is useful if you and your best friends use Echofon Pro, because you can use Twitter instead of SMS messages.

- *Twitterriffic*: Twitterriffic works as a universal app, meaning that if you also have an iPad, you can install the same app on the bigger device at no extra cost. The app is powerful yet doesn't try to do everything. Instead, it's a streamlined and easy-to-use app.

Many more Twitter apps are available, so be sure to search for Twitter in the App Store on your iPhone or in iTunes.

Summary

The iPhone can do much more than just make phone calls. In this chapter, you've read about how you can use built-in and third-party applications to communicate with the world using a variety of messaging and social networking systems. Here are some important things to remember about sending messages and updating social networks from your iPhone:

- SMS and MMS messages are not free. On AT&T's network, you need to either purchase a message plan or pay per message. If you're concerned about costs and already have an iPhone data plan, you may want to consider one of the other messaging tools described in this chapter.

- The iPhone processes all SMS and MMS messages in the Messages app. Once a conversation has begun with a contact, it appears in a threaded format that displays both sides of the conversation.

- While you're using the Messages app, you can reply to a text or MMS message, call a correspondent, look at contact information, or even add a new contact.

- Instant messaging (IM) is useful for real-time text conversations with others. Most IM services are free, and using the proper apps, your iPhone can communicate over those services. While SMS and MMS messages use the phone system as a transport medium for communication, IM operates on the data network.

- Internet Relay Chat (IRC) is a collection of online community forums that has been around for many years. Popular with developers and hackers, IRC is now accessible from the iPhone.

- Social networks Facebook and Twitter are at home on the iPhone. Although only a handful of Facebook apps are available (and, in our opinion, the only useful app is the official one described earlier), you can choose from many Twitter apps. Facebook is fabulous for keeping in contact with many people and companies, while Twitter is tops for succinct messages to a group of peers.

Chapter **5**

iPhone E-mail

Unlike many other smartphones, your iPhone can send, receive, and browse e-mail without getting weighed down with compromise. The iPhone doesn't settle for cramped, odd presentations. Your e-mail looks the way it should—the way it would if you were reading it on your home computer. That's because the iPhone provides an HTML-compatible rich-text client. Mail looks better because the client is better. It's made to work right.

iPhone mail works with most industry-standard e-mail systems. With it, you can send and receive photos; view Excel spreadsheets, PDF files, and Word documents; manage your accounts; and more. This chapter introduces you to many features of the iPhone Mail application. You'll discover how to set up and use your iPhone with new and existing e-mail accounts. You'll learn how to manage your mail, how to compose new mail, and how to get the most out of the iPhone's e-mail settings. If you have questions about using mail with your iPhone, this chapter is for you.

Compatibility

iPhone Mail is surprisingly compatible. It works with virtually all major e-mail providers, including Gmail, AOL, Yahoo!, and Comcast. For businesses, iPhone plays relatively well with Microsoft Exchange. This high level of provider support is because of the iPhone's support of industry-standard protocols. The iPhone understands the most popular e-mail standards, namely, POP, IMAP, SMTP, and Exchange. If you're not already familiar with these standards, here's a brief overview.

POP

POP (aka POP3) stands for Post Office Protocol. It's probably the most common e-mail retrieval protocol in use today. It allows mail clients to connect to a server such as Gmail or AOL, retrieve messages, and disconnect afterward. This usually happens on a set schedule, such as every ten minutes or every hour; you do not receive mail until your client connects to the server and requests that new mail.

POP works by checking in with a server, downloading your e-mail, and optionally leaving the original copies of your e-mail on the server. This leave-on-server option works well with the iPhone, because when you're on the go, you probably want to check your mail on the iPhone and retrieve it again later when you get back to the office or return home. POP also has its downsides. Unlike the newer and improved IMAP protocol, POP downloads entire messages all at once, so it's a bit of a space hog on portable devices.

> **NOTE:** The 3 in POP3 indicates the third version of the protocol standard; POP1 and POP2 are obsolete.

SMTP

Mail clients use one protocol for receiving mail and another for sending mail. Your iPhone uses Simple Mail Transfer Protocol (SMTP) to send outgoing messages. SMTP contacts a mail server and transmits messages you've written along with any attachments including text, photos, and so forth. A common kind of SMTP, called SMTP-AUTH (AUTH stands for authorization), allows you to send secure, authorized mail. You provide your account name and a password. Your mail client authenticates itself to the server, and your e-mail is sent on its way.

The iPhone makes sending authenticated e-mail easy. Enter your account name and password into the Mail settings pane. Once you've done this, just use outgoing mail to send a note, share a web page's URL, or pass along a photo that you've just snapped with the iPhone's built-in camera. The iPhone takes care of all the protocol issues. You decide what to send and to whom to send it.

IMAP

IMAP stands for Internet Message Access Protocol. Like POP3, it allows you to receive e-mail on the iPhone. It's a newer and more flexible protocol. As the name suggests, IMAP was built around the Internet. It introduces advanced ways to connect to the mail server and use the limited bandwidth of mobile connections in the most efficient way. The key to understanding IMAP is to recognize that messages are meant to live on the server rather than go through a retrieve-and-delete cycle. You manage your mail on the IMAP server. You read your mail on a client, like the iPhone.

When you download mail with POP, you download entire messages. When you download mail with IMAP, you download headers instead, at least initially. Headers are the bit that tells you who the mail is from and what it's about. You don't download the main body of the message until you explicitly request it from the server. Since the header occupies only a fraction of the space of the message, you can download IMAP data a lot faster than you download POP. The rest of the message stays on the server until you're ready to read it.

The same thing goes for attachments. Say that someone sends you a 10MB video. It doesn't get downloaded to your iPhone. It stays on the server until you're ready to watch it on your home computer. If you'd downloaded the message with POP, the entire video would have transferred with the message. With IMAP, you can read the message that came along with the video without having to download the video file itself until you're ready to watch it. The video attachment waits for you on the mail server.

IMAP also offers a feature that's called *push e-mail*. Geeks will tell you that *technically speaking* IMAP is not exactly the same thing as push e-mail. True push e-mail reaches out and tells your e-mail client whenever new mail arrives in the system. Instead, your iPhone IMAP client connects to and gently tickles the server until new mail arrives. This kind of always-on connection allows the iPhone to receive mail almost as soon as it arrives on the server. In practice, there's better intention there with push-style mail than actual results. Yahoo! and Gmail offer free IMAP accounts for iPhone users. To sign up for an account, point your browser to http://mail.yahoo.com or http://gmail.com.

Microsoft Exchange

Microsoft Exchange provides e-mail along with other enterprise-level services intended to support Outlook on the Web, personal computers, and mobile devices. Past versions of the iPhone did not support Exchange without, well, jumping through hoops. Exchange Server administrators had to open all sorts of security holes to get it to work, and they usually weren't too happy about doing that. Fortunately, iOS 4 provides much better compatibility with Microsoft Exchange, to the point that you can now configure multiple Exchange ActiveSync accounts on your iPhone for business use.

Exchange is more than just e-mail, though—it's also about sharing calendars and contacts. Since iOS 4, iPhones can receive push e-mail from an Exchange Server, access a company-wide global address list, accept or create calendar invitations, and even search e-mails that are stored on the server.

If you're using your iPhone in a corporate setting that uses Microsoft Exchange Server, it's best to work with your IT department to ensure that your device is connected to the server in the most secure way possible. If they're not familiar with how the iPhone works with Exchange, Apple has provided a white paper on Exchange deployment that is free to download: http://images.apple.com/iphone/business/docs/iPhone_EAS.pdf.

Adding Mail Accounts to iPhone

You can add accounts to your iPhone in two ways. First, you can synchronize with iTunes. The first time you connect your iPhone to your computer and sync, iTunes searches your computer for mail accounts and adds them to your phone. Second, you can add accounts directly on your iPhone using Mail settings. It takes a few more steps than using iTunes, but it's not at all complicated. Here are both ways to do this.

Adding Accounts with iTunes

iTunes takes most of the work out of setting up your iPhone with your existing mail accounts. It looks at programs on your computer like Outlook and Apple Mail, finds account information, and offers to synchronize those account settings with your iPhone (see Figure 5–1). This makes it really easy to get your iPhone up to speed. A single sync puts these account details on your iPhone, and you're pretty much ready to roll.

To select which accounts to add, launch iTunes, and connect your iPhone. Select your iPhone from the source list—that's the column at the left of the iTunes window; your iPhone appears under the Devices heading. The iTunes screen updates and displays a summary of your iPhone, including its name, its phone number, the software version, and so forth. Locate the tabs at the top of this window, and select the Info tab. Scroll down the Info pane to Mail Accounts.

The Mail Accounts settings area allows you to choose whether to synchronize your Mail accounts to your iPhone. Ensure the "Sync selected Mail accounts" check box is checked, and pick the accounts you want to use.

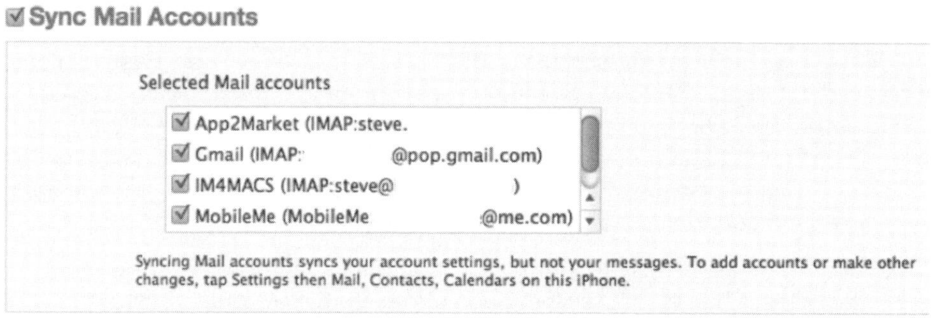

☑ **Sync Mail Accounts**

Selected Mail accounts

☑ App2Market (IMAP:steve.
☑ Gmail (IMAP: @pop.gmail.com)
☑ IM4MACS (IMAP:steve@   )
☑ MobileMe (MobileMe   @me.com)

Syncing Mail accounts syncs your account settings, but not your messages. To add accounts or make other changes, tap Settings then Mail, Contacts, Calendars on this iPhone.

Figure 5–1. *The Mail accounts settings appear on the Info tab in iTunes. Select your iPhone device, click Info, and scroll down to find the Mail Accounts settings.*

Next, scroll down further on the Info tab, below Mail Accounts and Web Browser, to the Advanced settings area (see Figure 5–2). As a rule, your iPhone won't add new accounts until you force things. Unlike normal syncs that just update data, when you select to replace your mail accounts on your iPhone, iTunes updates your iPhone with all the accounts you just selected in the Mail Accounts settings.

Replacing mail accounts isn't something you do all the time. You'll want to do this account replacement with new iPhones that you want to initialize, when you've moved your iPhone's home to a new computer, and after you've restored your iPhone's firmware to factory settings. If you just want to add a new e-mail account, add it directly on your iPhone rather than using iTunes. It's easier.

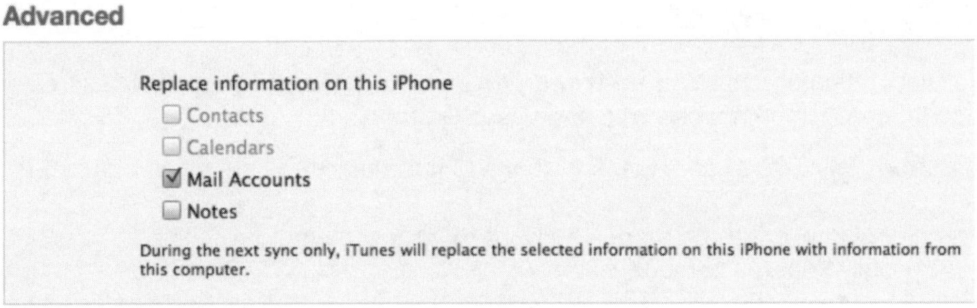

Advanced

Replace information on this iPhone

☐ Contacts
☐ Calendars
☑ Mail Accounts
☐ Notes

During the next sync only, iTunes will replace the selected information on this iPhone with information from this computer.

Figure 5–2. *Use Advanced settings to replace mail accounts during the next sync. You can also choose to update Contacts, Calendars, and Notes from this settings pane.*

Adding Accounts from Your Phone

It takes just a few steps to add a new account to your iPhone. It's especially easy when you use one of the preferred providers: a Microsoft Exchange Server, MobileMe, Gmail, Yahoo!, or AOL. Here are the steps to take, whether you're using a preferred provider or another provider that does not appear on the list:

1. From the Home screen, tap Settings, and navigate to **Settings ➤ Mail**.

2. Tap Add Account.

3. Select the kind of account you will use *or* tap Other if your provider is not listed (see Figure 5–3).

Figure 5–3. *When you use a preferred provider, the e-mail setup process is vastly simplified to entering a few items of information. Tap Other to set up e-mail with another provider.*

E-mail Provider Setup

Setting up account information for preferred providers is very easy. Your iPhone already knows how to contact the mail servers and which protocols they use.

1. Preferred providers require just four items of information, as shown in Figure 5–4.

    a. For Name, enter the name you want to appear in your From line, usually your full personal name.

    b. For Address, enter your full e-mail address (for example, yourname@yahoo.com).

    c. In the Password field, enter your password. Make sure to type carefully and slowly, and look at the key confirmations as you type. You will *not* be able to see the password itself as you type it. Try not to make mistakes.

    d. Finish by entering an account description. Your iPhone uses the text you type into the Description line as a label in the Accounts list, so enter something meaningful, such as "Work Yahoo! Account" or "Home AOL."

2. Tap Save, and wait as the iPhone verifies your account information. You automatically return to the Mail settings, and you are done setting up your account.

3. What if your e-mail provider isn't on the list? For example, we use Comcast Internet service, which provides e-mail accounts to customers. To add an e-mail provider that isn't listed on the main e-mail screen in Figure 5–3, tap the Other button. You'll be asked to enter the same information as in step 4, and when you're done, tap Save, and the iPhone verifies your account information.

4. If the iPhone's automated setup doesn't work for you, you have several options:

    a. If the account is set up correctly on your Mac or Windows computer, use the method described earlier in "Adding Accounts with iTunes" to sync the settings to your iPhone.

    b. Still no luck? Tap the recalcitrant e-mail account in the list of accounts in **Settings ➤ Mail**, Contacts, Calendars. On the screen that appears, tap Account Info. A display similar to Figure 5–4 appears:

Figure 5–4. *The Account Info screen is available for tweaking incoming or outgoing mail server settings and changing server port numbers.*

    c. On this screen, you can change the name of the incoming and outgoing mail servers. You may need to contact your e-mail provider for the details of your account. Some important settings to know are the host (server) name, your full username (sometimes it's the full e-mail address instead of just the first part of the e-mail address), whether or not SSL is enabled, the type of authentication used by the server, and the server port number.

> **TIP:** Setting up an Exchange account can be difficult, because no two Exchange Server configurations seem to be the same. We recommend contacting your IT department or mail service provider for specific instructions on the exact settings you should use to set up your Exchange account.

Removing Accounts from iPhone

To remove an e-mail account from your iPhone, go to **Settings ➤ Mail, Contacts, Calendars**, and tap one of the items in your Accounts list. Scroll all the way down to the bottom of the account screen, and tap the red Delete Account button. To be safe, the iPhone prompts you to confirm account deletion. Tap Delete Account one more time to remove the account, or tap Cancel to leave the account alone.

At times, you may want to disable an account without removing it from your iPhone. To do this, go to Settings ➤ Mail, Contacts, Calendars ➤ the name of the account. Locate the Mail switch at the top of the screen. Set this from on to off to disable the account or from off to on to reenable it.

E-mail Checks and Other Basic Settings

You're ready to start using Mail, but there are just a few more steps you'll want to take first. Navigate to Settings ➤ Mail, Contacts, Calendars, and scroll down to the Mail section (see Figure 5–5). Here, you'll find preferences that control the way your iPhone checks for and displays mail. You'll find that Mail works far more smoothly and predictably when you customize these settings *before* using your new accounts.

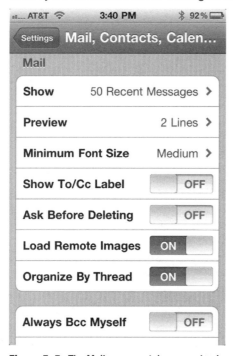

Figure 5–5. *The Mail pane contains many basic settings you'll want to configure before using your mail accounts.*

Here is a rundown of the settings you'll want to look over:

- *Show*: How many messages should the iPhone download and display at once? Choose from 25, 50, 75, 100, and 200 recent messages. Choosing fewer messages speeds downloads of messages from your server and saves space on your device, but if you get a lot of e-mail, you may want to see them all in one fell swoop.

- *Preview*: Your inbox, which you can see in Figure 5–9, displays information about each message. It shows who sent the message, the time it was sent, the message subject, and a brief preview of the message itself. In addition to all this information, you choose how many lines to show. Choices are None (no message preview), 1, 2, 3, 4, and 5 lines. The example in Figure 5–9 shows two lines per message. The more lines you choose to see of each message, the bigger the preview you get; however, fewer messages can fit on each screen.

- *Minimum Font Size*: If your eyes have issues with small print, the default font size on the iPhone might be difficult to read. The iPhone lets you choose a minimum font size, so you can make sure text displays no smaller than what you can read. Choose from Small, Medium, Large, Extra Large, and Giant. I use Large.

- *Show To/Cc Label*: By default, your iPhone does not show the To and Cc lines from e-mail. The iPhone normally hides them to save screen space. If you want to override this behavior for your mail, switch this option from off to on.

TIP: You can view the To and Cc lines even if you haven't enabled this option. Tap Details in the From line of the e-mail to reveal the extra information. Tap Hide to hide them again.

- *Ask Before Deleting*: You might think that asking for confirmation before allowing the iPhone to delete a message is a great idea. When working your way through 100 messages in your inbox, this idea quickly becomes less attractive. The iPhone allows you to delete e-mail without confirmation by default. If you want to add an extra layer of protection, switch this option on.

- *Load Remote Images*: Many e-mail messages contain images. These images are not actually sent with the e-mail; instead, the image is actually a link to an image file on a server. Enabling Load Remote Images ensures that the images are downloaded from the server and displayed within the body of the e-mail message when you open it. The trade-off is speed; loading images can slow down the receipt of e-mail.

- *Organize by Thread*: Do you ever get into e-mail conversations, with many e-mails flying back and forth? If so, enabling Organize by Thread can make some sense of your inbox. When it is enabled, e-mail conversations are signified by a number on the right side of the message indicating how many e-mails are in the thread (Figure 5–6, left). Tapping the number and arrow displays the messages in the thread (Figure 5–6, right).

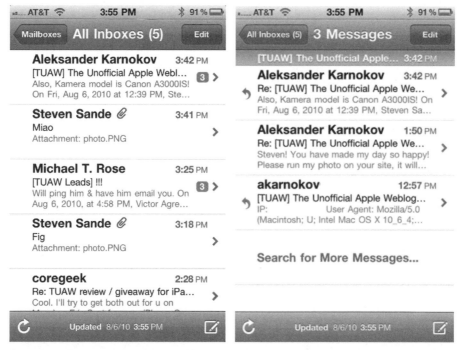

Figure 5–6: *Organize by Thread makes it easy to follow e-mail conversations by aggregating all similar e-mails into one easy-to-read thread.*

- *Always Bcc Myself*: Some mail services put a copy of sent e-mails into a Sent Mail folder. Others do not. Enable this option to send a blind carbon copy to yourself when writing letters. The "blind" part of carbon copy means that you won't be visibly added to the recipient list. When correspondents "reply to all," you won't (necessarily) receive multiple copies of those e-mails.

- *Signature*: By default, iPhones add the words *Sent from my iPhone* to all outgoing messages. To remove this tag, erase the text in the signature. You can also customize this message or replace it entirely. Perhaps you might add contact information or a favorite quote. To do this, tap the current signature. A keyboard appears and allows you to edit the text. After making your edits, tap Mail to return to the **Settings ▶ Mail, Contacts, Calendars** screen.

- *Default Account*: Choose the default account you want to use for sending mail. This applies only to non-Mail iPhone applications such as Safari or Photos. When you pass along a bookmark or a picture you've snapped, this option sets the account used to send that message.

Audible Mail Alerts

This final pair of settings appear in Settings ➤ Sounds, not Settings ä Mail, Contacts, Calendars.

- *New Mail*: Choose whether you want to hear an audible alert (YES) or not (NO) when your iPhone receives new mail. If you've enabled Settings ➤ Sounds ➤ Ring ➤ Vibrate, your iPhone vibrates when it plays the new mail sound.

- *Sent Mail*: When enabled, this option plays a whoosh sound that indicates your e-mail has been successfully sent on its way to the server. It's a good idea to leave this option enabled. Sometimes, it takes time for mail to get going. You won't be able to send a new message until the first one has fully gone. By listening for the whoosh, you know when you're ready to send the next message.

Getting Started with iPhone Mail

The iPhone Mail application is located on the Home screen on the bottom line, just to the right of the Phone application (see Figure 5–7). The icon is blue with clouds and a white envelope. Tap this icon to open the Mail application. As with the Phone and SMS applications, a red bubble appears to indicate the number of unread messages in all of your e-mail accounts.

Figure 5–7. *A red bubble superimposed on the Mail icon indicates the count of unread messages across all your e-mail accounts.*

When you enter Mail for the first time (and after reboots), you're greeted by the Mailboxes screen. This screen lists every inbox on your iPhone, as well as every account you've added to your iPhone. Each inbox and account displays the number of unread messages. Tap an inbox name to open any of the individual inboxes, or tap the account names to view individual folders within an account. Return by tapping the Accounts back button at the top-left corner of that screen.

Inboxes

Each e-mail account has a number of mailboxes; Inbox, Outbox, Drafts, Sent Mail, Trash, and Junk are some of the common mailboxes you'll find. In iOS 4, Apple began segregating the Mailboxes screen into a Inboxes list and an Accounts list. Most of the time, you're going to be working in the inboxes, reading and responding to mail, so they're listed on the Mailboxes screen first (Figure 5–8).

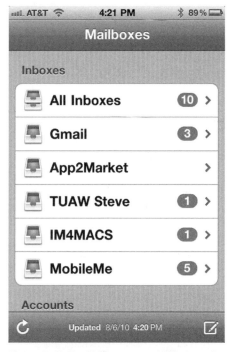

Figure 5–8. *The Mailboxes screen displays all e-mail inboxes first, followed by the accounts. All Inboxes is a global inbox that accumulates all incoming e-mail for all accounts. Numbers indicate how many unread messages are in each inbox. The Accounts section lists all the other mailboxes (including Drafts, Trash, and Sent Mail, among others), for each account.*

If you're looking for one place to read all your new e-mail, All Inboxes is that place. It is a global inbox for all of your accounts, containing all recent read and unread e-mail in a chronological order. To see only the e-mail that has come into a particular inbox, tap the inbox with the name of that account. The numbers that are listed on the right side of the inboxes indicate how many unread messages are contained in each inbox.

Accounts

Below the Inboxes list is a list of accounts. Each account may include some or many of the following standard mailboxes:

- *Inbox*: All new messages load into your inbox. You have an inbox for each account.

- *Drafts*: Messages that are written but not yet sent get saved to Drafts.

- *Sent*: If your mail account saves copies of outgoing mail, they're placed in a Sent folder.

- *Trash*: The iPhone stores deleted mail in Trash folders. Use **Settings ➤ Mail ➤ Account Name ➤ Advanced** to decide if and when to remove deleted messages from Trash mailboxes.

- *Other folders*: Additional folders such as Gmail's Starred folder are a feature of the mail provider and not of iPhone. At this time, you *cannot* add new folders to an e-mail account from your phone.

Using Mailboxes

When viewing an account's mailboxes, you can open a mailbox and view the messages stored inside by tapping the mailbox name. This links you to a new screen (see Figure 5–9) that displays the list of messages stored in that mailbox. From here, you can choose messages to display and manage your mailbox. Here are the actions you can take from this screen:

- *View a Message*: Tap an e-mail to open it for viewing.

- *Refresh Mail*: Tap the icon at the bottom left of the screen. It looks like a semicircular arrow. When tapped, your iPhone contacts your mail provider and requests new mail.

- *Compose new messages*: Tap the icon on the bottom right (a square with a pencil through it) to start writing a new message.

- *Edit messages*: Tap Edit to enter Edit mode. In Edit mode, you can tap the red circle next to any message to delete it. Confirm by tapping Delete, or tap anywhere else to cancel. Tap Done to leave Edit mode.

> **TIP:** Edit mode is actually pretty useless, because you don't need Edit mode to delete mail. Just swipe your finger through any message to instantly bring up the Delete button, or when displaying a message, tap the garbage pail at the bottom of the screen. Some people have trouble mastering the swipe at first—they open their messages instead of deleting them. Keep trying and persist. The swipe becomes second nature after a while.

- *Return to the mailbox list*: Tap the Back button at the top left of the screen to return from this mailbox to your account screen. The button name varies, but it's always shaped like a pentagon on its side, with the pointy bit facing left.

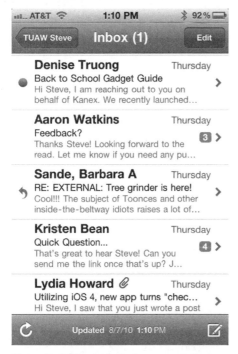

Figure 5–9. *The dot indicates an unread message on this inbox listing screen. Each message shows the recipient, the subject, and the date or time the message was sent. You control how many lines of text are shown for each message in* Settings ➤ Mail ➤ Messages ➤ Preview.

Reading and Navigating Through Mail

If you're used to reading e-mail on older portable devices, the iPhone's mail-viewing capabilities comes as a welcome relief. Instead of arbitrary word wrapping, missing attachments and odd formatting, mail on the iPhone just looks...right. This being the iPhone, you can scroll up and down your e-mail—flicking if needed to move more quickly—and zoom in and out using all the standard pinching and tapping tricks described in Chapter 2.

And, as with Safari, it's not watered-down, text-only e-mail. It is fully functional e-mail that behaves the way it should. Sure, there are some missing features; you can't add attachments at will, for example, and you can't play back video files sent to you by mail without saving them to your Photo library first, but iPhone mail viewing performs to a much higher standard than most other gadgets. Unfortunately, as Figure 5–10 shows, the mail-viewing screen is littered with a proliferation of buttons and unlabeled icons. Here's a quick-and-dirty guide to your screen.

Figure 5–10. *The message display screen offers many unlabeled icons for your mail management pleasure.*

Bottom Icons

The icons at the bottom of the message display screen, from left to right, are as follows:

- *Refresh*: The Refresh button appears at the bottom left of the screen and looks like a semicircular arrow. Tap this to request new mail from your provider.

- *File This Message*: The folder with a small down arrow allows you to move messages from one mailbox to another. When tapped, the iPhone prompts you to "Move this message to a new mailbox." Select the mailbox you want to transfer to, and the iPhone rewards you with one of its most adorable animations. The message flies from one mailbox to the other. If you'd rather not transfer the message, tap Cancel instead.

- *Trash Can*: Tap the small trash can in the bottom center to delete the currently displayed message. The trash lid flips up; your animated message moves down into the can. It's visually delightful. Your message moves from the Inbox mailbox (or whatever mailbox you're displaying) to the Trash mailbox.

TIP: To undelete, navigate to Trash (Back, Back, Trash), select the deleted message, and file it back to the original mailbox.

■ *Reply/Forward*: The Reply/Forward icon appears just to the right of the trash can icon. It looks like a backward-pointing arrow. Tap this, and a menu appears. Tap Reply to reply to the currently displayed message, or tap Forward to pass it along to a new recipient.

■ *Compose*: This rightmost icon looks like a square with a pencil on it. Tap this to compose a new message.

Top Icons

The icons at the top of the message display screen, from left to right, are as follows:

■ *Back button*: Tap the Back button in the top-left corner to return from the message display to the Mailboxes screen. The button looks like a pentagon on its side, pointing left. The text inside the button varies according to the name of the mailbox.

■ *Message number display*: This isn't, strictly speaking, an icon. The iPhone displays the number of the current message at the top of the screen (for example, 1 of 50).

■ *Next Message/Previous Message*: These two buttons appear at the top right of the screen. Tap the up triangle to move to the previous message in the current mailbox, and tap the down triangle to move to the next.

■ *Details/Hide*: This button appears just below the Next Message arrow. Tap Display to reveal your message's To and Cc lines. Tap Hide to hide them again. Details also reveals a Mark as Unread button, which does exactly what the name implies. It restores the blue dot to the message and updates the unread message count.

Embedded Links

iPhone Mail supports embedded links that you can tap from within a message. These allow you to automatically open web links in Safari or do a number of other tasks using information from message text:

■ *Embedded Web Address*: When someone sends you an embedded web address (also known as an URL), you can tap it to open it in Safari. Better yet, tap and hold that address for a second or two. A dialog box appears allowing you to either open the web page in Safari or copy it for pasting elsewhere.

- *Phone Numbers*: Mail is smart enough to recognize when someone has included phone numbers in a message. It underlines the number and displays it in blue—just like a normal web address link. To place a call, just tap the number. Tap and hold the phone number, and four buttons appear (Figure 5–11).

Figure 5–11. *Tap and hold a phone number in an e-mail message, and you can call that number, send a text message to it, create a new contact from the information, or add the phone number to an existing contact.*

- *Addresses*: If someone sends you a street address in an e-mail message, Mail can do a number of useful things. Tapping the address opens the Maps app to a map of the address, while a tap and hold displays the four buttons shown in Figure 5–12.

Figure 5–12. *Tap and hold an address in an e-mail, and you can open the address in the Maps app, create a new contact card, add the address to an existing contact, or copy the address for pasting elsewhere.*

- *Events*: One of the coolest things you can do with embedded links in e-mails is to automatically create events for your iPhone Calendar. The iPhone recognizes terms like "next Thursday at 7:30 PM" and displays them as links. A tap on that link displays a Create Event button to add the event to your calendar. It even gets the date and time from the e-mail and prefills that information in the Calendar app (Figure 5–13).

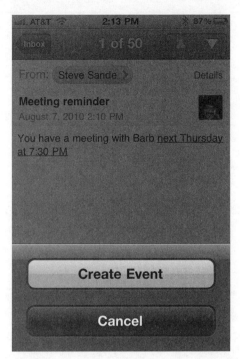

Figure 5–13. *Mail on the iPhone makes it a snap to add appointments to your calendar with a few taps.*

TRIVIA: The iPhone's ability to understand and act upon words like "next Thursday" is nothing new for Apple. The Apple Newton MessagePad (1993–1998) also understood similar phrases and would create calendar events from them. This feature is now also available in Mac OS X.

Viewing Attachments

iPhones support many e-mail attachment file formats including Word files (.doc, .docx), Excel spreadsheets (.xls, .xlsx), PowerPoint presentations, (.ppt, .pptx), Pages documents (.pages), Keynote presentations (.key), Numbers spreadsheets (.numbers), many image file formats (.jpg, .png, .gif), some video formats (.mov), and PDF documents. When a message arrives with a large attachment, the iPhone shows you that the attachment is available (see Figure 5–14) and lets you choose whether to download it. If you choose to do so, tap the attachment, and wait for it to load in a new screen. After, tap Message to return to the message from the attachment viewer.

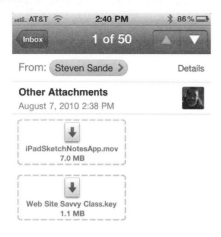

Figure 5–14. *Documents over about 1MB in size are not immediately downloaded to your iPhone. Instead, a download button appears. Tapping the button downloads the file and makes it available for viewing on your iPhone.*

Smaller documents are downloaded to Mail immediately, and they appear with buttons to tap for viewing (Figure 5–15).

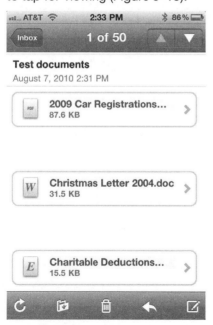

Figure 5–15. *Smaller documents attached to e-mails appear as buttons. Tap the buttons to view the documents.*

Attachments can be viewed in Mail, but if you want to edit the documents that have been sent to you, a compatible app must be installed on your iPhone. Fortunately, these apps register themselves to your iPhone, and if a compatible app is available for a certain document type, an Open In... button appears in the document viewer. Tapping the Open In... button displays buttons for any apps that can edit the document, and tapping one of those buttons launches a compatible app and opens the document for editing (Figure 5–16).

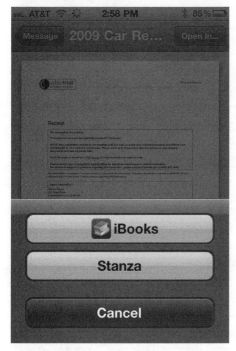

Figure 5–16. *Tapping the Open In... button displays a list of any applications that can open the document for viewing or editing. In this example, a PDF document is readable in Mail but can also be opened in the iBooks or Stanza e-book reader apps.*

Sending Mail

The iPhone offers many ways to send mail. Unfortunately, consistency is not a strong point here. You'd imagine Apple would have designed a single universally recognized compose e-mail button and placed it more or less in the same place for each application. You'd be wrong. Here's a quick rundown of the most popular ways to ask your iPhone to create a new message across several programs:

- *Compose button*: The Compose button, which looks like a square with a pencil through it, appears at the bottom right of many Mail screens (see Figure 5–10) and in the Messages application at the top right of the screen. In the Mail application, it creates a new letter. In Messages, it creates a new SMS text or MMS multimedia message.

■ *Reply/Forward button*: The Reply/Forward button appears just to the left of the Compose icon in open e-mail messages. Tap this to reply to a message or forward it on to another party.

■ *Envelope icon*: In the Notes application, an envelope icon appears on the bottom of the page, to the left of the trash can. Tap it to e-mail the current note.

■ *Share icon*: The Share icon appears at the bottom left of the screen in Photos and many other apps. It looks like a rectangle with an arrow jumping out of it—the arrow is basically a mirror of the Reply/Forward button. To send a picture, tap this, and then select Email Photo from the pop-up menu. As mentioned earlier, there isn't a consistent look for the icon, so in some apps, it may appear as an envelope.

Each of these (various, assorted, and inconsistent) methods requests Mail to open a new message, ready to be addressed, personalized, and sent.

Addressing E-mail

When you reach the New Message screen shown in Figure 5–17, you're ready to address your message. Start by tapping either the To or Cc/Bcc line on the New Message screen. The iPhone opens a keyboard so you can enter text. As you type, the iPhone searches its contacts list to match what you're typing to the contacts in its list. Tap in a few letters until you see the name of the contact you want to use. Tap that contact, and the iPhone automatically adds it to the field (To, Cc, Bcc) you selected.

You do not have to use an address from your contacts list. You can type in the full e-mail address (the iPhone helpfully provides you with the @ sign on the main keyboard for e-mail) and address your e-mail by hand. Also, it remembers the e-mail addresses you use. So, the second time you type *alex@nowhere.nomail.org*, the proper address pops up by the time you type *a* and *l*. As with normal contacts names, just tap an e-mail address to add it to your recipient list.

To remove a recipient from the message, select one of the blue recipient bubbles— they're labeled with a name or e-mail address—and tap Backspace.

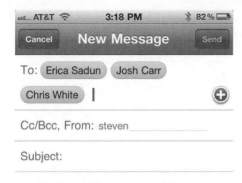

Figure 5–17. *The New Message screen allows you to address and personalize your e-mail.*

Entering a Subject

Tap the Subject line to move the cursor to that field. Use the keyboard to enter a meaningful subject for your message.

Editing the Message

Tap in the message area to begin editing your message. A blinking cursor indicates this where the keyboard will enter text. Use the typing skills covered in Chapter 2 to type your message. Remember to use the spyglass trick to move the cursor if you need to back up and make corrections.

> **TIP:** To remove an attached photo or other file from e-mail, position the cursor right after the picture, and tap Backspace.

Saving a Draft

At any time, you can take a break from editing a message and return to it later. To do this, tap Cancel. It's at the top left of the message-entry screen. A pop-up menu appears. Tap Save Draft to save the message for later, Delete Draft to abandon the message, or Cancel to return to the editing screen. When you choose Save Draft, the iPhone creates a copy of your message in the Drafts (or sometimes Sent) mailbox for your default account. Return to that mailbox when it's convenient to continue editing the message and/or to send it.

Sending E-mail

When you are done addressing and composing your letter, you can send it on its way by tapping Send. If you haven't disabled the feature, the iPhone alerts you with a whoosh sound to indicate that the message has been sent successfully to the outgoing mail server. You don't need to remain in the Mail app, because your message delivery will take place whether your phone is asleep or you are in another app. As soon as you've finished tapping Send, you can move on to another task.

Summary

iPhone's Mail program removes many burdens associated with checking and responding to e-mail on a portable device. It provides a fully capable e-mail client that displays messages the way your senders intended you to view them. With its powerful attachment handling, the iPhone brings you one step closer to the ideal of bringing along your work or home computer in your pocket. Here are a few key points from this chapter that you might want to think about:

- Make sure to use your full iPhone interaction vocabulary of touches, pinches, and so forth, to get the most out of viewing attachments.

- It's really easy to add preexisting mail accounts using iTunes and add new ones using iPhone settings.

- Many corporations use Microsoft Exchange Server for mail and other groupware tasks. Be sure to ask your IT department for access to your work e-mail system if you so desire.

- If you see an underlined blue link in an e-mail, be sure to take advantage of Mail's abilities to understand the information contained in the link. This makes it easy to add new contacts or update existing contact information with a tap.

- Remember that there are many different icons and buttons used to denote how to send messages. Become familiar with these buttons in your favorite apps, because it makes it much easier to share information with the world.

Chapter 6

Syncing Your iPhone with iTunes

Your iPhone is a media machine at heart. Whether you like watching movies or TV shows, listening to music, or checking in on your favorite podcasts, the iPhone is able to supply you with plenty of media in a pocket-sized box. Music and video content starts with iTunes. It doesn't matter whether you bought your songs and video at the iTunes Store or you imported them into the program from CDs and DVDs. iTunes can synchronize your iPhone to any content in its library. iTunes determines which music and video files transfer to your iPhone.

iTunes is also the place to organize your apps, change settings for accessibility, see what books and audiobooks are on your iPhone, and transfer documents from your computer to certain apps on your iPhone.

In this chapter, you'll discover how to bring all your content together in iTunes and transfer that information to your iPhone. You'll see how to choose which items you want to synchronize and how to keep your iPhone content fresh and up-to-date.

Managing Your iPhone in iTunes

Locate your iPhone in the Devices section of the sources list. This light blue column, shown in Figure 6–1, appears on the left side of the iTunes screen. Your iPhone is listed, along with any other devices you have connected, including other iPhones and iPods. Select your iPhone to open the iPhone Summary tab in the main iTunes screen.

Figure 6–1. *Your iPhone appears in the Devices section of the iTunes sources list.*

The Summary Tab

The iPhone Summary tab, shown in Figure 6–2, appears each time you connect your iPhone to iTunes. This tab provides your top-level iPhone summary. It tells you important information about your iPhone and offers some basic options.

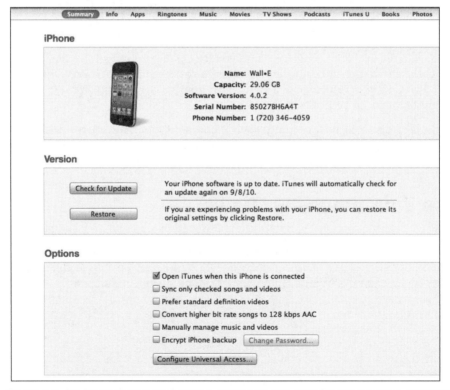

Figure 6–2. *The iPhone Summary tab offers a device overview, including serial number, current software version, and capacity.*

Here is a rundown of the items you'll find on the screen, what they do, and why they are important:

- *Name*: Your iPhone's name appears at the top of the Summary screen. It refers to whatever name you have given your iPhone. To rename it, click the iPhone in the sources list. This opens a text edit field around the name. Edit the name as desired, and then press Return or Enter to confirm your change.

- *Capacity*: This number indicates the actual data capacity of your iPhone. As with all data storage, the advertised capacity (32GB in this case) never quite matches the actual capacity (29.06GB).

NOTE: The difference between the actual data capacity and advertised capacity is because the advertised capacity uses base 10; Apple and other manufacturers talk about a gigabyte as 1,000,000,000 bytes. In computer terms, this decimal number is worthless. Computers use base 2. To a computer, a gigabyte is 1,073,741,824 bytes, so the advertised 32,000,000,000 bytes get cut down to about 29.8 computer-sized gigabytes. Add in some overhead for the operating system, and boom, you're down to those 29.1GB that your iTunes screen mentions for your 32GB iPhone. All sorts of useless lawsuits have been filed over this issue throughout the years, and this is still the way things are done in the mass-storage industry.

- *Software Version*: Unlike most cell phones, the iPhone regularly updates its software with bug fixes and improvements. iTunes indicates which firmware release is currently installed on your iPhone. To check whether your firmware is the latest available, click the Check for Update button.

- *Serial Number*: This unique serial number identifies your iPhone to Apple.

NOTE: The serial number shown on the Summary tab in iTunes should not be confused with your International Mobile Equipment Identity (IMEI) cell phone identifier or your Integrated Circuit Card ID (ICCID) SIM number. All three identifiers are printed on your original iPhone box.

- *Phone Number*: This is the phone number assigned to your iPhone and is retrieved from the SIM card inserted in your phone (see Chapter 1). When you change your SIM, you change the phone number.

Restoring Your iPhone

You may experience problems with your iPhone at some point and need to restore your unit to its factory-fresh settings. To do this, click the Restore button, and follow the prompts. The restore process wipes all information from your iPhone and reloads the most recent firmware. After restoring, you can use your backup data to reload your personal information and media to your iPhone. It may be advantageous to simply reload your personal information and apps through the sync process rather than doing a complete restore. Your iPhone loses the location of apps and folders, your scores and progress in games, and other similar data, but that's really about it.

The iPhone automatically backs up your data whenever you connect to iTunes. The backups are incremental; only changed items are copied. This saves space on your personal computer and makes the backup process more efficient. Backups are tagged with a date, and that date is shown both in iTunes and on the backup files. To check on the date and time of your most recent backup, open the iTunes preferences window (select **Edit ➤ Preferences** in Windows or **iTunes ➤ Preferences** on the Mac), and select the Devices tab.

> **TIP:** If you're on a Macintosh, you can find your backup files in your home folder in `Library/Application Support/MobileSync/Backup`. There's really not much you can do with those files without using iTunes or another external app.

Choosing Options

A number of options appear at the bottom of the Summary tab:

- *Open iTunes when this iPhone is connected*: Select this check box to have iTunes automatically launch when you connect your iPhone to your Windows or Mac computer. Disabling this option means you want to manually synchronize the iPhone. This allows your iPhone to connect to your computer more quickly, but you may forget to perform your backups on a regular basis.

- *Sync only checked songs and videos*: This option itemizes the features you want to sync. Instead of performing an exhaustive sync with each connection, this option limits synchronization to those items you have selected on the various tabs described in the next section. Despite what the name implies, you can sync podcasts, photos, and so forth, as well as songs and videos.

- *Prefer standard definition videos*: There are standard-definition and high-definition videos available for purchase in the iTunes Store. High-definition videos look great on the iPhone (particularly on the Retina Display of the iPhone 4), but they consume a lot more of your available storage. Select this box to make the smaller standard-definition versions of videos your preference.

- *Convert higher bit rate songs to 128 kbps AAC*: If you have a lot of music in your iTunes library, selecting this box can save a tremendous amount of storage space both on your computer and on your iPhone. What this setting does is take much larger music files and downconvert them to the very space-efficient 128 kbps AAC format. One caveat—it takes quite a while for a large music library to be converted, so make sure that you don't need your iPhone for a while if you choose this option.

- *Manually manage music and videos*: If you'd prefer to have total control over what media is transferred from your computer to your iPhone, select this box. To transfer music, movies, or TV shows, you can now drag songs, videos, and playlists to your iPhone.

- *Encrypt iPhone backup*: Although the files that make up your iPhone backup are rather cryptic anyway, you can choose to encrypt them to make them secure from most hacking attempts. If you carry sensitive information on your iPhone, it's a good idea to encrypt any backups that are made of the iPhone data. When you enable backup encryption, you'll be asked to enter a password to protect your iPhone backup file.

- *Configure Universal Access…*: The Apple iPhone is probably the most accessible smartphone on the market, providing features that can assist the sight and hearing impaired. Clicking this button provides a way for a person to set up the phone with the universal access assistance. In Figure 6–3, the iPhone functions for hearing and sight assistance are listed. VoiceOver reads all text that is on an iPhone screen, including buttons and other prompts. Zoom magnifies the entire screen, requiring a three-finger drag gesture to move around the screen. The white-on-black display provides extremely good contrast, which is important for many sight-impaired individuals. Speak Auto-text causes the VoiceOver function to automatically speak autocorrections and autocapitalizations.

  For the hearing-impaired, there are check boxes to use monaural audio instead of stereo and to show closed captions on videos when available.

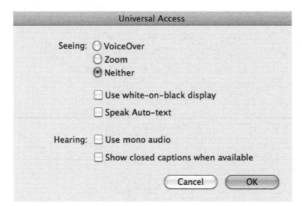

Figure 6–3: *Click the Configure Universal Access button to view this setup window.*

After selecting your iTunes options, click Apply to save your new settings.

> **TIP:** Sometimes it can be annoying to have your iPhone automatically sync every time you connect it to a computer. To turn off that feature, visit **iTunes ➤ Preferences (Edit ➤ Preferences** in Windows), click the Devices tab, and then check the box labeled "Prevent iPods, iPhones, and iPads from syncing automatically."

Ping and the iPhone

As this book was going to press, Apple introduced a new social networking tool to iTunes. Ping, as it is called, is designed for "music discovery." The idea is that by knowing what your friends are listening to, you'll learn more about different music and will be more willing to expand your potential music purchases. By enabling Ping in iTunes 10 or later, you also enable Ping on your iPhone. You'll need to have Ping up and running on your default iTunes account before you'll see it show up on the iPhone.

The Ping button appears in the center of the button bar at the bottom of the iTunes app on the iPhone. Tapping that button brings up a page with three tabs at the top: Activity, People, and My Profile. Activity lets you respond to Follow Requests, see who your friends are following, "like" an activity that a friend has performed, and add comments on those activities.

The People tab is broken into two lists: People I Follow and People Who Follow Me. Within these lists you can find out more about a person by tapping on their name or picture, and also see what albums, artists, or tracks they like. The final tab is all about you. The My Profile tab lists information about your activities and also lets you check on the information that is listed in your personal profile. To change the personal profile, you'll need to use the desktop version of iTunes.

Ping is just in its infancy at the time of printing, but should prove to be a huge and popular success for Apple.

Synchronization Choices

iTunes provides several tabs that allow you to select the items you want to sync with your iPhone. Most of the items are discussed in individual sections that follow:

- *Info*: The Info tab offers controls for synchronizing contacts, calendars, and mail accounts, as well as bookmarks and notes. These options are described further in Chapter 3 (contacts), Chapter 5 (mail), Chapter 9 (bookmarks), and Chapter 11 (calendars). The Info tab is longer than it first appears. Scroll down to find the Advanced settings.

- *Apps*: Select which apps you want to sync to your iPhone and how you want to organize them on the device.

- *Ringtones*: Select which custom ringtones you want to sync to your iPhone.

- *Music*: Use this tab to choose the playlists and music videos you want to sync.

- *Movies*: Use this tab to select the movies you want to sync.

- *TV Shows*: Whether you want to view individual episodes or an entire series, this tab provides a way to manage TV shows.

- *Podcasts:* Use these options to sync podcast episodes to your iPhone.

- *iTunes U:* Did you know that iTunes provides a way to learn about just about anything? iTunes U consists of videos and podcasts that contain educational content from a number of sources. Use this tab to set up synchronization of iTunes U collections and items.

- *Books:* The iBooks app on the iPhone turns your device into a very capable ebook reader. Use this tab to determine what books in your iBooks library are loaded onto your iPhone.

- *Photos*: This tab controls which photos and albums get synchronized to your iPhone. These options are described further in Chapter 8

After making changes to any of these items, click Apply to save your new settings. In most cases, your iPhone and computer will synchronize again.

The iPhone Capacity Meter

How much data is on your iPhone? With only a few gigabytes onboard, managing data is essential. The capacity meter at the bottom of your iTunes screen provides an important tool for keeping on top of this information. It creates a disk-usage thermometer, indicating how much space you've used, as shown in Figure 6–4. It's color-coded: blue is audio, purple is video, yellow means pictures, green designates apps, magenta shows books, and orange indicates other data (bookmarks, contacts, and so forth). The white portion is the remaining free space.

Figure 6–4. *The iPhone capacity meter indicates the space used by your iPhone.*

If you would prefer to see this information in terms of item numbers, click the bar. The meter updates to show you the number of songs, videos, and photos loaded on your iPhone. Click again to view the number of hours and minutes used by your audio and video. Click one last time to view the original size information.

The Apps Tab

The iPhone can become almost anything you want it to be, provided that you have installed an app to perform that function. The Apps tab (Figure 6–5) is where you select which apps to sync to your iPhone, and you can also use the tab to organize your Home screens.

Figure 6–5. *The Apps tab lists all your apps on the left side and displays them on the right side as they'll be viewed on the iPhone.*

To sync apps, make sure that the Sync Apps box has been selected. There's also a check box to automatically sync new apps. This is useful if you purchase apps on either your iPhone or your computer. If you've purchased them on your iPhone, it allows you to back the apps up on the computer and if you've purchased the apps on your computer, it installs them on your iPhone.

Perhaps you don't want to sync a certain app. To take it off of your list of installed apps on your iPhone, deselect the box next to its name in the apps list. If you want to delete the app from both your iPhone and your computer, go to Library in the sources list on the left side of iTunes, look for Apps, and click it. You'll see a full listing of all apps. To delete an app, right-click (or control-click) it, and select Delete from the pop-up menu.

The right side of the Apps tab for your iPhone is quite important, because it provides a quick and easy way to organize your apps into a convenient and logical layout on the Home screens of your device. As shown in Figure 6–5, your Home screens are displayed in full size as well as in small thumbnail images. Here are a few organizational tips:

- *Install apps*: You can install an app on a particular Home screen by dragging it from the list of apps on the left to the appropriate screen on the right and then dropping it where you want it to reside on your iPhone.

- *Create folders*: The iTunes Apps tab is a good place to organize your apps into folders. To create a new folder, simply drag and drop one app onto another app. When you do this, a folder is created (Figure 6–6).

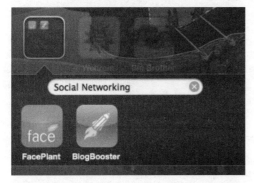

Figure 6–6. *A new folder is created by dragging and dropping one app onto another. You can put up to 12 apps in each folder, you can have up to 16 folders per Home screen and up to 10 Home screens.*

The folder gets a default name based on a common category for the apps (if one exists). To rename the folder, tap the Delete button (with the *x* in it) to clear the automatically generated name and type in the new name. Click anywhere on the pseudo-Home screen to save the folder name.

- *Move apps and folders*: While you're organizing your apps, why not consider moving more frequently used apps to your first Home screen? You can move apps and folders around by dragging them in the Apps tab Home screen or between any of the Home screen thumbnail images.

- *Use Command-Click to group apps*: Command+clicking an application icon adds it to (or if already added, removes it from) the currently selected group. You can move groups all at once between pages.

- *Use empty pages*: If you have the pages to spare, use the empty pages that iTunes makes available to you to help organize applications by "theme." For example, you can drag an empty page into, say, the page 2 position and then start filling that page with games from the other pages. Adding apps to that empty page causes another empty page to appear at the end of the list if there is room. You're limited to 11 pages total for your applications.

- *Use the Dock*: Your Dock provides a home for up to four applications that you use the most. Docked applications appear on every page, offering the quickest access to your most-used apps. Don't feel limited to the apps that the iPhone OS defaults to. It's your Dock. Use it the way that best suits you.

- *Use the Home screen*: If you have more than four apps that you need quick access to, don't forget that the first screen of apps is always just a Home button click away. Tapping the Home button when viewing apps automatically jumps you to the first page. Place your high-priority apps on this first page if they fall short of the urgency of the Dock items.

To apply all the changes you've made to your iPhone, sync by clicking the Apply button.

The Ringtones Tab

The Ringtones tab (Figure 6–7) provides a way to take control of the ringtones you have loaded onto your iPhone. As noted in Chapter 3, iTunes allows you to purchase and edit a music track for use as a ringtone. The ringtone must be purchased in addition to a track, so your minimum cost is actually about twice that of a single track.

- Use the check box to choose whether to synchronize ringtones.

- Choose "All ringtones" to sync every ringtone in your library.

- Choose "Selected ringtones" to pick individual ringtones you want to synchronize.

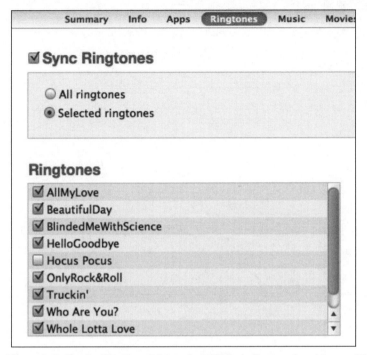

Figure 6–7. *Use the Ringtones tab to select which ringtones get sent to your iPhone.*

The Music Tab

The Music tab, shown in Figure 6–8, lets you select which items to sync to your iPhone's music library:

- Choose whether to synchronize your entire music library (select "All songs and playlists") or only selected playlists, artists, and genres. In the latter case, select only those playlists, artists, or music genres you want to sync.

- Decide whether you want to synchronize your music videos by selecting or deselecting the "Include music videos" option. As with any video data, music videos occupy a lot more iPhone space than audio tracks. Keep in mind that iTunes does not allow you to select which music videos to sync—it's all or nothing.

- If you use the Voice Memos app on your iPhone to record reminders or meeting notes, you can choose to synchronize those voice memos with your computer. Once the voice memos are on your computer, they can be synced to other iPhones and devices as well. Enable this capability by checking the "Include voice memos" box.

- Not sure what songs you want to copy from your computer to your iPhone? Let iTunes make the decision. Selecting the "Automatically fill free space with songs" box will fill up as much free space as you have on your iPhone with music.

Figure 6–8. *Use the Music tab to select which playlists get synchronized to your iPhone.*

TIP: iTunes also allows you to transfer purchased media from your iPhone into iTunes. Right-click or Control+click the iPhone in the sources list, and choose Transfer Purchases from the pop-up menu. To play these songs back, your computer must be added to your list of authorized machines. To make this happen, sign into your iTunes account (**Store ➤ Sign in**), and then authorize your computer (**Store ➤ Authorize Computer**).

The Movies Tab

Your iPhone can be your own personal movie theater, which is useful when you're stuck in an airport or trying to keep your kids busy. Load up the iPhone when you're at home or in the office with a fast Internet connection, and you'll always have entertainment at your fingertips. Movies are available from the iTunes Store in either high or standard definition, and you can either purchase them outright or rent them.

Once you've loaded them onto your computer, syncing movies to your iPhone is very straightforward. The Movies tab (Figure 6–9) should look familiar by now; it has a check box at the top for enabling the synchronization of movies, and you can choose to automatically sync all movies, the most recent movies, or only unwatched movies.

If you want to sync only certain movies to your iPhone, deselect the "Automatically include … movies" box, and then select those movies that you want to copy.

At the bottom of the Movies tab is a list of playlists that include movies. By default, iTunes creates a Recently Played playlist; other playlists may appear if you create them (for example, you might create a Clint Eastwood Spaghetti Westerns playlist).

As with all the other tabs, click Sync to apply your changes and synchronize movies with your iPhone.

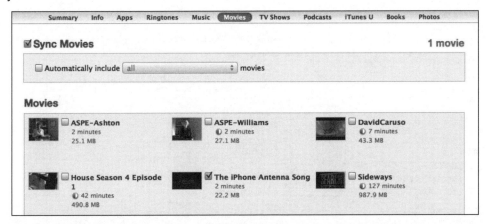

Figure 6–9. *The Movies tab is where purchased, rented, self-produced, or ripped movies are listed and selected for synchronization with your iPhone.*

> **TIP** If you own a collection of movie DVDs, you can prepare them for viewing on your iPhone by "ripping" them—that is, moving the movie to your computer in a compatible format. HandBrake (`http://handbrake.fr`) is an excellent open source application for converting your DVDs to an iPhone-compatible format.

The TV Shows Tab

Movies aren't the only visual entertainment you can watch on your iPhone. The iTunes Store also sells TV shows. Individual episodes are sometimes available shortly after a new show airs for the first time, or you can purchase a Season Pass to watch all current and future episodes of a series. It's a nice way of keeping up with your favorite shows when you want to watch them, not when the networks are scheduling them. We know people who have given up their cable or satellite service and get all of their shows through the iTunes Store and other online sources.

The TV Shows tab (Figure 6–10) is your conduit for moving TV shows that you've purchased from the iTunes Store onto your iPhone. Select the Sync TV Shows box to enable syncing, and then pick shows and episodes from the panes in the center of the tab. You can also choose to automatically include newest or unwatched episodes of all or just selected shows.

As with movies, if there are any TV shows that are part of a playlist, you can choose to include episodes in those playlists. To copy your selected shows from your computer to the iPhone, click the Sync button.

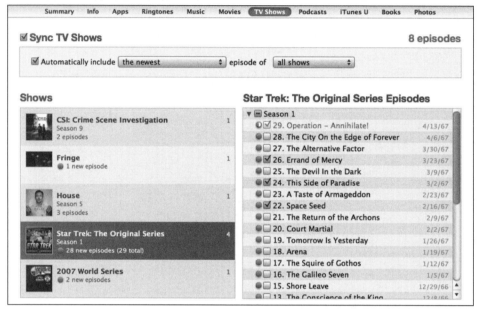

Figure 6–10. *The TV Shows tab is the place to set up syncing of individual show episodes or complete seasons of a TV series.*

The Podcasts Tab

Many people use iTunes to subscribe to their favorite podcasts. *Podcasts* are audio or video programs delivered over the Internet, much as TV shows are delivered over the airwaves or cable. Numerous podcasts are available these days, including entertainment, tech tips, advice, how-to shows, and much more. iTunes monitors your podcast subscriptions and automatically downloads new shows when they become available. Use the Podcasts tab to control which shows get synchronized to your iPhone.

- Select Sync Podcasts to include podcasts on your iPhone.

- To automatically include new, recent, or unplayed episodes of your podcast subscriptions, select the box just below Sync Podcasts. Use the pop-up menus to select how many recent, unplayed, or new episodes to copy to your iPhone.

- Want to include only certain episodes from your list of podcasts? Click the podcast title on the left side of the Podcast tab, and a list of episodes appears on the right side (Figure 6–11). Podcast episodes that have not been heard are denoted with a small blue dot. Select the box next to the episodes you want to listen to.

- As with all of the tabs, when you've changed the settings, click the Sync button to apply the changes and copy the new content to your iPhone.

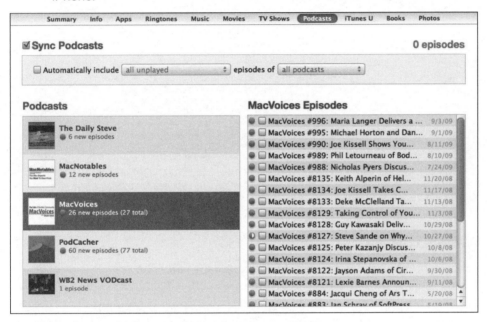

Figure 6–11. *iTunes lets you choose which podcasts you want to sync.*

The iTunes U Tab

Learning is no longer tied to a single spot like a university or library. iTunes U provides educational content from some of the world's top institutions of higher learning. If you've been yearning to learn more about nano-to-macro transport processes at M.I.T., there's no need to uproot yourself and move to Cambridge, Massachusetts. Instead, you can watch a series of lectures on the subject on your iPhone.

We recommend that you browse the iTunes U offerings in iTunes. There's not always a prominent link to iTunes U on the iTunes Store home page, but you can always find one at the bottom of that page.

Once you've decided which lectures or videos you'd like to watch on your iPhone and have downloaded the content to your computer, visit the iTunes U tab (Figure 6–12) to determine what items to copy to your iPhone.

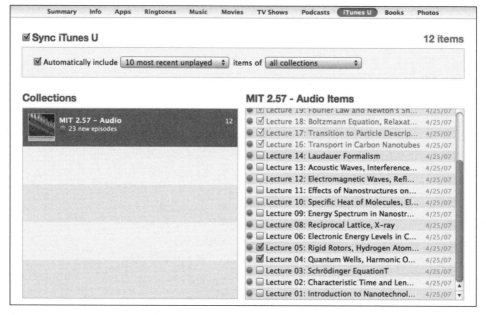

Figure 6–12. *The iTunes U tab is the entrance to your virtual university. Lectures are available in a variety of subjects in both audio and video formats, all free to the public.*

The Books Tab

In 2010, Apple introduced the world to the iBookstore, a virtual bookstore where you can purchase bestselling and classic books to be read on either an iPhone or an iPad.

The iBooks app, available for the iPhone, is probably the best way for iPhone owners to browse, purchase, and install electronic books. In keeping with the theme of organizing and syncing content with iTunes, Apple added a Books tab (Figure 6–13) to the iTunes application. The tab shows all books that have been purchased and installed on an iPhone.

Figure 6–13. *The Books tab is used to sync ebooks purchased on your iPhone in the iBooks app back to your computer for backup.*

As with the other tabs available in iTunes, the Books tab can be enabled to sync books between your computer and iPhone by selecting the box at the top of the page—in this case, Sync Books. You can choose to sync all books between your device and computer—ebooks are surprisingly small in size—or just selected tomes in your library. If you choose to select which titles will be synced, just check them in the list of books displayed on the tab.

The Books tab is also where you can choose to sync audiobooks. Unlike books, audiobooks can be purchased on your computer in the iTunes Store and then synced to your iPhone via iTunes. To enable syncing of audiobooks, make sure that the Sync Audiobooks box near the bottom of the Books tab is selected. There are radio buttons to specify syncing of all audiobooks or just your selections.

> **TIP:** How do you get current documents, formatted as EPUB or PDF files, into the iBooks app? Connect your iPhone to your Windows computer or Mac, and launch iTunes. Drag the book files to the Books icon in your iTunes library (you can edit the name and author(s) of the books if you don't like the way they are displayed). Click your iPhone in the Devices list in iTunes, and then click the Books tab. Make sure that the book title box and Sync Books are both selected, and then click the Sync button. The next time you open iBooks, you should be able to read the books. If you want to try converting other ebook file types to EPUB, try either the Calibre ebook management tool (`http://calibre-ebook.com`) or the 2EPUB online file converter (`http://2epub.com`).

Manually Synchronizing Your iPhone

Tap the Sync button at the bottom right of the iTunes screen to initiate a new sync with your iPhone at any time. On a Mac, you can also Control+click or right-click your iPhone in the sources list and choose Sync from the pop-up menu.

Creating Smart Playlists

iTunes offers a powerful feature called the Smart Playlist, which allows you to use rules to select content for your iPhone. When dealing with a device with limited storage space like the iPhone, Smart Playlists can make your life easier.

After highlighting a content source in your library or the store in the sources list of iTunes, choose File ➤ New Smart Playlist to create your Smart Playlist. A Smart Playlist dialog box opens, allowing you to define the rules for the playlist. Figure 6–14 shows a Smart Playlist that selects up to 25 songs that have not been played in the last 30 days. Creating this Smart Playlist ensures that you'll listen to new music every time you launch the iPod app on your iPhone.

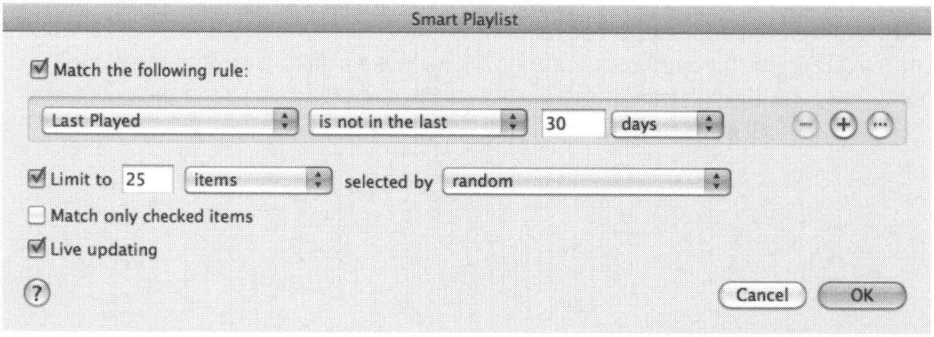

Figure 6–14. *Smart Playlists use rules to create playlists. This playlist selects up to 25 that haven't been played in the last 30 days.*

Once you've created Smart Playlists, you can select them for syncing to your iPhone. Do an online search for Smart Playlist ideas to discover more ways to create Smart Playlists for your iPhone.

Creating iPhone-Friendly Content

When items you've chosen fail to synchronize properly, it may be because they are incompatible with your iPhone. iTunes offers a built-in feature that converts audio and video files to iPod-friendly (and hence iPhone-friendly) formats. Click any audio or video item in iTunes, and select **Advanced ➤ Create iPod or iPhone Version**, as shown in Figure 6–15. Be aware of the following:

- You can import only QuickTime-readable media into iTunes. If QuickTime cannot read a file, neither can iTunes. The reverse is not true. Just because you can play back something in QuickTime does not mean it will necessarily work in iTunes. iTunes is limited in its ability to import and convert media.

- You can expand your "QuickTime vocabulary" to use a wider variety of video formats. To do this, download and install *codecs*, which encode and decode digital data. Macintosh users should download Perian from `http://perian.org`. It installs codecs for most major formats, including Xvid, Flash Video, and so forth. If you're using Windows, you must search for, find, and install individual QuickTime codecs on a format-by-format basis.

- You cannot convert protected audio or video. By *protected*, we mean media that uses digital rights management (DRM) encryption. Items purchased from iTunes are already in an iPhone/iPod-friendly format, even those using DRM.

- To load video from your DVDs onto your iPhone, download a copy of HandBrake from `http://handbrake.fr` (for Windows, Mac, and Linux), and convert your DVD content to an iPod/iPhone-friendly format.

Figure 6–15. *Use the iTunes built-in format converter, found under the Advanced menu, to convert movies and audio tracks to an iPhone-friendly format.*

Ejecting Your iPhone

Before disconnecting your iPhone from your computer, tap the Eject button next to the iPhone name. It looks like a tiny triangle sitting atop a rectangle. Alternatively, right-click (Control+click) the iPhone name, and choose Eject from the pop-up menu.

Summary

This chapter introduced the basics of iTunes media management. It's important to recognize the role of iTunes in organizing and selecting the media you want to synchronize to your iPhone. By putting your library in order on your personal computer, you ensure that the media you want and need arrive properly on the iPhone. Here are a few tips to take away from this chapter:

- Ambrosia Software's iToner2 software is another way that you can create custom ringtones for your iPhone.

- If you want to sync audiobooks, be sure to add them to a playlist first.

- Fans of life-long learning have access to a huge variety of educational content in Apple's iTunes U.

- You don't need a TV to watch many popular TV series. Instead, you can purchase a Season Pass and download the new episodes to your iPhone as soon as they've been aired.

- Video files are *big*. Pick only the ones you want to watch right away. You just can't fit an entire library of video on the iPhone the way you can store video on an 80GB or 160GB iPod Classic.

- Smart Playlists offer the best way to keep your on-phone library fresh and exciting. Take the time to learn how to set up your own so you don't get tired of your iPhone music.

Chapter **7**

It's Also an iPod

Your iPhone can do a thousand different things, given the right apps. One of the roles that it performs very well is that of media player, and given the family lineage of the iPhone, that's not surprising. The iPhone does this through the iPod app, which provides it with the ability to play music, show videos, function as an audiobook and podcast player, and even act as a portal to iTunes University. This chapter introduces you to the iPhone-as-iPod and shows you how to get the most use out of it.

iPod as Application

The iPod in your iPhone is not a device—it's an application. It brings all the functionality and ease of use you expect from an iPod, but it delivers that functionality in a distinctive iPhone package.

Figure 7–1 shows the iPod application icon. By default, it's on the bottom right of your iPhone screen. It's easy to spot, since it's colored bright orange. Tapping this icon launches the iPod application on your iPhone.

Figure 7–1. *The familiar profile of the original iPod graces the iPod app icon on the iPhone (at right).*

In Figure 7–1, the iPod app has been grouped with several other music apps in a Music folder. If your current iPod experience is with an "old" classic model, an iPod shuffle, or an iPod nano, expect to be pleasantly surprised. If you're new to the world of iPods, expect to be blown away. The iPhone iPod app uses the best possible iPod interface, one that is also used on its phone-less siblings, the iPod touch and iPad. The touch interface simplifies browsing, locating, and playing music and videos, and it will most likely find its way to many future Apple devices. For users of older iPod models, here are just a few ways the iPhone will change your iPod experience:

- *Touch screen*: With the iPhone's touch screen, there's no need for scroll wheels. Flick through your lists, and tap the items you want to play.

- *Cover Flow*: If you like Cover Flow in iTunes, you'll love it on the iPhone.

- *Alphabetical index tool*: The iPod application uses the same kind of alphabetical index you saw in Chapter 2 (see Figure 2-1). It makes searching through long alphabetized lists a breeze.

- *Customizable button bar*: Do you prefer to search by genre and album, rather than artist or song? Just drag the items you use the most onto the configurable button bar.

- *Widescreen video playback*: There's no need to settle for cramped video on the iPhone. Flip your iPhone to its side and view your videos using a wider, side-to-side landscape orientation.

And that's just a taste of the ways the iPhone changes the way you use your iPod. Read on for more details on how this program works.

Browsing Media on the iPhone

To launch the iPod app, tap the orange iPod icon. This application gives you access to all the media files you have synchronized to your iPod, both audio and video. Locate the More button at the bottom right of the screen, and tap it to load the screen shown in Figure 7–2.

NOTE: Do not confuse the iPod and iTunes applications on your iPhone. iPod is used to play back your music tracks and videos, while iTunes is an app for browsing and purchasing digital content such as music, videos, movies, and TV shows. Although you can listen to short samples of music in the iTunes app, it's not designed to be a general music player.

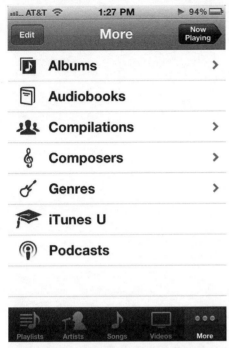

Figure 7–2. *The More screen provides an excellent jumping-off point for exploring your media. When you're playing a track, the Now Playing button appears in all category screens, including this one, and instantly takes you to the track currently playing.*

The More screen offers the best place to start exploring your media collection. From here, you can see every kind of category used to sort your songs and videos: Playlists, Artists, Songs, Videos, Albums, Audiobooks, Compilations, Composers, Genres, iTunes U, and Podcasts. Some of these appear in the black bar at the bottom of the screen. Some appear in the list in the center of the screen. Tap any item to open that collection. For example, tap Artists to see a list of your media sorted by artists, or tap Audiobooks to view the audiobooks loaded on your system.

The black bar is your shortcuts bar, also known as your browse buttons bar. The difference between the items in the black bar and the items in the list above it is that these shortcuts appear universally in every category view. Your iPhone lets you select which items you want to keep handy in that bar, as described next.

Editing Your Browse Buttons

From the More screen, tap the Edit button to open the Configure screen, as shown in Figure 7–3. This screen allows you to customize your browse buttons bar.

Figure 7–3. *Use the Configure screen to choose which items appear in your browse buttons bar at the bottom of the screen.*

To replace any item on the browse buttons bar, drag an icon from the center of the screen onto the item you want to replace in the bar at the bottom. Say you listen to podcasts and audiobooks more than you watch videos. Drag those two icons onto your bar, and you'll see them in every category view. Add whichever icons you use the most. You can also rearrange the icons in the bar by dragging them left or right within the bar.

The bar must always contain four—and only four—icons. You cannot drag icons off the bar, and you cannot set the bar to contain fewer than those four icons. You cannot add more than four shortcuts, and you cannot replace the More button with another item.

Here are the items you can choose from:

- *Songs*: Every song on your iPhone.

- *Video*: Every video on your iPhone.

- *Audiobooks*: Every audiobook on your iPhone.

- *Albums*: Every album on your iPhone.

- *Playlists*: A list of all the playlists that you've chosen to sync to your iPhone.

- *Artists*: A list of your media sorted by the artist who recorded them. This list includes many kinds of media: songs, podcasts, music videos, and so on. You might be surprised to see "artists" like Dora the Explorer listed next to The Beatles and Green Day.

- *Compilations*: A list of all media belonging to compilations—that is, albums that have been contributed to by various artists.

- *Genres*: A list of every genre—such as Classical, Rock, Pop, Country, and so on—that appears on your iPhone. Each genre leads to a list of media that belongs to that genre.

- *Composers*: A list of media sorted by their composers. Your iPhone might contain listings for George Harrison, Wolfgang Amadeus Mozart, and more.

- *iTunes U*: A list of all iTunes U content that you have downloaded from iTunes to your iPhone.

- *Podcasts*: A list of podcasts that you have chosen to sync to your iPhone.

When you are finished making changes, tap Done to return to the More screen.

Navigating the Category Screens

Each category screen works much the same way. It lists its members—whether podcasts, videos, artists, or songs—as an alphabetically sorted scrolling list. If the list is long, you'll see an alphabet control on the right side of the screen, as in Figure 7–4. Tap a letter or scroll your finger down the alphabet to move to the section you want to view.

> **TIP:** A category screen may offer a Shuffle option as the first item. Tap it to start playing back that category in random order.

When the items listed are individual songs or videos, tap any name to play your selection. When the items listed are collections, like genres or albums, tap to open a screen that displays each item of that collection. For example, you can tap an album to list its tracks and then tap a track name to play it.

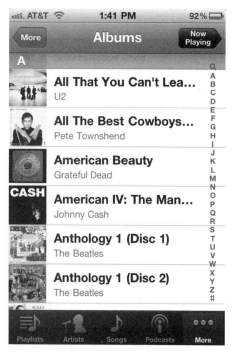

Figure 7–4. *The Albums screen lists albums in alphabetical order. When you've downloaded album art, it appears in the squares to the left of the album name. To save space on your iPhone, you can delete album art.*

> **TIP:** Tap Now Playing to jump to the currently playing item. The Now Playing button is visible only when a song is being played.

Playing Audio

Figure 7–5 shows the iPhone's Now Playing screen. You arrive at this screen whenever you start playing a song. You can also jump to this screen from any category by tapping the Now Playing button at the top-right corner (see Figure 7–4).

Figure 7-5. *The iPhone's Now Playing audio playback screen*

Here are the items you'll find on the Now Playing screen and what they do:

- *Play indicator*: The right-pointing play indicator at the top right of the screen (just left of the battery status) appears universally when you're playing back music. This tells you at a glance that music is playing, even when you have headphones plugged in. You'll find this especially helpful when you've removed your earbuds and placed the iPhone on a table. It alerts you that your iPhone is gleefully playing music that no one is hearing. Fortunately, the iPhone doesn't use much power when it's playing music, so this shouldn't affect your battery unless you leave it playing overnight.

- *Back button*: Tap the Back button at the top-left corner (the arrow pointing left) to return to the most recent album or playlist screen. Tapping Back does not stop playback. Your song continues to play as you browse through your categories or press Home to do other things on your iPhone.

- *Artist, song, and album*: These items appear at the top middle of the screen and are for information only. Tapping them does nothing.

- *Album View button*: This button looks like a three-item bulleted list and appears at the top right of the screen, just below the battery indicator. Tap this to switch between your Now Playing screen and its Album view (discussed in the next section).

- *Album art*: When you've downloaded album art, the cover image appears just below the top bar and occupies most of your screen. (When the iPhone cannot find album art, it displays a light gray music note on a white background instead.)

  - Tap the art area to open the gray playback controls that appear just below the black header in Figure 7–5.

  - Tap again to hide the controls.

  - A double-tap on the album art sends you to the Album view.

  - Swipe to the right to return to the most recent category screen.

- *Loop control*: This control, which looks like a pair of arrows pointing to each other in a circle, appears when you tap album art.

  - Tap once to loop the currently playing album or playlist, and the loop turns from white to blue to indicate that looping is enabled. After the last song plays, the first song starts again.

  - Tap a second time to loop just the current song. The number 1 appears on the loop, telling you that the loop applies to just this song.

  - Tap once more to disable looping. The loop returns to its initial white color.

- *Scrubber bar:* The scrubber bar appears to the right of the loop control. Tap the album cover to make this control appear; tap again to hide it.

  - The number at the left of the bar shows the elapsed playback time. The number at the right shows the remaining playback time.

  - Drag the playhead to set the point at which your song plays back. You can do so while the song is playing, so you can hear which point you've reached.

  - Look just above the scrubber bar to see which album or playlist track is playing back. In Figure 7–5, the iPhone owner has a playlist that contains everything he wants to listen to on his iPhone. This is track 222 of a total of 1,246 tracks in the playlist.

- *Genius:* The Genius button looks like a stylized drawing of an atom, with electrons swirling about. It's the same icon that's visible at the Genius Bar in Apple retail stores, and like the human Apple geniuses, it is there to give you advice. In this case, your iPhone Genius is providing a list of songs that are somehow similar to the song that is currently playing.

■ Tap the button to create a Genius Playlist based on the current song (Figure 7–6). A Genius Playlist uses a sophisticated algorithm to create a list of songs that are somehow matched to the first song, whether they are of the same musical era or a similar genre.

Figure 7–6. *A Genius Playlist contains songs that are similar to the song from which it was generated. If you're in the mood for early 1970s music, creating a Genius Playlist from a Doobie Brothers song will make your day.*

■ If you didn't mean to create a Genius Playlist based on the song that was selected, tap the New button. You'll be asked to choose a song from which to create a Genius Playlist.

■ Like the song, but don't like the selections that the Genius made? Tap the Refresh button, and the list will be rebuilt. This works best when your song library contains a large number of songs.

■ Do you like the Genius Playlist that was created? Tap the Save button to save it for future use. The playlist is given the name of the song that was used to create it. Once you've saved a playlist, Refresh and Delete buttons appear at the top of the list to let you reshuffle the playlist or delete it altogether.

■ *Shuffle*: The shuffle control looks like two arrows making a wavy *X*. It appears to the right of the scrubber bar, and like the loop and scrubber controls, displays only after tapping the album cover.

- When the shuffle control is off (white), album and playlist songs play back in order.

- When the shuffle control is selected (blue), the iPhone randomly orders songs for shuffled playback.

- *Rewind*: The Rewind button looks like a vertical line followed by two left-pointing triangles.

  - Tap to move back to the beginning of the currently playing song.

  - Double-tap to move to the previous song in the album or playlist. If you are at the start of the song, tap to rewind. If you're already at the first song, this works as if you had pressed the Back button.

  - Touch and hold to rewind through the current song. You'll hear very short snippets as you move backward through the song.

- *Play/Pause*: Play looks like a right-pointing triangle. Pause looks like a pair of upright lines. Tap this button to toggle between playback and pause.

- *Forward*: The Forward button looks like the Rewind button in a mirror. The vertical line is to the right, and both triangles point right instead of left.

  - Tap once to move to the next song in the album or playlist. If you're at the last song, tapping Forward moves you back to the album or playlist.

  - Touch and hold to fast-forward through your song.

- *Volume*: Drag along the slider at the bottom of the screen to adjust playback volume. You can also use the physical volume buttons on the top left side of your iPhone unit to adjust volume.

NOTE: The Mute/Ring button has no effect on song playback volume.

Album View

Tapping the Album View button at the top-right corner of the Now Playing screen switches you to an overview of the current album or playlist, as shown in Figure 7–7. This screen shows a track list with item names and durations.

Figure 7–7. *The Album view shows a list of tracks and durations for the current album or playlist.*

Several items on this screen overlap with the Now Playing view and work in the same way. Here's a quick screen rundown:

- *Return to Now Playing*: The icon at the top right (it looks either like a music note or, if you have album art, like a wee version of the album cover) switches you back to the Now Playing screen.

- *Rating stars*: Use the stars control to rate the current song, from zero to five stars. Drag your finger along the stars to set your rating. The rating syncs back to your computer, and you can use your rated songs to make a Smart Playlist in iTunes on your computer. As an example, you might choose to create a Smart Playlist containing only five-star rated tracks. These ratings are not sent to the iTunes Store.

- *Track list*: Scroll up and down the track list to see all items on the current playlist or album. Tap any item to start playback.

> **TIP:** When there's empty space on the track list—for example, when you have only one or two tracks—double-tap the empty areas to return to the Now Playing screen. Alternatively, double-tap either side of the rating stars display.

Cover Flow

Tilt your iPhone onto its side when browsing or listening to music, and you instantly enter Cover Flow mode. Cover Flow is the iPhone feature that allows you to view your media collection as a series of interactive album covers, as shown in Figure 7–8.

Figure 7–8. *Cover Flow presents your media library as a series of album covers.*

To use Cover Flow, simply flick your way through your collection to the left or right. The iPhone provides animated, interactive feedback.

Here's what you can do in Cover Flow mode:

- *Album selection*: Tap any album to bring it to the front. Tap again to enter Album view.

- *Play/Pause*: Tap the small Play/Pause button at the bottom left of the Cover Flow screen to pause or resume the currently playing track.

- *Album view*: To enter the Cover Flow version of Album view, tap the small *i* (Info) button or the album cover. The cover flips and displays a list of tracks.

- Tap a track name to start playback.

- Tap Play/Pause to pause or resume playback.

- Tap anywhere on the screen (other than the Play/Pause button or a track name) to leave Album view.

Turn your iPhone back to portrait orientation to exit Cover Flow mode. Note that if you're used to using the normal mode, it can be irritating to toss your iPhone into the car seat next to you and have it automatically switch to Cover Flow.

Add Playlists

Add Playlists allow you to build a playlist on your iPhone when you're away from your computer. This feature lets you select songs, add them to the playlist, and then edit the playlist to keep or remove items.

What exactly would you use a playlist for? They allow you to put together a selection of related songs that you can listen to without interruption. You might want to create an exercise playlist with fast-paced energetic music, a rainy day playlist of sad or depressing songs, or a playlist of songs that just make you smile whenever you hear them.

To get started, tap Playlists, and then tap Add Playlist. You will be prompted to name the new playlist (Figure 7–9, left); in this case, we're creating a playlist that consists of favorite depressing blues-like songs. When you've named the list, tap Save. The song list appears, as shown in Figure 7–9, right. Navigate through your entire collection and pick which songs you want to add by tapping the plus (+) sign to the right of each track name. After making your selections, tap Done.

Tapping Done sends you to the newly created playlist itself. From here, you can tap Shuffle to begin a random playback of your playlist songs, tap Playlists to go back to the previous screen, tap Edit to add or remove items from your playlist, tap Clear to remove the songs from the playlist but still retain the empty playlist, or Delete to get rid of the playlist.

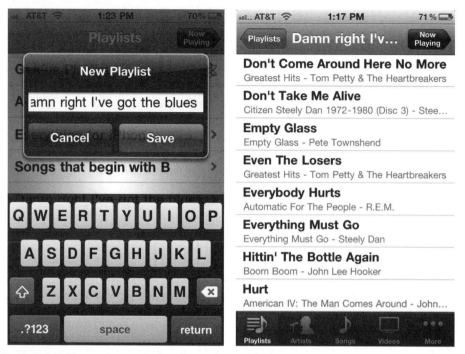

Figure 7–9. *Add songs to your playlist with the Songs selection screen shown on the right. Tap the blue button with the + to the right of each name to add a song.*

The Edit mode, shown in Figure 7–10, provides all the tools you need to manage your new playlist:

- Tap the plus (+) sign at the top left to add songs to your playlist. After adding items to your playlist, you'll have an opportunity to edit, clear, or delete the playlist.

- Tap Clear Playlist to remove all songs from the playlist. A confirmation dialog box appears. Confirm by tapping the red Clear Playlist option, or tap Cancel to leave your songs unchanged.

- Tap the minus (–)sign in the red circle to the left of any name to begin deletion. Tap Delete to confirm, or tap anywhere else to cancel.

- Drag the move bars (the three parallel gray lines to the right of each track name) to reorder items within your playlist. Grab a move bar, drag it to a new position, and then release.

- Tap Done to leave Edit mode and return to your playlist.

NOTE: Unlike other iPhone screens, the Edit playlist screen does not allow you to delete items by swiping.

Figure 7–10. *In Playlist Edit mode, tap – to delete a song or + to add a song. Use the grab bars to the right of each song to change its order in the playlist.*

Playing Video

On the iPhone, video is a widescreen-only feature, unlike audio, which plays back both in portrait orientation and the widescreen Cover Flow mode. You must flip your iPhone on its side to view TV shows, video podcasts, movies, and music videos. Select any item in your Videos list to begin playback, and then flip your iPhone on its side to watch. The Home button goes to your right.

NOTE: If you own an iPod touch, you know that there are separate apps for music and video on that device. On the iPhone, they're combined into one seamless iPod app.

Video Playback Controls

The iPhone automatically hides your video controls. Tap the screen to reveal them. Figure 7–11 shows the controls.

Figure 7–11. *The iPhone's video playback controls. The video is from "The iPhone 4 Antenna Song" byJonathan Mann (*`http://jonathanmann.bandcamp.com/track/the-iphone-4-antenna-song`*).*

The video playback controls work as follows:

- *Play/Pause*: Tap to pause or resume video playback.

- *Rewind*: Tap to return to the start of the show, or press and hold to scan backward.

- *Fast-forward*: Press and hold to scan forward.

- *Scrubber bar*: Drag the playhead along the scrubber bar to set the current playback time. The scrubber bar is the one at the top. The volume control is the larger bar at the bottom.

- *Zoom*: Either double-tap the screen or tap the Zoom button (two arrows pointing toward or away from each other, at the top right) to switch between full-screen and the original aspect ratio. When viewing in full-screen mode, the entire iPhone screen is used, but some video may be clipped from the top or sides of the video. In original aspect, you may see either letterboxing (black bars above and below) or pillarboxing (black bars to either side) to preserve the video using its native aspect.

- *Volume*: Drag the volume control at the bottom of the screen to adjust playback volume.

Tap Done to exit video playback and return to the Videos list. Press the Home button to quit and move to your Home screen.

Deleting Videos on the Go

The iPhone allows you to recover space on the go by deleting videos after you've watched them. To take advantage of this feature, go to the Videos screen and swipe through the name of any video. A red Delete button appears to the right of the video name (Figure 7–12). Tap Delete to remove the video, or tap anywhere else on the screen to cancel and keep the video.

Figure 7–12. *Removing videos after viewing can save space on your iPhone. Swipe through the name of the video, and then tap the Delete button.*

Going Beyond the iPod App

Now that you've seen how to browse through your media and play back both audio and video, here's a quick run-through of some ways you can work with playback that go beyond the iPod application itself.

Conserving Battery Power

Although iPhones keep getting consistently better battery life with each new generation, having enough power available for a long trip without a charge can still be a concern. One fast solution is to put your phone to sleep during playback to conserve battery power. Press the Sleep/Wake button once. This locks your phone and turns off the screen but allows your music to keep playing.

To peek at the current album cover during playback, press the Sleep/Wake button. When you've loaded album art for the track, the cover appears on your lock screen instead of your normal wallpaper, as shown in Figure 7–13. If your track has no art, you still see the current time and track name. Double-tap the Home button to view your playback controls: Play/Pause, Volume, Next Track, and Previous Track.

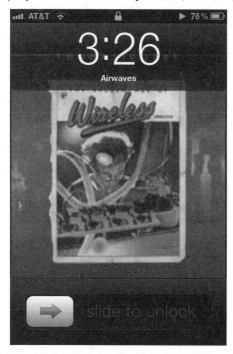

Figure 7–13. *During audio playback, your iPhone lock screen displays the currently playing song and, if album art is available, the album cover. The small triangular play icon just to the left of the battery indicates that audio is playing back.*

Adding a Sleep Timer

Unlike the Sleep/Wake button, which switches off your iPhone screen without interrupting music playback, the Clock application allows you to put your iPhone to sleep and tell it to end playback after a set interval.

To set the sleep timer, on the Home screen, tap Clock. Then tap the Timer icon at the bottom right of the Timer screen. Scroll the hours and minutes wheels to select a period of time after which you want the iPhone to sleep. Tap When Timer Ends and choose Sleep iPod from the options list, as shown in Figure 7–14. Tap Set to set your sleep timer, and then tap the big green Start button.

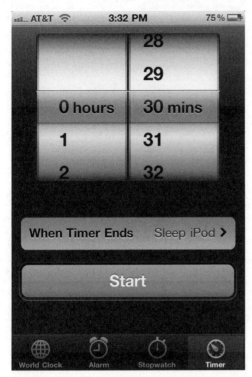

Figure 7–14. *The Sleep iPod function automatically ends iPod playback and locks your iPhone.*

The iPhone begins a timer countdown. When it reaches zero, it automatically stops iPod playback and locks your iPhone.

During Playback

During playback, you have several handy controls and can receive phone calls:

- *Volume controls*: Normally, those two physical volume controls on the top-left side of your iPhone casing control how loud your phone ringer sounds. During playback, they control audio level instead. Use them to raise and lower audio volume.

- *Headphone playback controls*: The headphone squeeze control makes it a snap to control audio playback without taking the iPhone out of your pocket. Squeeze once to pause; squeeze again to resume playback. A double-squeeze fast-forwards to the next track.

- *Phone calls*: When you receive a phone call during playback, your audio fades out, and your selected ringtone plays. Use the techniques described in Chapter 3 to answer your call. After hanging up, your music fades back in.

■ iOS 4 brought a form of multitasking to the iPhone, and with that came another way to control your music playback. Double-click the Home button, and swipe right from the first set of apps to reveal a playback controller (Figure 7–15).

Figure 7–15. *With iOS 4 and later versions of the operating system, double-clicking the Home button displays this small playback controller in any application. Here we're accessing the playback controller from within the Dropbox app.*

This controller contains the familiar rewind, play/pause, and forward buttons, as well as the iPod app button (right) and another button that isn't too familiar. The button on the left is used to lock your iPhone into portrait orientation, which is one easy way to keep the iPod app from switching to Cover Flow mode when you turn the device on its side.

Listening to Music

Unless you enjoyed listening to music on monaural (nonstereo) AM transistor radios in the 1960s, you won't want to listen to your music over the iPhone speaker. It's not stereo, and it's really designed to work best with speech, not music.

What's the best way to listen to music with your iPhone? With headphones. The iPod app supports the use of the iPhone headset, including use of the microphone/switch to play or pause music and change the volume. We commented on the use of Voice Control for controlling music in Chapter 2, but let's go into a bit more detail about the specifics when you're using the iPod app. Some of the Voice Control commands you can use during music playback include the following:

■ *Next/Previous Track:* Squeeze and hold the headset button for two seconds. When the Voice Control screen appears, say "Next track" to immediately jump to the next track in the playlist, or say "Previous track" to skip back to the previous track.

■ *What song is this/What is this song called?:* Ask this question, and you shall be answered! A voice tells you the name of the song as well as the artist performing the track.

■ *Play songs by:* If you only want to hear songs by a specific artist, tell Voice Control to "play songs by <artist name>." It will respond with the phrase "Playing songs by <artist name>" and then start with the first song by that artist in the current playlist.

■ *Play/Pause music:* This is identical to tapping the play/pause button on the iPod app screen.

■ *Play album <album name>:* You can listen to an entire album by telling Voice Control to play it.

Remember, Voice Control commands are visible when you enable the function, so if you can't recall a specific voice command, just wait, and it may float by on the iPhone screen.

If you're not fond of the standard iPhone earbuds, you might want to consider Apple's In-Ear Headphones with Remote and Mic ($79). Some people find the earbuds to be loose in their ears and prefer the tighter and customizable fit of the In-Ear Headphones. There are also over-the-ear headphones like the Bowers & Wilkins P5 Mobile Headphones ($300) that include the remote and microphone, add noise isolation, and are amazingly comfortable to wear.

You don't need to stick with wired earbuds or headphones; many Bluetooth headsets that support the A2DP standard will work as well. The online and retail Apple Stores sell a variety of Bluetooth stereo headsets from Senneiser, Sony, Plantronics, and Motorola. Although they're made for listening only and don't have built-in microphones, these headsets provide a wire-free listening experience that many people find to be much more comfortable.

Shopping at the Mobile iTunes Store

One app that is supplied with every iPhone shipped is the iTunes app. This software allows you to browse the iTunes Store on the go and make purchases directly to your iPhone. When you return to your computer, your purchases are copied from the iPhone to your computer. Read more about using the iTunes app in Chapter 10.

Adjusting iPod Settings

Surprisingly, for a feature-rich application like iPod, the iPhone provides just a few settings. You'll find these in **Settings ➤ iPod**, and they work as follows.

Music

- *Shake to Shuffle:* When you're listening on the go and don't want to unlock your screen, open the iPod app, and press Shuffle to randomize your music playback, just shake your iPhone. This setting is turned on by default and can sometimes cause issues if you're running or engaging in other physical activity while listening to music with the iPod app. If you find that Shake to Shuffle is changing your songs every few seconds, change the setting to Off.

RECOMMENDATION: Shake to Shuffle can be very annoying, especially if you're not expecting it. Since this is a default setting for the iPod app, we recommend turning it off

- *Sound Check*: Say you're listening to a song that was recorded way too low so you crank up the volume during playback. Then when the next song starts playing back, boom! There go your eardrums. Sound Check prevents this problem. When you enable Sound Check, all your songs play back at approximately the same sound level.

TIP: You can also use Sound Check in iTunes. Choose **Edit ➤ Preferences ➤ Playback ➤ Sound Check** (Windows) or **iTunes ➤ Preferences ➤ Playback ➤ Sound Check** (Mac).

- *Audiobook Speed*: Your iPhone allows you to slow down or speed up audiobook playback so you can choose how you want to listen. When you're paying close attention or transcribing notes or so forth, choose **Settings ➤ iPod ➤ Audiobook Speed ➤ Slower**. This elongates each word and makes the speech easier to follow. When you're impatient and just want to hear the book a little faster, choose Audiobook **Speed ➤ Faster**. **Audiobook Speed ➤ Normal** is the default setting.

    EQ: The iPhone offers a number of equalizer settings that help emphasize the way different kinds of music play back. Select **Settings ➤ iPod ➤ EQ** and choose from Acoustic, Dance, Spoken Word, and many other presets. To disable the equalizer, choose Off.

- *Volume Limit*: Face it: personal music players bring your audio up close and very personal—so up close, in fact, that your hearing may be in peril. We strongly recommend that you take advantage of the iPhone's built-in volume limit to protect your ears. This setting affects only playback through headphones and has no effect on speaker playback.

  Navigate to **Settings ➤ iPod ➤ Volume** Limit (Figure 7–16), and adjust the maximum volume using the slider. All the way to the left is mute—sure, you'll protect your ears, but you won't be able to hear anything. All the way to the right is the normal, unlimited maximum volume. If you're super paranoid or, more typically, if children have access to your iPhone, tap Lock Volume Limit to open a screen that allows you to set a volume limit passcode. No one may override your volume settings without the correct passcode.

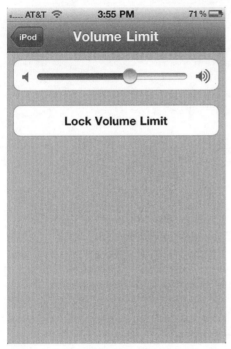

Figure 7–16. *Set the maximum volume for your iPhone by dragging the slider in the settings pane. Tap the Lock Volume Limit button to password-protect the settings and keep the kids from blasting their ears with your iPhone.*

Video

- *Start Playing:* There's nothing more annoying than watching a movie on an airplane and then having to shut off your iPhone before landing without completing the movie. Tap **Settings ➤ iPod ➤ Start Playing**, and select Where Left Off to restart the movie at the point you were so rudely interrupted, or choose From Beginning if you never got all that far into the film anyway.

- *Closed Captioning:* Many videos and movies that you can view on the iPhone are close-captioned. If you are hearing-impaired or in a situation where it's impossible to hear the movie soundtrack, set **Settings ➤ iPod ➤ Closed Captioning** to On. Note that the closed captioning can be difficult to read on the small screen of the iPhone.

TV Out

The iPhone 4 and later models can use the same Apple Dock Connector to VGA adapter that works with the iPad to connect to projectors, monitors, and properly equipped TVs. Not all iPhone apps support TV Out, so be sure to check with the app developer prior to buying an app that you're hoping to display on the big screen. You can use the Apple Component AV Cable or Apple Component AV Cable with all models of iPhone as another way to display iPod app videos and movies on a big screen, once again with the same caveat about the app that you're using to "feed" the TV. There are several settings to consider:

- *Widescreen:* To display your iPod videos and movies in widescreen (16:9 aspect ratio) mode while using TV out, be sure that **Settings ➤ iPod ➤ Widescreen** is set to On.

- *TV Signal:* Television sets worldwide used to come in two flavors: NTSC and PAL. These acronyms refer to the analog broadcasting protocol used by TV stations in various countries. In most countries, NTSC and PAL have been replaced by other new digital protocols, but most televisions still support NTSC or PAL. Your iPhone needs to be aware of what protocol the TV set expects to be receive, so you can make your choice at **Settings ➤ iPod ➤ TVSignal**.

Summary

This chapter introduced all the ways you can browse and play back media using the iPod application. With the iPhone, you can flick through your entire collection of music, video, and other media, and then tap to play the media you want to enjoy. Here are a few points to think about before you move on to the next chapter:

- Cover Flow makes browsing through your media a simple visual pleasure. Tip your iPhone on its side while using the iPod app to enter Cover Flow mode.

- Don't be afraid to fill your browse buttons bar with the items you use the most. It's easy to customize. It's also easy to put it back the way it started.

- Take the time to learn your headset controls. It's a lot easier to squeeze or double-squeeze your way through songs than to pull out your iPhone, double-tap Home, and tap Pause/Play.

- Genius playlists are a fast way to hear a group of songs that are all from the same era or genre. If you're in the mood to listen to the blues, create a Genius playlist while listening to a blues tune. You'll be impressed with how often the Genius playlists make excellent selections from your collection.

- Choose your videos wisely. Even with newer iPhones with expanded memory, videos can quickly eat up your free space. And don't be shy about deleting your videos on the go. You can always sync them back on your home computer.

iPhone Photos and Video

All iPhones have featured a built-in digital camera, but the iPhone 4 brought increased power and performance by adding a VGA (640x480 pixel) front-facing camera to a very good 5-megapixel camera with an LED flash. Every iPhone comes with software for managing, viewing, and sharing your photos. With the iPhone, you can snap your friend's picture, e-mail it to her, assign it to her contact information, or even use it for your wallpaper. The iPhone makes it easy to use your photos in many applications.

Your iPhone isn't just a still camera, though. Since the iPhone 3GS, iPhones have had the ability to capture video as well. The iPhone 4 can actually capture high definition (720p) video at 30 frames per second, perfect for recording everything from weddings to roller-coaster rides.

In this chapter, you'll discover how to use your iPhone's camera and the built-in photo software to snap, view, and enjoy your pictures. You'll find out how to capture, view, and share video of the world around you. You'll learn how to download your photos and videos to your computer, upload existing photo albums and video clips to your iPhone, and perform many basic tasks related to capturing stills and videos. By the time you finish reading this chapter, you'll encounter both new and familiar ways to take advantage of your iPhone for photography and videography.

One App, Two Icons

On an iPhone fresh from the factory, Photos and Camera icons appear on the top row of your Home screen. Using what you've learned so far in this book, you may have moved them to another Home screen on your iPhone or perhaps collected all your photo apps into one folder (Figure 8–1). Regardless of where they're located, the two built-in apps we're interested in are very easy to find. The Photos icon is marked with a cheerful yellow sunflower. The Camera icon is a lens. Tap Photos to view your photo album collection. Tap Camera to snap new pictures and video.

Figure 8–1. *The Photos and Camera icons are located in the bottom row of this folder that is chock-full of photography apps for the iPhone. Many apps are available that act as a "digital darkroom" for your photos, providing touchups and effects that can turn a plain picture into something special.*

What these icons don't tell you is that they're hiding a secret. Both actually belong to the same iPhone application. MobileSlideShow.app handles all photography services, including taking pictures and video, managing albums, displaying slide shows, and so forth. But that's all beneath the surface. As far as you're concerned, you can pretty much treat the two icons as two separate applications. Use Photos for viewing pictures and captured video, and use Camera for taking your videos and photos.

Locating (and Removing) the Camera

The iPhone camera is embedded onto the back of your iPhone. You can see its small, plastic circle by flipping over your iPhone and looking about an inch up and to the left of the Apple icon. It's placed behind clear plastic for protection. The iPhone 4 has a second camera located on the front of the phone next to the earpiece. It's primarily used for FaceTime chats, although it also works very well for taking self-portraits. The iPhone 4 also added an LED flash, perfect for taking photos at night.

If you work on a military base or at any other secure, restricted facility, you can pay to have your camera(s) removed from your iPhone. For about $100, a service called iResQ (http://www.iresq.com) will send you a postage-paid, preaddressed, overnight shipping box. Place your iPhone in the box and send it off to iResQ. Your phone will be returned a day or so later, with the cameras removed.

Camera: Shooting Pictures

When the first iPhones appeared in 2007, they came with a 2-megapixel camera that really wasn't all that good. The iPhone 3GS introduced a 3-megapixel autofocus camera, and the iPhone 4 upped the photographic ante with a 5-megapixel autofocus camera with LED flash. The lower-resolution cameras on the older iPhones have some limitations, since they work badly in low light and compress images to conserve storage space on the phone. For these phones, you'll want to make sure that you take photos in situations where there's a lot of light available. Even then, when you get your pictures back to your computer, take advantage of the numerous tutorials around the Internet that show you how to enhance cell phone images with photo editors such as Photoshop or GIMP.

The iPhone 4 camera is actually pretty good as cell phone cameras go. It still has about half the resolution of many inexpensive point-and-shoot digital cameras, but as the saying goes, "The best camera is the one that is always with you." Chances are very good that you'll have your iPhone in your pocket or purse for almost any occasion while that digital camera is sitting on the shelf at home.

The iPhone 3GS and 4 both have digital zoom capabilities built in. Digital zoom means that the camera essentially crops an image down to a centered area and then interpolates the result back up to the size of the original image. It's has the same effect as using a zoom lens to zoom in on details of a faraway item but is all accomplished digitally. Unfortunately, without special post-processing, digitally zoomed photos don't have the same quality as those taken with an optical zoom lens.

Getting Started

To launch your photo-capture software, tap Camera. As the camera starts up, the iPhone displays an animation of an iris opening before transferring you to a live display (see Figure 8–2). Note that you can hold your iPhone in either portrait (vertical) or landscape (horizontal) orientation while taking photos. Frame your picture using this display, and then tap the Camera button to snap your picture.

Figure 8–2. *Tap the Camera button (the button that, not surprisingly, looks like a camera) to snap a new photo. Tap the Camera Roll button (bottom right, displaying the last photo in the camera roll) to switch to the Camera Roll in the Photos app. The Switch Cameras button (upper left) switches between the back- and front-facing cameras on the iPhone 4, the Flash button (lower left) is used to set the flash mode or turn the flash off, and the photo/video slider (upper right) is used to switch between still photos and video capture.*

Continue snapping pictures as long as desired and as long as you have space available on your unit. The iPhone plays a cheerful snapshot noise each time it captures an image. When you're finished, tap the Home button to return to the Home screen, or tap the button at the Camera Roll button (lower right in Figure 8–2) to switch to the current Camera Roll. Your Camera Roll contains all the digital pictures you've snapped on your iPhone, just like a physical film roll in a nondigital camera.

Picture-Taking Pointers

Here are a few pointers for taking pictures with your iPhone camera:

- To zoom in or out on a subject, tap the screen. A zoom slider with a plus sign on one end and a minus sign on the other appears. To zoom in, slide the button on the slider from minus to plus. To zoom out, slide in the opposite direction.

- The iPhone is not set up for use with a tripod right out of the box. You'll achieve better photographic results when you steady your hand on a wall or shoulder, rather than just holding the camera out at arm's length. There are also adapters that hold the iPhone in a vertical or horizontal position and include a standard tripod screw mount. Google *iPhone tripod mount* for a number of commercially available and do-it-yourself products.

- You can shoot your pictures in either landscape or portrait mode. The iPhone remembers the way each image was composed. Don't forget; you can also lock your iPhone orientation by double-clicking the Home button, swiping right, and then tapping the lock button.

- You can use selective focus to obtain sharp images with some depth of field. To do this, tap the screen in approximately the location of the item you want to focus on. A square appears on the image preview, flashes briefly as the camera focuses on the item you're pinpointing, and then disappears when the subject is in focus. This is particularly useful when taking macro close-up shots.

- How do you set the exposure on a picture? The selective focus also acts as a pinpoint exposure meter. The camera bases its exposure on the subject that you're focusing on. This is a handy thing to remember when you're taking portraits: focus on the face of your subject, and the face will always be properly exposed.

- The iPhone captures photos when your finger leaves the Camera button, not when you first touch the screen. To capture better images, touch your finger to the screen, frame your shot, and *then* snap the photo by removing your finger from the button. This gives you greater control and simplifies the trigger movement.

- While the cameras on the iPhone 3GS and 4 provide digital zoom, there's no way to take wide-angle or extreme telephoto pictures. You may want to consider something like the OWLE Bubo (http://www.wantowle.com), which is an aluminum casing that holds an iPhone 3GS or 4 and features a threaded mount for camera lenses and filters. It comes with .45x wide-angle/macro combination lens.

TIP: Have you ever wondered how we get these great screenshots for the book? To take a screenshot, press and hold the Home button, and then press the Sleep/Wake button. The screen "flashes," and the photo is saved to your Camera Roll in the Photos app.

Photos: Viewing Pictures

The Photos app display is shown in Figure 8–3 (left). If you're used to iPhoto, this display will look familiar, because it uses the same terms and structure. The Camera Roll includes all the images you've recently shot on your iPhone, and your Photo Library includes every image synchronized to your iPhone (see the "Synchronizing Pictures from Your Computer" section later in this chapter for details).

Figure 8–3. *The Photos application lists all albums that you've synchronized to your iPhone, as well as the current roll you've been shooting on your camera. People who regularly use iPhoto may have a lot more albums than shown here. The number of buttons on the bottom toolbar varies depending on whether you choose to sync events and faces from iPhoto to your iPhone.*

The Events and Faces buttons on the bottom toolbar in Figure 8–3 appear or disappear depending on whether you've chosen to sync any Faces or Events groups from iPhoto to your iPhone. Events are photos that are grouped by a particular event or time (such as a vacation or a wedding), while Faces are collections of photos with a certain person's face in them.

The iPhone's geolocation features can tag each of your iPhone pictures with the location where they were taken. To do this, you must have location services enabled on your iPhone and must give the Camera app permission to tag the photos that it takes. Make sure that Settings ➤ General ➤ Location Services is turned on; then scroll down the list of apps shown on the Location Services settings screen, and make sure that the button next to Camera is set to On.

As you can see in Figure 8–3 (right), tapping the Places button at the bottom of the Photos screen displays a map with a pin at each location where photos were taken. This iPhone had taken photos in Southampton, England, New York, and Denver, and tapping the pin shows not only how many photos were taken in that location but provides an arrow to tap to view the photos taken at that place.

Working with Photo Albums

Photo albums are collections. They contain groups of photos you've saved together on your personal computer or photos all shot at around the same time. It all depends on how you've organized your collection and how you've synchronized that collection to your iPhone.

Tap the name of any photo album to select and display it. As Figure 8–4 shows, album screens display their photos as rows of thumbnails. These small versions of your photos are displayed four per line. To find a particular photo, scroll up and down the library. Flick longer libraries to move quickly through your collection.

From your photo album, you can view your images:

- Tap any image it to display it full-screen.

- Tap the Play button at the bottom to start a slide show.

- Tap Photo Albums to return to the albums list.

Figure 8–4. *Each photo album screen contains image thumbnails tiled four across. Scroll this screen to see your entire album. Tap an image to open it, and then tap the Play button that appears at the bottom of the image to start playing a slide show.*

Working with Slide Shows

As the name suggests, iPhone slide shows display the contents of a photo album one image after another. Slide shows display each slide for a set period of time. To get started with slide shows, go to your Home screen and navigate to **Settings ➤ Photos**. As shown in Figure 8–5, this Settings screen allows you to specify exactly how you want your slide shows to display:

- *Play Each Slide For*: Here, you can set the slide duration. Your choices are 2 seconds, 3 seconds (the default, which works really well for most people), 5 seconds, 10 seconds (which starts to get boring fast), and 20 seconds.

- *Transition*: Give your slide show a visual style by specifying how the iPhone should replace each image with the next. In our opinion, it's best to stick with Dissolve, which softly fades one image into the next. Cube, Ripple, Wipe Across, and Wipe Down offer alternative transition styles. Of these four, Wipe Across and Wipe Down are the least annoying visually.

- *Repeat*: Set this to On to make your slide show loop.

- *Shuffle*: Show your pictures in a random order by switching Shuffle from Off to On. When disabled, your pictures display in album order.

Figure 8–5. *Navigate to* Settings ➤ Photos *to customize your slide shows.*

TIP: There's no "official" way to add music to your slide shows. If you like, just start some music playing in the iPod application, and then run your slide show. You cannot synchronize a track to your slide show or have your music start playing when the slide show begins.

To end a slide show, tap an image. This stops the slide show, places you in the full-screen photo display, and displays controls to start up the slide show again.

Working with a Full-Screen Image

Remember all the gestures covered in Chapter 2? When viewing an image full-screen, the iPhone allows you to interact with that photo using a number of these gestures:

- Pinching allows you to zoom into and out of the photo.

- Double-tap to zoom into the photo. Double-tap again to zoom out.

- When your image is displayed at the normal zoomed-out size, flick to the left or right to move to the previous or next image in the album. When zoomed into an image, dragging the photo pans across it.

TIP: If you start your zoomed-in drag at the very edge of an image and drag toward the center, you can actually see bits of the next image in the sequence until you release your finger. Then your image springs back to its original position.

- Tap any image once to bring up the image overlay, as shown in Figure 8–6. The image overlay allows you to navigate between images (the left and right arrows), delete the current image (garbage can), start a slide show (the Play button), or use your photo in some way (the rectangle with the arrow), as discussed in the next section.

- Flip your iPhone onto its side to have your photo reorient itself. If the photo was shot using landscape orientation, it fits itself to the wider view.

Figure 8–6. *Tap any image to display this control overlay. If you do not use the controls, the overlay fades away after a few seconds. The garbage can appears only when viewing the Camera Roll.*

Using a Photo

The image overlay has a Share button for using your photos in many ways. This button, represented by a rectangle with an arrow, is found all the way to the bottom left of your screen. After tapping it, you can choose what to do with the photo (Figure 8–7, right):

- *Email Photo*: The iPhone opens a new message screen and attaches your photo to the message. Address the message, add a note, and send it. Instantly, your photo travels across the ether to your recipient. On the iPhone 4 and newer models, photo file sizes are much bigger, so you may see a set of buttons displayed that allow you to scale the photo before sending it.

- *MMS*: Remember our discussion about MMS messaging in Chapter 4? You can immediately send any photo in your photo library by selecting the MMS button. The photo is scaled down to a small size and then placed in a blank MMS message ready for addressing and sending to a friend.

- *Send to MobileMe*: Want to share your photographic prowess with more than just one or two people? If you're a subscriber to Apple's MobileMe service, you can choose to post your photos to a MobileMe gallery for viewing (Figure 8–7, right). There's a place to add a title and a description of the photo, and a list of all available galleries appears at the bottom of the screen. Unfortunately, you can't create a new gallery from your iPhone.

- *Assign to Contact*: When you tap this button, your Contacts list opens. Select a contact name and set the photo, or tap Cancel to return without using the photo. This is a useful thing to do, because the contact's photo appears on the screen of your iPhone when they call you. At a glance, you can see who's calling.

- *Use as Wallpaper*: The iPhone prompts you to move and scale your image and then set it as wallpaper on your Lock screen, on your Home screen, or on both.

Figure 8–7. *The Share button is your gateway to sharing or using a photo in a number of ways. If you're a MobileMe subscriber, you can publish your photos to a MobileMe gallery complete with a title and description.*

Uploading Pictures by E-mail

Many photo-hosting and printing services allow you to upload pictures using e-mail. Check with your host or printing service to see whether it offers this option.

For Flickr, visit `http://flickr.com/account/uploadbyemail`. Flickr will assign you a "secret" e-mail address. Mail photos from your iPhone to that address, and they automatically load into your Flickr account.

For Costco, mail your images to `save@mycostcophotos.com`. You'll receive a confirmation letter at the address you used to send the message. The confirmation includes a link to the Costco Photo Center web site, where you can order prints, gifts, and share your photos with friends.

The American drugstore chain Walgreens does a very good job of printing photos quickly and inexpensively. Set up a free account at `http://walgreens.com`, and then send the photos to `save@mywalgreens.com` from the e-mail address associated with your account, and the photos are saved into your album at the Walgreens Photo Center web site for printing.

These are just a handful of the many locations where you can upload your photos. When uploading pictures by e-mail, remember to send them at their highest resolution. That's the largest file size, but it ensures that printed photos are going to look their best.

Photo-Sharing Apps

E-mail isn't the only way to share your photos with others. There are plenty of iPhone apps available in the App Store specifically written to let you share your pictures through common photo-sharing and social networking sites.

For Flickr fans, there's an official app (Figure 8–8) available for free just for uploading your pics (`http://itunes.apple.com/us/app/flickr/id328407587?mt=8`). You can apply tags to the photos that you upload, set them as public or private, and choose which set you want to add the photos to.

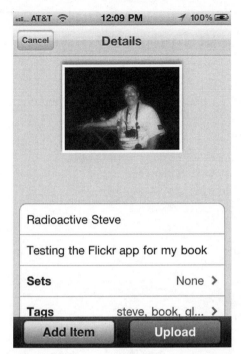

Figure 8–8. *The official Flickr app provides a quick and easy way to send photos directly to Flickr. You can take new photos (or video) to send or upload photos from your library.*

The free Pixelpipe app (http://itunes.apple.com/us/app/pixelpipe-hd-post-upload-to/id290648828?mt=8) pushes your photographic endeavors to Facebook, YouTube (videos), Picasa, Flickr, and many other sites or blog services. It's able to upload your pictures to as many sites as you want, all with one tap on the iPhone.

Facebook users can use the official Facebook app (free, http://itunes.apple.com/us/app/facebook/id284882215?mt=8) to whisk photos fresh from the camera or the photo library up to their Facebook page.

If you're a Twitter fan, you'll want to know about TwitPic (http://www.twitpic.com). It's an online service for hosting photos you can upload from most Twitter clients or post via e-mail.

Many more apps are available in the App Store, so be sure to browse the Photography category for additional apps that can both improve your photography and let you share your photos.

Synchronizing Pictures from Your Computer

iTunes synchronizes your iPhone with pictures stored on your computer. You can bring your photo collection with you and share it through the iPhone. To make this happen, connect your iPhone to your computer and launch iTunes. Select your iPhone from the sources list (the blue column at the left side of the iTunes screen), and open the Photos tab. Your choices depend on your operating system:

■ *Windows*: iTunes can sync your iPhone photos with Adobe Photoshop Elements 3.0 or newer on a Windows computer (Figure 8–9).

Figure 8–9. *On Windows, choose whether to synchronize photos to Pictures or to another folder.*

■ *Mac OS X*: Choose whether to synchronize to iPhoto, to Aperture, or to a folder (such as Photos in your home directory), as shown in Figure 8–10. When synchronizing to iPhoto, you may sync your entire photo and album collection or choose just those albums you want to include.

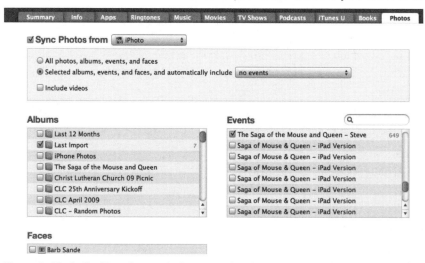

Figure 8–10. *On the Mac, choose whether to synchronize photos to iPhoto or a specific folder on your computer.*

Your iPhone as a USB Camera

Your iPhone identifies itself as a standard USB digital camera when you connect it to computers. This allows you to offload your images to the computer without using iTunes. On Windows, your iPhone works like any other digital camera. You can set it up to automatically download its pictures each time it connects. On Macs, you can download photos using iPhoto, Image Capture, Preview, or any other software that communicates using the USB digital camera standard.

The iPhone and Windows XP

Windows allows you to choose what happens when you connect your iPhone to your computer. To make that choice, follow these steps:

1. Open the Control Panel, select **Printers and Other Hardware** ➤ **Scanners and Camera** ➤ **Apple iPhone** (Windows XP).

2. Right-click Apple iPhone, and pick Properties from the context menu.

3. Click the Events tab, and choose the "Camera connected" option from the "Select an event" pop-up list, as shown in Figure 8–11.

Figure 8–11. *The Apple iPhone Properties dialog box allows you to automatically save your iPhone pictures to a folder you specify.*

4. Pick one of three options for when you connect your iPhone to your computer:

    ■   *Start this program*: By default, this option launches the Microsoft Scanner and Camera Wizard and guides you through the process of choosing whether to download your images.

■ *Take no action*: Choose this option when you want to manage your photos through iTunes or when your iPhone is hosted on another computer. It tells Windows not to do anything automatically when you attach your iPhone.

■ *Save all pictures to this folder*: Select this option to automatically download your images to a folder you specify whenever you connect your iPhone. This makes photo downloads simple. Connect your iPhone; offload your pictures.

The iPhone and Windows Vista/Windows 7

For Windows Vista and Windows 7, changing the default action when you attach an iPhone to the device is done in a different manner than with Windows XP. When the iPhone is connected to the Windows computer with a USB cable, two actions take place. First, iTunes is launched if it has been installed on the computer. The second action is to launch the AutoPlay window (Figure 8–12). When Windows detects that the iPhone has a built-in camera, AutoPlay gives you the option of importing pictures using Windows or opening the device to view files with Windows Explorer.

Figure 8–12. *When your iPhone is attached to your Windows Vista or Windows 7 computer for the first time, the AutoPlay dialog box appears. Check "Always do this for this device" if you want to have it always import pictures into the Pictures folder or if you want to use Windows Explorer to view, copy, or move the image and video files on the iPhone to the computer.*

You can set other AutoPlay defaults by clicking the Set AutoPlay defaults in Control Panel link at the bottom of the dialog box. Doing this opens a window (Figure 8–13) that, among other things, displays devices that have been attached to the computer. This window lets you also choose the option to take no action when you attach your iPhone to the computer (helpful if you plan to use iTunes to sync photos to your PC) or ask whether you want to import pictures or browse files each time the iPhone is connected.

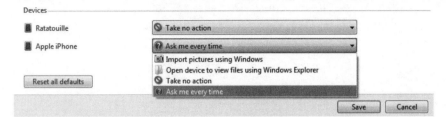

Figure 8–13. *If you're going to use iTunes to sync photos between a folder on your computer and your iPhone, then you may want to set AutoPlay to take no action when you connect your iPhone via the USB sync cable.*

The iPhone and Mac Image Capture

By default, iPhoto is your iPhone's natural sync partner, but you do have a choice. If you want to just download your pictures to a folder, rather than import them into iPhoto, use Image Capture instead, as follows:

1. Launch **Applications ➤ Image Capture**.

2. In the sidebar on the left side of the app window, select your iPhone from the list of Devices. Below, you'll see the name of the device and the words "Connecting this iPhone opens:". You can make a choice to open iPhoto (the default), Image Capture, Preview, or AutoImporter.

Now you're ready. Connecting your iPhone launches Image Capture instead of iPhoto, as shown in Figure 8–12. To download your entire photo roll, select the folder where you want to save your photos and video, and then click Import All. The iPhone sends over its pictures, and the Mac stores them in the selected folder.

What's that AutoImporter setting? If you select this, connecting your iPhone to your Mac automatically opens Image Capture and imports all photos without intervention on your part. It's perfect if you take a lot of photos with your iPhone and don't want to be hassled with choices or dialog boxes on your Mac every time you connect the iPhone.

Image Capture provides more than just another way to pull photos off your iPhone. As you can see in Figure 8–14, it also displays a huge amount of information about every picture. You can view a time and date stamp, the size of the file, the aperture at which the photo was taken (it will always be f/2.4 on an iPhone 4), the color depth of the image (in bits), the color space (which helps reproduce the image colors on your computer), the physical dimensions of the image in pixels, the resolution in dots per inch, the Exchangeable Image File Format (EXIF) version, the focal length of the lens (4mm on iPhone 4), the shutter speed, the "film" speed (ISO), the latitude and longitude for the location where the photo was taken, the flash settings, the maker of the camera (Apple), and the model (iPhone).

Figure 8–14. *Image Capture allows you to download your iPhone photos directly to any folder on your Mac. A small portion of the image information displayed by Image Capture is shown in this illustration.*

The iPhone and Mac Preview

The Preview application that comes with every Mac is an extremely useful program. You can view most image formats, annotate images, do some minor color tweaking, and rotate or crop pictures. It shouldn't come as a surprise that it can also be used to import and display images from your iPhone.

Launching Preview on your Mac when your iPhone is attached to it, select **File ➤ Import from <name of your iPhone>**. What you'll see is essentially Figure 8–14 without the sidebar on the left side of the window. Clicking Import or Import All copies the photos on your iPhone and then opens them for editing or viewing in Preview.

A Selection of iPhone Photo Apps

The iPhone makes it very easy to take photos and share them with the world, but sometimes your "best" photo of a subject could stand a little improvement. That's where photo-editing apps can be useful in making your photos perfect before your share them. Here are a few of our favorites, all available in the App Store:

- *Adobe Photoshop Express (free)*: It won't do photo retouching, but with this free app you can adjust colors, add frames, apply focus effects, and more.

- *Photogene ($1.99)*: This app features many professional-quality editing tools. It adds artistic filters, text bubbles, frames, special effects, resizing of your photo to a different resolution, and you can share your edited project with Facebook, Twitter, or Flickr directly from the app.

- *Lo-Mob ($1.99)*: This highly rated photo-editing app is great for adding special filters and effects to your iPhone photos. It's a popular and well-designed app for creatively editing your photos.

- *You Gotta See This! ($1.99)*: This app doesn't edit your photos but instead allows you to create a photo collage by simply waving your iPhone 4 (or newer) around. It produces very artistic collages in a number of styles.

Camera: Recording Video

As mentioned earlier, every iPhone since the iPhone 3GS not only has the ability to take great photos but to also capture video. With the advent of the iPhone 4, high-definition (HD) video can be captured at 720p resolution. That means that the video is captured at a resolution of 1280x720 pixels and that your iPhone's video capabilities are remarkably good. Several filmmakers have taken advantage of this fact to film advertisements and even short movies using nothing but a handheld iPhone 4.

Getting Started

Capturing video on your iPhone isn't that much different from taking photos. For both activities, you use the Camera app. On the Camera toolbar is a small toggle switch with two icons next to it: a camera and a stylized movie camera (Figure 8–15). To prepare to shoot video, slide the switch button to the movie camera icon.

Figure 8–15. *Before capturing video, make sure that you've moved the toggle switch (upper right) to the video capture setting. You'll know that you're in video mode when the camera button turns into a red LED light button (right center). Toggles to switch between cameras (upper left) and set the LED light settings (lower left) to visible.*

When the Camera app is in video capture mode, you won't be able to use the digital zoom feature that we discussed earlier in the chapter. However, the icons for the LED flash and the toggle between forward- and back-facing cameras still appear. As with taking still photos, you can also tap the screen to get an initial focus on your subject before you start to film.

What does the LED flash do when you're filming video? The app simply turns the light on, and it serves as a small camera-attached studio light for your video work. Just make sure that your subject is properly lit by the diminutive light, or move to a better location. Sometimes the light can be too bright, in which case you may want to turn off the light and just use natural lighting.

To start capturing video, tap the Camera button. In video capture mode, it features a simulated red LED light rather than a camera icon. When filming is taking place, the light (known as a *tally light* in the videography business) flashes on and off, and an elapsed time counter is displayed on the screen.

Although the length of the video you capture is limited only by the amount of memory in your iPhone, there are practical limits. If you're planning on sharing your video via e-mail or MMS messaging, keep your masterpiece short. If the movie is going to be any more than about 45 seconds long, any attempt to share your video from the iPhone is met with an unhappy message (Figure 8–16).

Figure 8–16. *Video taken with your iPhone must be about 45 seconds in length or less if you want to share them from the iPhone.*

TIP: When recording video using an iPhone, move the camera slowly when panning or tilting to keep your subject in view. Moving too quickly tends to blur the video and make it difficult to watch.

When filming is completed, tap the Camera button one more time to stop the recording. The segment you just captured is stored on the iPhone in the Photos app.

Trimming Your Video

The best home videos and movies aren't composed of one long, unending shot. Instead, they're made of many shorter shots that are spliced together. Within the Photos app, Apple provides a way for you to do a first-cut edit of your video.

Tapping any video segment in Photos displays a screen that looks like Figure 8–17. At the bottom of the image are the familiar buttons for sharing or deleting the video, but there are three other buttons as well. The triangular play button in the center of the toolbar is used to begin playing the video clip. It turns into a pause button while the video is playing, and tapping it again pauses the video at once. There are also left and right arrows. Those are used to navigate to the video or photo immediately before (left) and after (right) the existing video clip. If you're currently perusing the last item in your photo library, there won't be a right arrow.

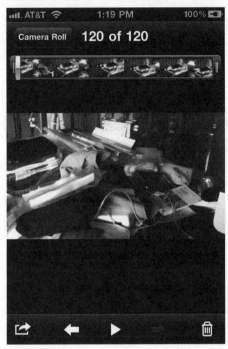

Figure 8–17. *Your video appears in the photo library along with snapshots you've taken. Tap the image to display the timeline at the top of the screen, or play the video by touching the triangular play button in the toolbar at the bottom.*

To view your cinematic masterpiece, tap the play button or the larger play button that appears on the video clip itself. A video timeline at the top of the image displays a "scrubber button" that moves from left to right as the video plays. To view an earlier part of the current scene, drag the scrubber button to the left; to "fast-forward" through the rest of the scene, drag the scrubber to the right.

You can be extremely accurate with your placement of the scrubber button. Tapping the button and dragging down zooms into the timeline, showing only a small portion of the total video segment instead of the whole segment from start to end.

This fine control of the scrubber button comes in handy when you're trimming your video. Let's say that someone coughed at the beginning of a video shoot, and you want to cut three or four seconds from the start. Tapping one of the handles at either end of the timeline enables a Trim button, and the timeline border turns bright yellow (Figure 8–18).

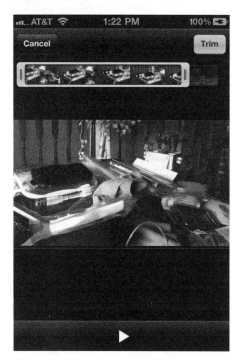

Figure 8–18. *Tapping the timeline above a video clip enables the trimming handles. Drag them to mark the starting and ending points for your video clip.*

Drag the left handle to the right slowly to begin editing. You'll see an image of the video at any point in the timeline, and the image will jump by a few seconds as you drag the handle progressively further to the left. If you need more control over the trim point, use the trick we described earlier and drag down toward the toolbar. This gives you even more control over the start and end points.

When you're ready to trim, press the Trim button. Some buttons appear on the iPhone screen (Figure 8–19).

If you're sure that you've picked the proper start and end points and you want to get rid of the offending material that is about to be left on the cutting room floor, tap the Trim Original button. However, if you're concerned that you might be cutting out something that would have significance or value at some future point, tap Save as New Clip. It retains your old video clip and produces a new, trimmed clip as well.

Figure 8–19. *The Photos app provides a choice of either trimming your original clip or creating a new clip while retaining the original.*

Sharing Your Video

Most iPhone owners make video clips for one reason. They want to share them with others. As with photographs, your iPhone provides a variety of ways to share your videos.

Tapping the Share button at the bottom of any video brings up a short list of sharing options (Figure 8–20). There are buttons that e-mail the video, send it as an MMS message, send it to MobileMe, or send it to YouTube.

Figure 8–20. *The sharing options for video in the Photos app provide a handful of ways to show your work to the world.*

Let's see what these buttons do:

- *Email Video*: Tapping this button inserts the video into a blank, unaddressed e-mail for sending. Note that you won't be able to e-mail any videos that are more than about 45 seconds in length because of file size restrictions.

- *MMS*: As expected, tapping the MMS button inserts the video into a blank and unaddressed MMS message. The same length and size restrictions that apply for e-mailing videos also apply here.

- *Send to MobileMe*: If you have MobileMe subscription, you can easily share your iPhone videos by sending them to your MobileMe account. If you've already set up MobileMe syncing or e-mail, the app knows where to send your video file. Unlike e-mail and MMS, videos sent to MobileMe can be as long as you like, provided that you have sufficient storage space for the video file.

■ *Send to YouTube*: YouTube is probably one of the most widely recognized video-sharing sites on the planet. To post a video to YouTube, you'll need to have an account set up (visit http://youtube.com to create an account). With a tap to this button, your video is compressed and uploaded to your YouTube account. YouTube videos can be up to 15 minutes in length, which is perfect for short vacation movies.

Editing Your Video

Trimming your video isn't the end of your ability to edit your movies on an iPhone. In 2010, Apple released iMovie for iPhone ($4.99, http://itunes.apple.com/us/app/imovie/id377298193?mt=8). iMovie for iPhone contains a subset of the capabilities of iMovie on the Mac and is no substitute for desktop applications like Final Cut Pro on Mac; Adobe Premiere Pro on PC or Mac; or PowerDirector, Corel Video Studio Pro, or Sony Vegas Movie Studio for Windows.

So, what can you do with iMovie for iPhone? With this app, it's quite easy to stitch together a number of short video takes into a professional-looking movie. You can have beginning and end credits using one of several themes, add transitions between your takes, and even put titles anywhere in your movie (Figure 8–21). We won't go into how to use iMovie for iPhone in this book, but if you're interested in creating movies on an iPhone, the app well worth the $5.

Figure 8–21. *iMovie for iPhone turns your iPhone into a pocket-sized video-editing suite. The app requires an iPhone 4 or newer model.*

A Dozen Oddball Uses for Your iPhone Camera

Here are some creative ways to use your iPhone camera that you might not have thought of, but which might come in handy:

- *Record receipts*: When your company permits, snap photos of your receipts rather than carrying them around stuffed into your wallet. The iPhone camera's resolution is good enough to capture most receipt details. There are a number of apps in the App Store that will even adjust the receipt pictures to make them look just like you placed them on a copy machine.

- *Remember where you parked your car*: Snap a photo of the aisle number and row where you parked. This can really help when you're late for a trip and running to make that shuttle at the airport.

- *Remember how you got to where you are*: If you're navigating your way through a strange city, snap pictures whenever you make a major turn. That way, you can keep an iPhone trail of visual bread crumbs to get you back to where you started.

- *Record meeting notes*: Sure, there may be one of those automatic copying whiteboards at a meeting you attend—but then again, there may not be. If not, whip out your iPhone and snap pictures of the whiteboard. As with receipts, iPhones have enough resolution that you should have no problem reading the photographed notes, especially if you take a series of close-up shots.

- *Go shopping*: Not sure whether you like that dress or that futon? Snap a picture with your iPhone so you can use it later for comparison shopping.

- *Look at the back of your neck*: Sometimes it's just a relief to know what's going on back there.

- *Look behind furniture*: Shine a flashlight down behind your furniture or under your car and let the iPhone do the work. There's no need to force your eyeball into position when your iPhone can look for you. Open the Camera application and appreciate the easy-to-watch screen.

- *Identify people*: When meeting new contacts, snap a photo as well as taking down names, e-mail addresses, and phone numbers. The iPhone makes it simple to assign pictures to your contacts list, and a photo can help you remember just who that contact is.

- *Bring your "catalog" with you*: If you're offsite and you cannot bring everything along, snap pictures to travel with you. It doesn't matter if you're showing off your garden, your children, or your business equipment. A few photos can offset a lot of describing when you plan and snap in advance.

- *Play "visual" scavenger hunt*: Bored and looking for something to do with a friend? Instead of just texting back and forth, challenge your partner to a scavenger hunt, with snapped photos as proof.

- *Take time-lapse photos*: Apps like iTimeLapse Pro allow you to take time-lapse photos using your iPhone camera ($2.99, http://itunes.apple.com/us/app/itimelapse-pro-time-lapse/id335866860?mt=8)

- *Carry your own photo booth with you*: Nothing says fun quite like snapping pictures of you and your friends making appalling faces. One of our favorite silly apps is Incredibooth ($0.99, http://itunes.apple.com/us/app/incredibooth/id378754705?mt=8), which emulates one of those old "four for a quarter" type photo booths.

Summary

This chapter introduced the iPhone Camera and Photos applications. Despite the usual limitations of smartphone cameras, the iPhone makes it particularly easy to snap, share, and enjoy your photos and videos. Here are some final thoughts for this chapter:

- While the cameras on newer iPhones provide an ever-increasing number of megapixels, don't expect the cameras to meet or exceed the photographic quality of digital point-and-shoot or SLR cameras. Yes, some pro photographers are shooting all of their photos on iPhone cameras, but there were professionals who used Polaroid cameras for their work back in the 60s.

- iPhone's Camera and Photos applications offer some of the most instantly appealing ways to show off the power of your iPhone: scroll through your albums; zoom in and out with a pinch or double-tap; flip the unit on its side; and e-mail photos you've just snapped and videos you've captured. These features all deliver the iPhone wow factor.

- Don't forget that the iPhone is a USB-enabled camera in its own right. You don't need to limit yourself to iTunes to download photos to your computer. Image Capture and Preview are helpful Mac apps that make it easy to move photos and video from your iPhone, and Windows has the built-in ability to import photos or let you manually move them.

- The iPhone slide show settings are in a different place from the Photos application itself. Don't forget that they're available via **Settings ➤ Photo**.

- Uploading your photos by e-mail is a really great way to integrate your iPhone with Flickr. Once you set up a Flickr contact on your iPhone using your "secret" e-mail address, you'll be able to send your photos to Flickr with just a few taps. There are also a number of Flickr apps for iPhone, including the official Flickr app, that ease the transfer of photos from your device to Flickr sets.

Chapter 9

Browsing with Safari

More than any other application, the Safari web browser sets the iPhone apart from most other phones. With it, you can view web pages just as their designers intended. Web sites look like web sites and not like approximations of web sites. Sure, there are still limitations; the lack of Adobe Flash support is one glaring example, as well as the ability to search individual web pages for words or phrases. Yet when it comes to browsing, there's nothing else like Safari in the smartphone market.

In this chapter, you'll discover how to get the most from Safari with all its awesome full-browser powers. You'll learn how to navigate to pages, manage bookmarks, and use both portrait and landscape orientations. You'll also discover some great finger-tap shortcuts, useful Safari web sites, and handy bookmarklet utilities. Read on for all this and more.

Getting Started with iPhone Safari

Tap the Safari application icon to launch the program. On a newly purchased iPhone, you can find Safari in the bottom bar on your Home screen, marked with a white compass on a blue background (see Figure 9–1). Once tapped, the Safari application opens a new window.

Figure 9–1. *Launch Safari from the bottom bar on your Home screen.*

Safari's Browser Window

Many elements on the Safari window may look familiar, especially to anyone experienced using web browsers. Familiar elements include the address field, the search field, the Reload button, and the previous and next page arrows. Figure 9–2 shows a typical Safari browser window.

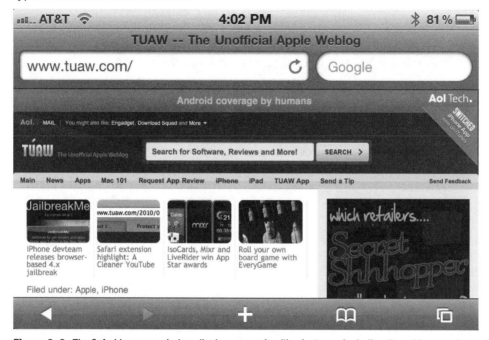

Figure 9–2. *The Safari browser window displays many familiar features, including the address and search fields, Reload button, and the previous/next page buttons. As you can see from this image, Safari works equally well in both portrait and landscape orientations.*

Here are interactive elements you'll find arranged around the screen and what they do:

- *Address field:* Use the address field at the top left of the Safari window to enter a new web address.

- *Search field:* When you need to do a web search using the Google, Yahoo!, or Bing search engines, type your search word or phrase into this field using the iPhone keyboard, and then tap Search. A results page from the search engine appears in the browser window. You can change your default search engine by selecting **Settings ➤ Safari ➤ Search Engine** and then choosing one of the three engines.

- *Reload button:* The arrow bent in a semicircle in the right corner of the address field is the Reload button. Tap it to refresh the current screen.

- *Stop button*: As a page loads, Safari replaces the Reload button with a small *X* (you cannot see this in Figure 9–2). When you change your mind after navigating to a page, tap this. It stops the current page from loading any further.

- *Previous/next page buttons*: The two triangles, facing left and right, navigate through your page history. When they're grayed out, you haven't yet created a history. The arrows turn from gray to white once you start browsing, and you can move back and forth through your history to the previous and next pages. Each page maintains its own history. You can't use these buttons to go back to a page you were viewing in another window (use the Pages button to select another window).

- *Add Bookmark button:* Found just to the left of the address bar, this plus sign–shaped button adds the current page to your bookmark collection. You'll read more about bookmark creation and management later in this chapter.

- *Bookmarks button*: Tap the book-shaped icon to open your Bookmarks screen.

- *Pages button*: The button at the bottom right that looks like two squares superimposed on one another allows you to open the page selection browser and select one of your Safari sessions. You can open up to eight browser windows at a time. With more than one session active, a number appears on this icon. It indicates how many sessions are in use.

> **NOTE:** Although iPhone Safari allows you to browse the web in full resolution, some web sites detect that you're surfing with an iPhone and present a lighter, mobile version of their web pages.

Navigation Basics

iPhone Safari lets you do all the normal things you expect to do in a browser. You can tap links and buttons. You can enter text into forms and so forth. In addition, Safari offers iPhone-specific features you won't find on your home computer: tilting the iPhone on its side moves it from landscape to portrait view and back. The following how-tos guide you through Safari's basic features.

Entering URLs

Tap the address bar to open the URL-entry field (see Figure 9–3). The navigation section appears at the top of your screen, and a keyboard opens from below. Between these, the screen dims, and you can still see part of the page you were on.

Tap the white URL field, and use the keyboard to enter a new URL. Apple provides both the forward slash (/) and a .com key to help you type but not a colon (:). Safari is smart enough to know about http://; you don't have to type it each time.

When you are done typing, tap Go, and Safari navigates to the address you've entered. To return to the browser screen without entering a new URL, tap Cancel instead.

As you type, Safari matches your keystrokes to its existing collection of bookmarks. The space between the top of the keyboard and the bottom of the Google field turns white and displays a list of possible matches. To select one, just tap it. Safari automatically navigates to the selected URL. This matching ability is much more useful in portrait orientation than in landscape orientation. There's more space to view matches.

> **TIP:** When you see a white *X* in a gray circle in a text entry field, you can tap it to clear the field.

Figure 9–3. *The URL entry field allows you to enter the address that you want Safari to visit.*

Performing Web Searches

In Figure 9–2, we pointed out a search field. To perform a search for a keyword on the Web, tap the search field, and it expands to fill the location where the URL entry field is. You can tell the difference between the URL entry field and the search entry field—the search entry field has rounded ends, while those of the URL entry field are more square (Figure 9–4).

Figure 9–4. *The search field is used to enter search terms into one of the available search engines—Google, Yahoo!, and Bing.*

If you haven't yet typed a search term into the search field, you'll see the name of your default search engine (Google, Yahoo!, or Bing) in gray. Type in your search term, and then tap Search to retrieve a list of possible hits. Remember, if you would like to change your default search engine from the default of Google to something else, **Settings ➤ Safari ➤ Search Engine** provides a list of search engines you can choose from.

Entering Text

To edit the contents of any text entry other than the address bar, tap a text field. Safari opens a new text-entry screen. Although this screen is superficially similar to the URL-entry field, it presents a few differences. These differences include a Done button, which you may tap after editing to return to the web page, and previous and next buttons that search for other text fields on your web page. These buttons let you fill out forms without having to go through tedious tap/edit/Done cycles. Simply enter text, tap Next, enter more text, and so forth.

To submit a form after you've entered all the text, tap Go or Search instead of Done. This is like pressing the Enter or Return key on a normal computer.

You'll notice that there's also an AutoFill button. AutoFill enables Safari to fill in fields in forms with your contact information and enter names and passwords that it has saved. To use AutoFill, you need to turn it on first in **Settings ➤ Safari ➤ Autofill** (Figure 9–5).

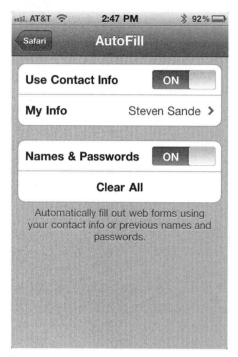

Figure 9–5. *AutoFill settings can speed up the process of filling out forms or entering passwords online when you're using Safari.*

When you enable Use Contact Info by sliding the switch to the on position, you can choose whose contact information you use to fill out forms. By default, My Info is set to your default contacts card.

Since AutoFill makes filling out forms and entering passwords so easy, why wouldn't you want to use it? If your iPhone is ever lost or stolen, the person who picks it up could log into web sites, personal information online, and even bank accounts with your saved usernames and passwords. Be sure to use a passcode (see Chapter 2) to lock your iPhone if you plan on using AutoFill.

Following Links

Hypertext links are used throughout the World Wide Web. Text links are marked with underlines and usually involve a color change from the main text. Image links are subtler, but they can also move you to a new location.

Tap these links to navigate to new web pages or, for certain special links, to open a new e-mail, place a phone call, or view a map. When a link leads to an audio or video file that the iPhone understands, it will play back that file. Special links include `mailto:` (to create Mail messages), `tel:` (for phone calls), and automatic recognition of Google Maps URLs.

NOTE: Supported audio formats include AAC, M4A, M4B, M4P, MP3, WAV, and AIFF. Video formats include h.264 and MPEG-4.

To preview a link's address, touch and hold the link for a second or two. A window with four buttons appears (see Figure 9–6). To open the link in the same window you were just viewing, tap Open. If you prefer to open the link in a new browser window, tap Open in New Page. To simply copy the URL to send to someone in an e-mail, for example, tap Copy. You can also tap the Cancel button if you decide to stay on the current page.

TIP: To detect image links on the screen, tap and hold an image. A window similar to that in Figure 9–6 appears, with an additional button—Save Image—that provides a way to save an image to your photo library. If an image does not have a link associated with it, the only three buttons that appear are Save Image, Copy, and Cancel.

Figure 9–6. *Touch and hold either an image or text link for a second or two to view the URL preview window shown here. This window reveals the link's full URL and allows you to choose whether to open the link in the current browser window, open it in a new browser window, or copy it for pasting elsewhere. Images with links add a Save Image button to this window.*

Changing Orientation

One of the iPhone's standout features is its flexible orientation support. When you turn your unit on its side, the iPhone flips its display to match, as you can see in Figure 9–7. A built-in sensor detects the iPhone's tilt and adjusts the display. Tilt back to vertical, and the iPhone returns to portrait orientation. It takes just a second for the iPhone to detect the orientation change and to update the display.

The iPhone's landscape view offers a relatively wider display. This is particularly good for side-to-side tasks such as reading book-width text. The wider screen allows you to use bigger fonts and view wider columns without scrolling sideways. The portrait view provides a longer presentation. This is great for reading web content with more narrow columns, such as news feeds. You don't have to keep scrolling quite as much as you do in landscape view. Whether in landscape or portrait view, Safari features work the same, including the same buttons in the same positions. In landscape view, you enter text using a wider, sideways keyboard. In portrait view, the smaller keyboard provides more space for you to view possible address completions while entering URLs.

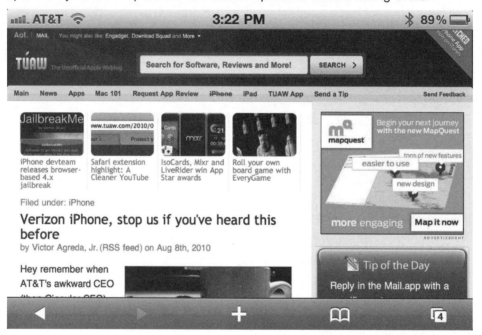

Figure 9–7. *Safari can display web pages using both landscape and portrait orientations.*

Scrolling, Zooming, and Other Viewing Skills

Safari responds to the complete vocabulary of taps, flicks, and drags discussed in Chapter 2. You can zoom into pictures, squeeze on columns, and more. Here's a quick review of the essential ways to interact with your screen:

- *Drag:* Touch the screen, and drag your finger to reposition web pages. If you think of your iPhone as a window onto a web page, dragging allows you to move the window around the web page.

- *Flick*: When dealing with long pages, you can flick the display up and down to scroll rapidly. This is especially helpful when navigating through search engine results and news sites.

- *Double-tap*: Double-tap any column or image to zoom in, autosizing it to the width of your display. Double-tap again to zoom back out. Use this option to instantly zoom into a web page's text. The iPhone recognizes how wide the text is and perfectly matches that width.

- *Pinch*: Use pinching to manually zoom in or out. This allows you to make fine zoom adjustments as needed.

- *Tap*: Tap buttons and links to select them. Tapping allows you to move from site to site and to submit forms.

- *Page down*: When zoomed-in onto a column, double-tap toward the bottom of the screen while staying within the column. The page recenters around your tap. Make sure not to tap a link!

- *Jump to the top*: Tap the status bar at the very top of the screen to pop instantly back to the top of the page.

- *Stop a scroll:* After flicking a page to get it to scroll, you can tap the page at any time to stop that movement. Don't forget, you can also manually drag the screen display to reset the part you're viewing.

Page Management

Safari allows you to open up to eight concurrent browser sessions at once. To review your open windows, tap the Pages button at the bottom-right corner of your browser. Safari's pages viewer opens, as shown in Figure 9–8.

Figure 9–8. *The pages viewer allows you to select which of eight possible browser sessions to display.*

This viewer allows you to interactively select a browser session:

- To select a window, scroll horizontally from one window to the next. The brightest dot along the line of dots shows which item you're currently viewing. In Figure 9–8, this is third of eight open pages. Either tap the window or tap the Done button to select that window and display it full-screen.

- To close a window, tap the Close button—the red circle with an *X* in it at the top-left of each page. The page viewer slides the remaining pages into the gap left by the closed window. You cannot close the last remaining window; Safari insists on keeping at least one browser session open at all times.

- To add a new page, tap New Page. Safari creates a new session and opens the new, blank page for you to work with. Add up to eight pages, after which the New Page button no longer works.

Working with Bookmarks

One of the great things about iPhone is that it lets you take your world with you: contacts, calendars, e-mail accounts, and bookmarks. You don't have to reenter URLs for all your favorite pages on the iPhone. It loads these bookmarks whenever it syncs. The secret to this lies in iTunes. As Figure 9–9 reveals, iTunes allows you to enable syncing of Safari bookmarks. To find these settings, tap the Info tab, and scroll toward the bottom of the screen. Check Sync Safari bookmarks to turn on syncing, and if you'd like the bookmarks on your Windows computer or Mac to overwrite those on the iPhone, make sure that Bookmarks is checked under Advanced as well.

> **NOTE:** As Chapter 5 discussed, use the Advanced replace information settings only when you transfer your iPhone to a new host or when you want to completely overwrite your iPhone bookmarks.

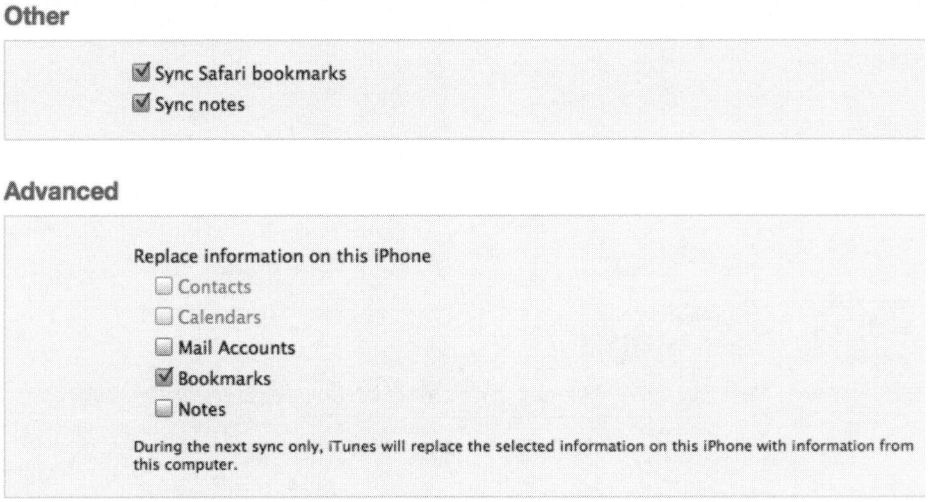

Other

☑ Sync Safari bookmarks
☑ Sync notes

Advanced

Replace information on this iPhone

☐ Contacts
☐ Calendars
☐ Mail Accounts
☑ Bookmarks
☐ Notes

During the next sync only, iTunes will replace the selected information on this iPhone with information from this computer.

Figure 9–9. The Info tab in iTunes lets enable syncing of Safari bookmarks with your iPhone. Unfortunately, you cannot sync your iPhone with other browsers.

Selecting Bookmarks

Many people have bookmark collections containing hundreds and hundreds of individual URLs. That's one reason we really appreciate the iPhone's simple bookmarks browser (see Figure 9–10). It uses the same folders structure that that you may have set up on your personal computer. You tap folders to open them and tap the Back button (top-left corner) to return to the parent folder.

Identifying bookmarks is easy. Folders look like folders; each bookmark is marked with a small open book symbol. Tap one of these, and Safari takes you directly to the page in question.

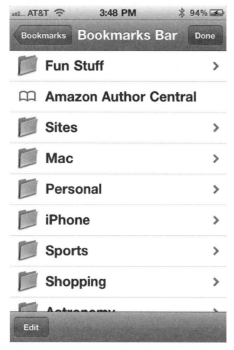

Figure 9–10. *Use iPhone Safari's interactive Bookmarks navigation to locate and open your favorite bookmarks.*

Editing Bookmarks

As Figure 9–10 shows, an Edit button appears at the bottom right of the bookmarks screen. Tap this to enter Edit mode (see Figure 9–11).

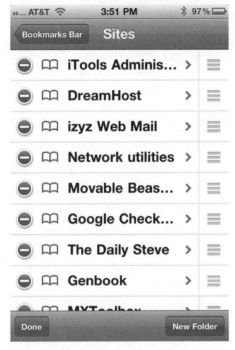

Figure 9–11. *Safari contains a built-in bookmark management system that allows you to edit and reorder your bookmarks.*

Edit mode allows you to manage your bookmarks on your iPhone just as you would on your personal computer:

- *Delete bookmarks*: Tap the red delete circle to the left of a bookmark to delete it. Tap Delete to confirm, or tap elsewhere on the screen to cancel.

- *Reorder bookmarks*: Use the gray grab handles (the three lines on the far right) to move folders and bookmarks into new positions. Grab, drag, and then release.

- *Edit names*: Tap the gray reveal arrow (the sideways *V* symbol to the right of each name) to open the Edit Bookmark or Edit Folder screen. Use the keyboard to make your changes, and tap the Back button to return to the bookmarks editor.

■ *Move bookmarks*: You can move bookmarks from one folder to another by tapping the gray reveal arrow and selecting a new location from the bookmark folder list (just below the name editing field). Select a folder to move to, and you'll be returned to the Edit Bookmark screen. Unfortunately, you don't get the same wild animation you do in Mail when you send an item to a new folder, but at least it works reliably.

■ *Add folders*: Tap New Folder to create a folder in the currently displayed bookmarks. The iPhone automatically opens the Edit Folder screen. Here, you can edit the name and, if needed, move your new folder. You'll be returned to the Edit Bookmarks screen automatically.

■ *Finish*: Return to the top-level Bookmarks list (tap the Back button until you reach it), and then tap Done. This closes the editor and returns to Safari.

Saving Bookmarks

To save a new bookmark, tap the add (+) button at the bottom center of any Safari web page. An Add Bookmark window opens (Figure 9–12) asking you to choose between adding a bookmark, adding a button to the Home screen, or mailing a link to that page to somebody. Let's see what those buttons do:

Figure 9–12. *Tapping the Add Bookmark button gives you a choice of adding a bookmark to your iPhone's bookmark list, adding a button to your Home screen, or mailing a link to a web page to someone else.*

- *Add Bookmark:* Tapping Add Bookmark opens an edit screen where you can change the name of the bookmark, edit the URL of the bookmark, and specify the location of the bookmark in your folders. Tap Save to finish adding the bookmark to your collection.

- *Add to Home Screen:* A screen appears with a default icon that will be displayed on your Home screen, as well as a title for the icon. When you tap the Add button on the Add to Home screen, an icon is added to your Home screen so you can quickly access the web site.

- *Mail Link to this Page:* To send an e-mail containing a link to the page you're currently viewing, tap this button. A standard e-mail entry screen appears, containing the title of the web page as a subject line, the URL as the body of the message, and with an open address field so that you can address the e-mail before tapping Send.

iPhone Settings

Customize your Safari settings by navigating to **Settings ➤ Safari**. This screen, shown in Figure 9–13, allows you to control a number of features, mostly security related.

Figure 9–13. *The Safari Settings window is primarily concerned with security features.*

Here's a quick rundown of those features and what they mean:

- *Search Engine*: This setting determines which search engine is used for the search field you saw in Figure 9–4. Choose from Google, Yahoo!, and Bing.

- *Autofill*: We discussed this feature a few pages ago. Remember that enabling the feature provides automatic fill-in of forms and sign-ins but that it doing so can result in security issues if your iPhone is ever stolen or lost.

- *JavaScript*: JavaScript allows web pages to run programs when you visit. Disabling JavaScript means you increase overall surfing safety, but you also lose many cool and worthy web features. Most pages are safe to visit, but some, sadly, are not. To disable JavaScript, switch from on to off.

- *Block Pop-ups*: Many web sites use pop-up windows for advertising. It's an annoying reality of surfing the Web. By default, Safari pop-up blocking is on. Switch this setting to off to allow pop-up window creation.

- *Accept Cookies*: Cookies refer to data stored on your iPhone by the web sites you visit. Cookies allow web sites to remember you and to store information about your visit. You can choose to always accept cookies, never accept cookies, or accept cookies only "From visited" web sites.

- *Databases*: Certain web sites, Yahoo.com being one example, support local database storage on the iPhone. This is a feature of HTML5, the latest and most robust version of the HyperText Markup Language used to build most web sites. Tapping this button provides a look at which web sites have requested local database storage and how much memory they are taking. You can delete the databases by tapping the Databases button and then tapping Edit on the Databases screen. Tap the Delete buttons to clear out the databases.

- *Clear History:* Tap and confirm to empty your page navigation history from your iPhone. This keeps your personal browsing habits private to some extent, although other people might still scan though your bookmarks.

CAUTION: Clearing your history does not affect Safari's page history. You can still tap its Back button and see the sites you've visited.

- *Clear Cookies:* Tap and confirm to clear all existing cookies from your iPhone.

- *Clear Cache:* Your iPhone's browser cache stores data from many of the web sites you visit. It uses this to speed up page loading the next time you visit. As with cookies and history, your cache may reveal personal information that you'd rather not share. Tap Clear Cache and Confirm to clear your cache.

> **TIP:** Clearing your cache may also help correct problem pages that are having trouble loading. By clearing the cache, you remove page items that may be corrupt or only partially downloaded.

- *Developer:* If you're an iPhone developer, then you probably already know about this button. Tapping Developer allows you to enable the debug console, a tool that is used by developers to resolve web page errors.

iPhone-Specific Web Sites

When Steve Jobs announced the iPhone in January 2007, he made it clear that the iPhone would not be opened to third-party native development at that time. Instead, he offered developers the "sweet" solution of using iPhone Safari to deliver advanced Web 2.0 interactive applications. These applications are known as *web apps* and are still actively developed, although they have been mostly supplanted by native iPhone apps.

Many web developers took Jobs up on that solution, producing a wealth of useful and varied web sites geared specifically for iPhone use. Visit `www.apple.com/webapps,` and you'll find thousands of iPhone-specific and iPhone-supporting web sites that allow you to do everything from balancing your budget to playing games to creating to-do lists.

> **NOTE:** The obvious downside to Jobs' "sweet" solution in the early years of iPhone was that you lost access to these applications when you were out of range of Wi-Fi or 3G. The Apple Software Development Kit (SDK) for iOS made it possible for developers to create apps that are not reliant on a network connection and has resulted in an App Store filled with hundreds of thousands of useful (and some not so useful) apps. The new HTML 5 standard used in Safari on the iPhone does provide the ability to run web apps offline, and there's even a web app store now (`OpenAppMkt.com`).

Summary

iPhone Safari puts the power of a real Internet browser into your pocket. There's nothing half-cocked or watered down about it. You can browse the real Web and read real sites without major compromise. Sure, Safari doesn't support Flash—and that's a pretty major failing—but many web developers are beginning to throw their support behind HTML5, which means that your iPhone and other iOS devices won't need Flash.

Here are a few tips to keep in mind as you move on from this chapter:

- iPhones work in more ways than just vertical. Go ahead and flip your phone on its side. Your Safari pages will adjust.

- Nope, there's no Flash support. Adobe and Apple have gone back and forth about this, and there appears to be no solution in sight.

- There are no in-page "find" features in Safari.

- Lost your address bar? Tap the status bar at the top of the screen to pop up to the top and reclaim your lost address bar.

- Bookmarks are a powerful tool for browsing favorite web sites efficiently. Use them to your advantage.

Chapter **10**

The Shopping Mall in Your iPhone

You might think of your iPhone as an Internet-connected computer, but it's much more than that. It's also a software store, a bookstore, a music store, and a place to buy or rent videos and movies.

The iPhone stores build upon Apple's history of building electronic storefronts that make it easy to purchase digital content. This started with the iTunes Music Store on April 28, 2003, resulting with Apple becoming the number-one seller of music in the United States just five years later. Now known as the iTunes Store, Apple's digital store accounts for 70 percent of all worldwide digital music sales.

Through the iTunes Store, you have access to more than 11 million songs available worldwide. Your iPhone, if it is using the U.S. iTunes Store, provides access to more than 1 million podcasts, 40,000 music videos, 3,000 TV shows, 20,000 audiobooks, 2,500 movies, and 225,000 iPhone apps in the App Store.

Starting on April 3, 2010, Apple opened the virtual doors of a new store, the iBookstore. At the time this book was being written, it didn't have the selection of Amazon's Kindle Bookstore, but a large number of classic and new titles are available.

In this chapter, we'll take you on a virtual shopping spree buying apps, music, movies, videos and TV shows, and books, all while sitting with your iPhone in front of you.

The App Store

The App Store opened its doors on July 11, 2008, and as of the printing of this book, more than 7 billion apps have been sold. Most of those apps were written for the iPhone and iPod touch, while a growing number are universal apps that can also run on the iPad. Many apps have been written especially to take advantage of the Retina display and faster processor of the iPhone 4 and newer models, and some apps run on any device but have improved capabilities that appear only when viewed on the newer iPhones.

When you activated your iPhone in Chapter 1, you were asked either to enter an existing Apple ID (iTunes or MobileMe account) or to sign up for one. By doing this, Apple set up both the payment and authorization mechanisms that are used by all the on-device stores. That means that you're ready to make purchases in any of the Apple stores directly from your iPhone.

When you launch the App Store on your iPhone, you're greeted with a screen that looks something like Figure 10–1.

Figure 10–1. *The iPhone App Store*

By default, the App Store initially displays Featured Apps. How can you tell? There are five icons at the bottom of the App Store page: Featured, Categories, Top 25, Search, and Updates. The first time you launch the iPhone App Store application, the Featured icon is highlighted.

When you're reading this chapter, be aware that the App Store may look different from what you see in the images in this chapter and elsewhere in the book. Apple is constantly changing the layout and content of the App Store to make browsing more enjoyable and provide additional information to help you make a purchasing decision.

Featured Apps

At the top of the store you'll see three buttons: New, What's Hot, and Genius. Each one of these buttons displays a slightly different view of the inventory of the App Store. We'll start by looking at the New view.

On top of the page are several buttons that highlight either a specific program or a group of apps. In Figure 10–1, three of the four buttons go directly to categorized groups. For example, tapping Hot New Games displays a list of five subcategories: New & Noteworthy, Made for iOS4, Best Undiscovered, Best First-Person Shooters, and Gripping Stories. As we mentioned earlier, these buttons, categories, and subcategories change frequently, so don't expect to see exactly what we're talking about here. Below the big buttons is a list of new apps that have caught the attention of the App Store team. When you see an app that you'd like more details about, just tap it, and a detailed app description appears (Figure 10–2):

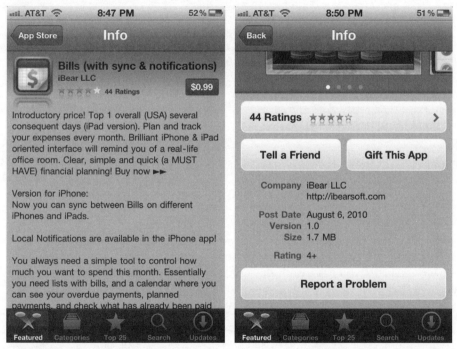

Figure 10–2. *Detailed description of an app in the App Store. Here we see the top of the description (left), as well as the buttons at the bottom (right).*

The app description screen displays the icon that appears on your iPhone screen, as well as the price, the category that the app is in, information about the latest release, compatibility, and customer ratings. There are also screenshots that show you special or fun features of the app. The screen shots displayed on the screen scroll, so to see all of them, just drag the visible picture to the left.

Want to tell a friend about the app that you found? Tap the Tell a Friend button, and the App Store creates an informative e-mail that you can send to your buddy. Even better, tap the Gift This App button to buy the app for your friend.

> **NOTE:** If you have purchased an app and have problems with it, tap the Report a Problem link, and you can let both Apple and the developer know about the issue. To report a problem, choose the appropriate type of problem (a bug, something offensive in the app, or something else), fill in the Comments section, and then tap the Report button to send the information.

We recommend reading the customer ratings and reviews at the bottom of the app description page, although they can sometimes be misleading. We find that the reviews often point out common issues that other users may be having with the app, so you can decide whether to purchase the app now or wait for a revision. After you buy an app, you can also rate it and leave a review for others to read.

When you've decided to purchase an app, all you need to do is tap the price. If it's a free app, the Free button turns into a green Install button. For those apps that are available for sale, the price turns to a green Buy Now button , which you then tap. A dialog box appears on your iPhone screen asking you to enter your iTunes password and then tap OK. Once that's been completed, the app is downloaded and installed onto your iPhone. You'll receive an e-mail receipt from Apple outlining your purchase within a few days.

> **WARNING!** When you tap OK and the download begins, the App Store closes and the Home screen of your iPhone appears. Don't be alarmed; this is normal. This also happens when you're updating apps.

You may notice tiny plus (+) signs next to the price on apps (Figure 10–3). Those indicate that the apps are universal and run on both iPhone and iPad devices. These apps can be worthwhile if you have both devices, since you pay once to run the app on both devices. On the other hand, some developers optimize the app for one device and not both, so the user experiences are totally different between the devices.

Near the bottom of the New tab in the Featured section of the App Store you'll find two very important buttons. The first, Redeem, is used to redeem iTunes gift cards, gift certificates, or promotional codes that you may receive from a software vendor. Tap the Redeem button, type in the code, and tap the Redeem button. You may be asked to enter your Apple account information for verification, after which time you'll be ready to download the app you had the promo code for, or you can start shopping with the proceeds from your gift card or certificate.

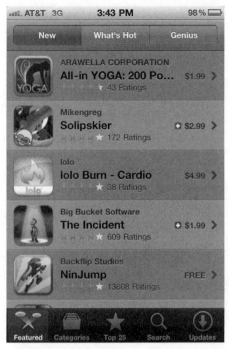

Figure 10–3. *Do you see those little white plus signs next to the price on Solipskier and The Incident? Those are universal apps for iPhone and iPad.*

The second button is marked with the word *Account* and the current Apple account you're using. If you have more than one Apple account, tapping this button will let you either view account information for the current account or sign out of the account.

Sometimes you may want to check credit card information or enter a different credit card into your account. It's good to know that you can do that from the App Store app and don't need to wait until you're using a "real" computer.

Moving on to the What's Hot tab in the Featured section of the App Store, you'll see another list of applications, this time sorted by the current popularity of the apps. As with the New tab, the Account button appears at the bottom of the page for those spur-of-the-moment account changes. There's not much different about this tab, other than the way the apps are displayed.

The Genius tab in the Featured section of the App Store is quite different. The first time you tap the Genius tab, the App Store app displays an explanatory screen (Figure 10–4). The explanation on that page is perfect: "introduces you to apps you'll love by learning about the apps you already have." Enabling this capability is just a tap away. Tap that Turn On Genius button, enter your Apple account password, and then agree to the Apple Store terms and conditions.

Figure 10–4. *Turning on the Genius feature is like having a shopping assistant in your iPhone who is constantly suggesting new apps that may fit your personal tastes.*

The Genius tab displays apps that the Genius thinks you'd like. For each item that is listed, there's a note explaining why the app is in your list. If you don't like a specific suggestion, just swipe across it, and a red Delete button appears. Tap that, and the suggestion is removed from your list. This is a good thing to do, since the Genius fine-tunes its suggestions based on how you react to its initial picks. We didn't like the fact that it was trying to suggest every Twitter client app in the App Store simply because we had one similar app on our iPhones; the suggestions died off after deleting the bad suggestions. Still, the Genius feature is an interesting way to find out about apps that you may have otherwise overlooked.

Categories

There may be times that you're not interested in knowing what the most popular or new apps are. You just want a specific type of app, and you'd like to find out everything in that category quickly.

That's where the Categories section of the App Store comes in handy. At the time of publication of this book, Categories was divided into 20 main areas of interest, from Games to Medical (Figure 10–5).

Figure 10–5. *Categories list large groupings of apps, some of which are sub-categorized for easier searching.*

Some of the categories listed in this section of the App Store are divided into subcategories to provide an easier way to search through thousands of apps. For example, tapping the Games category button displays a set of subcategory buttons, from Action games to Word games.

Usually, though, tapping a category button will display a list of the 25 Top Paid and Top Free apps in that category. There's also a listing of the top 25 apps by release date so that you can see what is new in any specific category.

At the bottom of each list is a Twenty Five More... button, which does exactly what it advertises and displays 25 more apps in that section.

Top 25

In the previous section, we described how each category or subcategory button displays the top 25 paid, free, or recently released apps for that section of the App Store. But what if you want to see the "crème de la crème" of the App Store, in other words, the top 25 overall apps? That's what the Top 25 section of the store is all about.

Tapping the Top 25 button displays three tabs (Figure 10–6): Top Paid, Top Free, and Top Grossing apps. Each tab displays the top 25 apps in those three areas, with a Show Top 50... button at the bottom of each list. The Top Paid apps are, naturally, the apps that you need to pay for, while the Top Free apps are very popular free or ad-supported apps.

The Top Grossing apps are the applications that are pulling in the most money in the App Store. At the time of publication, Madden NFL 2011 was taking in a lot of money, both because of the popularity of this football simulation game and the relatively high price ($7.99) of the app.

Figure 10–6. *Looking for the cream of the crop? The Top 25 section of the App Store is the best place to start.*

Search

Sometimes you just can't afford the time to browse around the App Store looking for a specific app. That's where Search can help you by providing a single point of entry into a focused text-based search of the App Store.

As an example of how search works, let's look for a text editor that works with the Dropbox (http://dropbox.com) online storage service. Tapping Search at the bottom of the App Store displays a search field and a blank screen. Not knowing the name of the text editor that we'd like to find, we'll enter the search term **Dropbox** into the search field (Figure 10–7).

Figure 10–7. *Searching for a Dropbox-compatible text editor using the term dropbox displays these two apps.*

Not knowing the name of the app, we could either tap the listing for "elements" or search further. Let's see what happens when we enter the term **text edit dropbox** into the same search field and tap the Search button. This search displays the information for three apps that both perform text-editing functions and support Dropbox. Sure enough, one of the apps is Elements (`http://secondgearsoftware.com/elements/`). A quick review of the app reveals that it is the one we were looking for, and with a few taps, it's downloaded to our iPhones to start writing a new book.

Updates

As writers, we test and review a lot of apps. Application developers are constantly improving their apps as well as fixing bugs, so there are a lot of updates that are published. Instead of needing to physically check each and every app for updates, the App Store displays the number of apps that are currently ready to be updated (Figure 10–8).

Figure 10–8. *There's one update awaiting us in the App Store, and since it's probably a fun new theme in Doodle Jump, it's time to tap the Update All button.*

The number of apps that have updates ready to install is listed in a tiny red circle next to the Updates icon at the bottom of the App Store. If you have more than one update waiting, tap the Update All button. You'll be asked to enter your Apple account password, after which the app update is downloaded and installed.

If you're on a 3G connection rather than in a location with Wi-Fi when attempting to install apps or updates, you may see a message informing you that the size of the file is too large to install over 3G. In that case, try again when you're connected to a Wi-Fi network. Apple has set a 20MB file size limit for over-the-air installations, so any file that exceeds this limit generates the error message described here.

> **NOTE:** Although we've brought it up before, it bears repeating: the App Store layout is constantly changing, so do not expect it to look exactly like what you've seen here in the screenshots. The App Store is essentially a web site that is run by Apple, and changing layouts to enhance usability or attract sales is done frequently. Feel free to just poke around the store as much as you'd like, and see what new and exciting features Apple has added to the world's top App Store.

The iTunes Store

The App Store is the place to shop if you're looking for games or other software, but what if you want to buy music, movies, or TV shows? That's the purpose of the iTunes app on your iPhone (Figure 10–9).

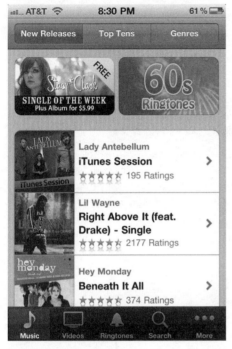

Figure 10–9. *The iTunes Store. Just tap the iTunes app icon on your iPhone to enter a world of songs, videos, movies, ringtones, and more.*

The first thing you may notice is the similarity in the design of the iTunes Store and that of the App Store. The iTunes Store came first and was refined over many years, so Apple took the same concept and applied it to the App Store and the new iBookstore. The iTunes store has one nice feature the App Store doesn't: 30-second previews. To preview any song, video, or movie in the store, or listen to a ringtone, tap it.

Both stores have a set of buttons across the top and bottom of the screen. In the iTunes Store, the buttons are titled New Releases, Top Tens, and Genres. As with the App Store, everything you see in the screenshots here are subject to change at any time.

Along the bottom of the screen are buttons for all the different types of media that you can download from iTunes. The media consists of Music (single tracks or albums by musical artists), Videos, Ringtones, Podcasts and several items you'll find listed under More: Podcasts, AudioBooks, and iTunes U.

Music

In the beginning, iTunes was all about the music, and this on-iPhone store still revolves around the recording industry. As with the App Store, the iTunes app Music section has three tabs for you to tap at the top of the screen. New Releases features recent songs or albums by a variety of artists.

In the list you see in Figure 10–9, some of the buttons are for new albums, and some are for singles that have just been released (the title will always be followed by the word *Single* in this case). Tap the name of any track to play a preview of the song.

You don't have to buy a complete album just to get one song that you really like. Most albums have each individual track listed, and a favorite track can be purchased just as easily as an album (and with less impact to your wallet). However, sometimes artists add special tracks or videos that can be purchased only as part of an album.

The Top Tens tab lists the Top Ten hits in a number of music genres (Figure 10–10). Whether your music tastes veer toward Country or Classical, Hip-Hop or Rock, you'll be treated to a list of the Top 10 Songs and Top 10 Albums in that genre. In this Top 10 Songs, tapping a listed track plays a preview of the song, while double-tapping delivers a list of all the songs on the associated album.

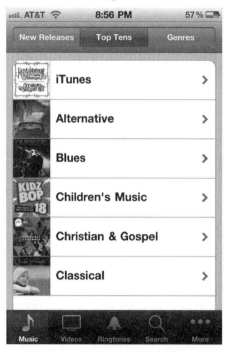

Figure 10–10. *Music Top Tens provides the top songs in a number of music genres. This tab is a great way to keep up with the latest music from just about any artist.*

As with the App Store, tap the price button to view a Buy Now button. Tap that button, enter your Apple account password, and your music is downloaded immediately.

NOTE: The next time you sync your iPhone to your computer, the music you just purchased is copied to iTunes on your Mac or Windows computer. In the iTunes sidebar under Store is a list of all the Music, Videos, Books, or other non-App items that you've purchased on a specific device.

The final tab in the Music section of the App Store lists music by genre. As with the Top Tens, if you like a particular genre, from Alternative to World Music, the Genre section highlights music by your favorite artists. There's a difference between this list and the Top Tens list; in one genre, you may see a list of new releases, while tracks in other genres appear to be randomly selected.

Videos

With the beautiful, bright images that the Retina display on the iPhone 4 provides, your iPhone can be a portable TV or movie theater. Tap the Videos button at the bottom of the iTunes app window, and three primary tabs are displayed at the top of the windows: Movies, TV Shows, and Music Videos.

Tapping the Movies button displays a screen similar to that shown in Figure 10–11. At the top of the screen are large buttons displaying individual movies of note, specials such as the "Dog Days of Summer" $4.99 movie purchase offer or the 99¢ movie rentals, and then a list of new movies that have just hit the iTunes Store.

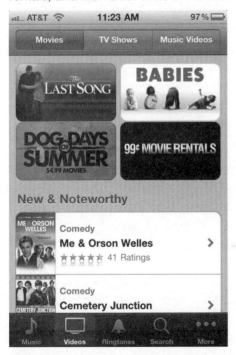

Figure 10–11. *The iTunes Videos button opens a world of movies and video to every iPhone owner.*

By tapping any specific movie in the list (Figure 10–12), you can see the price of the movie or movie rental (usually the price of the high-definition version), tap a preview button for a short trailer of the film, see reviews that have been left by other iTunes customers, and in some cases view a "Tomatometer" rating from the popular RottenTomatoes.com website. If the movie comes in both high-definition and standard-definition versions, there is an Also Available In Standard Definition link at the bottom of the description page.

Figure 10–12. *The detailed description of a movie displays purchase or rental options, previews, reviews by other iTunes customers, and (in some cases) reviews by professional film critics.*

> **NOTE:** Even though some movie rentals and purchases are offered in HD, they are not viewable in HD on your iPhone. It's better to take the less expensive SD version of a movie, which can be viewed on almost any device. One very cool feature of movie rentals is that you can begin to watch a rental on one device (like your iPhone), stop watching, and then begin watching at the same point on a computer, iPod, iPad, or even a TV using an Apple TV or similar device.

To buy a movie, tap the Buy button, which also displays the price of the purchase. A green Buy Now button is displayed confirming your intent to purchase the movie, and tapping the button commits you to the purchase.

When you buy a movie, it's yours in digital form forever. You can watch it on your iPhone, your iPad, your Windows computer, and your Mac—basically any device that is running Apple's iTunes software and that syncs to the online store.

Rentals, however, are different. When you commit to a rental of a movie in the iTunes app, the movie starts downloading immediately. You don't have to watch it right away. In fact, you have 30 days in which to watch the movie, so if you want to load up your iPhone before traveling out of the country for a while, you can have entertainment for those cold nights on the trains in Siberia. Once you've clicked the Play button, however, you have 24 hours to finish viewing the movie. You can watch the movie as many times as you want in that 24-hour period, but once the time limit is up, the movie is no longer available for viewing.

If you think you might want to split your movie watching into a couple of nights, you should consider either purchasing the movie for your iPhone or (if you're near a DVD player) just getting a DVD from your local library, from McDonald's Redbox, or from Netflix.

CAUTION: When renting movies, make sure you're on a fast Wi-Fi network. The movie files are quite large, so a spur-of-the-moment decision to rent a movie on your iPhone at a hotel on Saturday night can turn into an all-weekend ordeal of waiting for the download to finish.

At the very bottom of the Movies screen are buttons for Top Ten and Genre lists. The Top Ten section lists the Top Ten movies for a variety of movie genres, so it's easy to find the best movies in your favorite genre. There's also the familiar Account button at the bottom of the screen, in case you need to log in as another iTunes user.

Not a movie fan? The iTunes store also provides a wide selection of TV shows, either complete seasons or individual episodes. You can even purchase a season pass that allows you to watch new episodes as they become available online, usually within a day or two of the initial airing on the networks.

Unlike movies, there's no option to rent TV shows. You purchase either a single episode or a season. Seasons, especially of popular TV shows, can be quite expensive, as you can see in Figure 10–13. If the show was originally broadcast in HD, you'll get the HD version on your iPhone (although you can only watch it in SD), and the SD version will be available for download when you sync to your computer.

You might not want to watch the movie on your iPhone screen but still use it as a movie player. In Chapter 1, we discussed the accessory cables (iPad Dock Connector to VGA Adapter, Composite AV Cable, and Component AV Cable) that work with the iPhone 4 and some earlier phones. These cables can be used to watch your iPhone movies on a big display or TV.

Finally, the Music Videos tab takes you to the MTV of your iPhone. If you're a fan of music videos by your favorite stars, you'll love the Music Videos tab (Figure 10–14). Occasionally you'll find a free music video available for download as promotion for a new album or single being released by a musician. New releases are listed vertically on the screen, and with a tap you can watch a preview and buy the video.

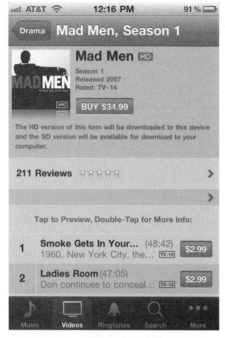

Figure 10–13. *TV series are available for purchase only, with no rentals. Complete seasons can be relatively expensive to purchase.*

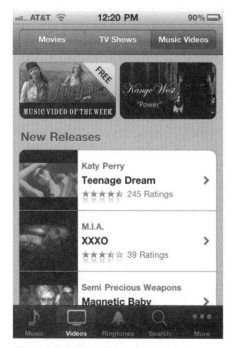

Figure 10–14. *The Music Video tab is one area where you might occasionally find a free download available for your viewing pleasure.*

Ringtones

We talked about selecting and making your own ringtones in Chapter 6. There's a very easy way to purchase ringtones featuring your favorite songs by hot artists, and it's available in the iTunes app.

Tap the Ringtones button to display a list of ringtones available for download (Figure 10–15, left). Some are 30-second bites of new songs, while others take on the classics. Similar to the tabs available in the other sections of the iTunes app, the Ringtones section is divided into Featured, Top Tens, and Genres.

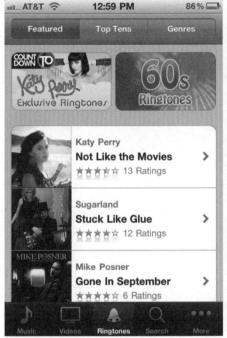 

FIGURE 10–15. *Thousands of iTunes tracks can be purchased and installed as ringtones on your iPhone (right). When you purchase a ringtone, you need to specify whether it is going to be your default ringtone or whether you're going to assign a song to a particular person (right).*

Like before, you can listen to a preview of the song by tapping on the name. All the ringtones have a small bell icon next to them in case you forget what you're buying. Tapping the price button displays the now familiar Buy Now button, and with a tap the ringtone will be ready to download. There's just one more thing you need to do—either assign the ringtone as your default ringtone or assign it to a contact (Figure 10–15, right).

> **CAUTION:** Although purchasing a ringtone directly from iTunes is generally less expensive than buying a song, when purchasing the rights to edit and create your own ringtone as described in Chapter 6, the iTunes ringtones cannot be edited. That means that the best part of some songs is left out of the ringtone!

Search

With the huge number of songs, movies, TV shows, ringtones, and other media that are available in the iTunes Store, there has to be an easy way to find items by name. The Search button, which looks like a magnifying glass, can be tapped to do text searches in iTunes (Figure 10–16).

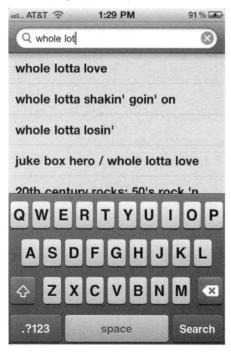

Figure 10–16. *The iTunes Search button displays a blank screen with a search field at the top of it. Start typing your search criteria into the search field, and possible hits for the search appear in a list below.*

If you're looking for a particular track or video, just start typing the name of the song or movie into the search field at the top of the screen. As you type, appropriate answers are listed below the search field. Tap any one of the answers to open a more detailed listing of individual media files that are listed in the iTunes Store (Figure 10–17).

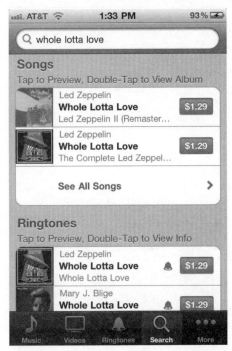

Figure 10–17. *Details of a search are organized by type of media—Songs, Videos, Ringtones, and more. The bell icon indicates that you can purchase the item as a ringtone.*

More...

At the far right of the button bar in iTunes is the mysterious More... button. What does it do? As Figure 10–18 shows, it is the gateway to other media—Podcasts, Audiobooks, and iTunes U content. You can replace the Music, Videos, or Ringtones buttons with any of these media types by tapping **More ➤ Edit** and then dragging any of the icons listed to the button bar and dropping it into place where you'd like it to be. Tap Done, and your changes are saved.

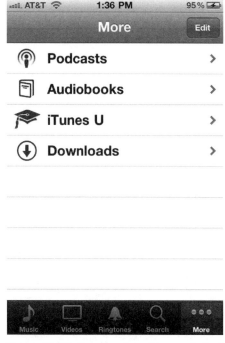

Figure 10–18. *There's not enough room in the button bar at the bottom of the iTunes app to display all the different types of media, so the More... button is your portal to those lesser used media types.*

iBooks and the iBookstore

If you love to read books, you'll love iBooks and the iBookstore. iBooks is a free app available from Apple, and when downloaded, it turns your iPhone into a pocket library and bookstore. iBooks displays your books, usually with a facsimile of their "real" bookstore covers, on a nice wooden bookshelf called the Library (Figure 10–19). You can choose to view your books on the bookshelf or in a list format by tapping the icons that are just to the right of the search field on the bookshelf.

To read a book, just tap it. There are icons at the top of the page to let you go back to the Library, display a table of contents or bookmarks, adjust the brightness of the screen, change the font size of the text (try that with a printed book!), search for key words or phrases, or set a bookmark. There's a beautiful animation of a turning page (Figure 10–19, right) when you slowly drag the lower-right corner of the page to the left, and it's as close to reading an actual book as you can get with any electronic book reader or application.

Although reading a book in the Library is fairly well self-explanatory and easy to pick up, the iBookstore needs a bit of clarification. It's part of the iBook app, and you enter the iBookstore by tapping the Store button in the Library. The first time you enter the iBookstore, you're plopped into the Featured section (Figure 10–20). Here you'll find new books that have excited the readers and editors at the store.

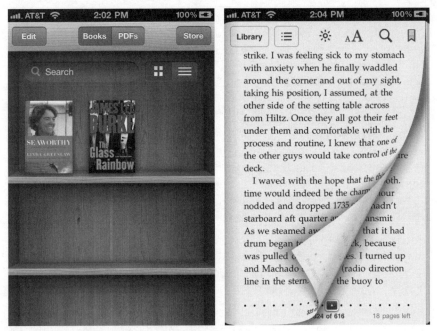

Figure 10–19. *The iBook app is an attractive and functional e-book reader. To visit the iBookstore, just tap the button in the top-right corner. Turning a page in the book is almost like turning a page in a real book, with the paper curling as you flip to a new page (right).*

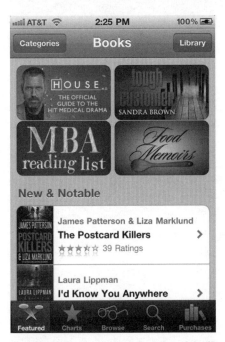

Figure 10–20. *The Featured section of the iBookstore is where to find all of the new books that have just arrived, as well as lists created by Apple tying a number of books by an author or a subject into a single area.*

Tap a title to get a description of the book, the price of the book, and in some cases, download a sample of the book. You can read reviews by other readers, and if an author page has been created, you can see a list of all books written by the author of the book you're perusing. As with the other stores, tapping the price button reveals a Buy Book button; tapping the BuyBook button commits you to a purchase. Your purchase is charged to the same credit card that you use to pay for music, movies, apps, and other media.

The Charts button lists the top books in two ways: Top Charts, which are the most popular paid and free books in the iBookstore, and New York Times, which lists the current *New York Times* bestsellers for fiction and nonfiction. If you like a particular category of book more than others, you can tap the Categories button to get an alphabetical list of book genres from Arts & Entertainment to Travel & Adventure. This button appears on the top of most lists in the iBookstore.

The Browse button is different from most buttons in the various stores on the iPhone. It produces a list of authors by paid or free books, and the list can be further defined by choosing a category from the Categories button. Once you've selected an author, tapping the author name generates a list of his or her books.

Search is used like the Search button in the iTunes Store. If you want to find a specific author or title, tap the Search button, type in your search criterion in the field at the top of the page, and a list of possible search results appears in a list below the search field. Finally, a tapping Purchases displays a list of all books you've purchased in the iBookstore, whether on your iPhone or another device (Figure 10–21). Each displays a button showing whether it is currently downloaded onto the device or can be redownloaded onto your iPhone. That's a great way to keep your library "stocked" with books without having to take up a significant amount of storage on your iPhone.

The iBooks app and the iBookstore represent Apple's take on the electronic book market. There are many other stores for e-books, most of which have their own app associated with them. Amazon's huge Kindle e-bookstore has an app, as does Barnes and Noble. The Stanza and eReader apps provide a way to read e-books on your iPhone that are formatted for other devices.

> **NOTE:** iBooks can read both EPUB- and PDF-formatted files. PDF files aren't formatted as nicely (in our opinion) as EPUBs, and the pages simply slide back and forth instead of using the book-like page-turning animation. There are Windows and Mac applications available to convert from PDF to EPUB. One popular free application for doing the conversion is Calibre (http://calibre-ebook.com).

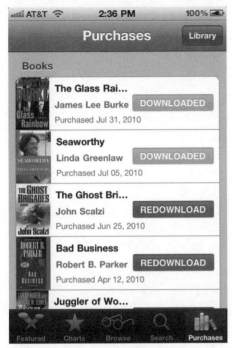

Figure 10–21. *The Purchases button displays a list of all e-books you've purchased from the iBookstore and offers a way to redownload them to your device if they're not currently installed.*

The Apple Store

Although this feature isn't available in all iPhone markets, the Apple Store app, free from the App Store, brings the ultimate in shopping convenience to your iPhone. It's an app with a lot of power. You can buy a number of Apple products and accessories from the App without ever leaving your home. You can find out where the nearest Apple Store is located, view a calendar of upcoming events at the store, and even make reservations for hard-to-get products, appointments at the Genius Bar, one-to-one training sessions, personal shopping, workshops, or meetings with the Apple Business Reps at a store. Launching the app for the first time displays a list of featured products (Figure 10–22).

Tapping the Products button shows a list of the major product categories in the Apple Store: iPhone, iPad, Mac, and iPod. Tap any one of those product categories, and a list of the products and major accessories is displayed. For example, tapping iPhone shows the current models of iPhone being sold at the Apple Store, followed by a list of accessory categories. By tapping one of the category buttons, like Car Accessories, a further list of items is listed (Figure 10–23).

Figure 10–22. *You don't need to live near an Apple Store to have the fun of purchasing new Apple products. The Featured button in the Apple Store app displays recently released products to tempt you.*

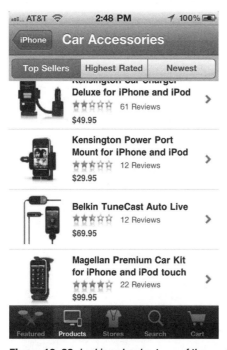

Figure 10–23. *Looking closely at any of the product categories, you can see the variety of items for sale in the Apple Store.*

Each item shows ratings by people who have purchased it, along with reviews. Tap an item, and you'll see a much more detailed description as well as a Question and Answer (Q&A) section, photo gallery, a list of features and technical specifications, and information about the manufacturer and what comes in the box. Just like with any of the other stores on your iPhone, tap the price if you want to buy an item. In the Apple Store, a green Add to Cart button appears. Tap that button to add the product to your virtual shopping cart.

When you're ready to check out, there's a Cart button at the lower-right side of the screen that is used to let you pay for your items and set up shipping.

If you want to visit an Apple retail store, the Stores button is going to be a big help. When you tap the Stores button for the first time, your iPhone will ask for permission to use your location. Once your iPhone knows where you are, it lists nearby stores either in a list format with the name of the store and the distance to it or as pins on a map. We're lucky in that we have six Apple Stores within a 42-mile distance.

As soon as you choose the Apple Store by tapping its name or pin, you see a detailed Store Home page (Figure 10–24). This page offers a map, store hours, and buttons for featured items, upcoming events at the store, and making reservations at the store.

Figure 10–24. *The Store Home page in the Apple Store app is your one-stop location for finding out what's going on at the store and for setting up appointments.*

The Apple Store app has proven to be very popular with Apple customers who want to make an appointment to visit the Genius Bar. They can book an appointment without calling anyone or needing to use a computer, and they can even do it on the way to the store.

Summary

The iPhone makes keeping up with your favorite TV shows, finding new music and applications, buying books, and watching your favorite movies as easy as tapping your finger on a button. Through the App Store, you have access to a large and expanding selection of software written to take advantage of the features of the iPhone. The iTunes Store brings a wide variety of audio and visual entertainment to your iPhone, while the iBookstore is sure to give traditional paper books a run for their money. Finally, the Apple Store app serves as a portable way to purchase Apple products and accessories, as well as a virtual concierge for setting up appointments at Apple's retail stores.

These are the key points of this chapter:

- The App Store, iTunes Store, iBookstore, and Apple Store all require an iTunes account for billing and validation purposes. Although you can set up the account on your iPhone, it's usually much easier to accomplish this feat on your home computer.

- All the stores require an Internet connection over Wi-Fi or 3G.

- The free apps that are portals to the digital App and iTunes Stores come preloaded on every iPhone. The iBookstore is accessible through iBooks, which is a free download from the App Store, and the Apple Store app can also be downloaded for free from the App Store.

- Do you need a hand in picking out movies to watch, music to listen to, or TV shows to follow? The iTunes Genius provides recommendations that get better the more you use iTunes to buy or rent media.

- Be sure to consider the amount of storage in your iPhone when purchasing or renting videos and movies from iTunes, because video content consumes much more space than music, books, or apps. Use the iTunes application on your computer to offload movies from your iPhone and keep the purchased content for future viewing.

- Take advantage of the free previews of music and books in the iTunes Store and iBookstore. Although they provide only snippets of tracks and a chapter or two of books, the previews may be enough to make you tap the Buy button or keep you from making an unnecessary charge on your credit card.

Chapter 11

Google Maps and Other Apps

As software goes, the iPhone heavy hitters have been covered in previous chapters. Now it's time to turn your attention to the other applications on your iPhone—those small but extremely useful utilities that occupy the rest of your Home screens. This chapter provides a run-down of those applications and how to use them. You'll also find tips on how to get the most from these utilities.

Google Maps

Google Maps interactively finds and displays locations using map and satellite imagery. With Google Maps, you can get directions, view traffic, and more. Launch the app by tapping the Maps icon. The icon looks like a small map and actually shows the location of Apple's headquarters at 1 Infinite Loop in Cupertino, California. This takes you into the Google Maps application, where you can view and explore geography from around the world.

If you've used Google Maps on a desktop or laptop computer, you'll find the iPhone app experience to be both different and similar to what you're used to. It's different in that you're able to find locations and get directions from a handheld device you have at your disposal at almost any time. In terms of functionality, the iPhone Google Maps app actually exceeds many of the capabilities of the desktop app in that it "knows" exactly where you are and even the direction you are facing at any time.

Maps Screen

Figure 11–1 shows the basic Google Maps interface, which consists of the following:

- *Search field*: Marked with a spyglass, the search field allows you to enter addresses and other queries. You can type an entire address (*350 Fifth Avenue, New York, NY*) or search for contacts (*Bill Smith*), landmarks (*Golden Gate Bridge*), or even pizza places in your local zip code (*Pizza 80126*).

- *Bookmarks*: The Bookmarks icon at the right side of the search field links to saved locations. From the Bookmarks screen, you can edit your bookmarks (tap Edit), see recently viewed locations and search results (tap Recents), or choose a location from your contacts list (tap Contacts). Tap Done to return to the main Maps screen.

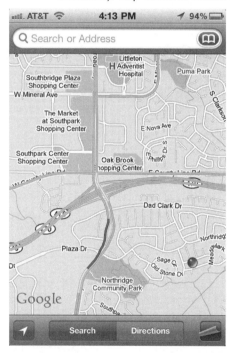

Figure 11–1. *The basic Google Maps interface, showing a map, place names for locations, traffic on major streets, and a number of buttons*

TIP: To add new bookmarks, tap a pushpin on the Maps screen, tap the blue > icon, tap Add to Bookmarks, and then tap Save.

■ *Map*: The map takes up most of the space on the Maps screen and is fully interactive. You can scroll by dragging your finger along the map, or you can zoom in and out using pinches and double-taps. (Use a single-fingered double-tap to zoom in and a double-fingered tap to zoom out.) Your current location, as determined by the onboard GPS receiver, is indicated by a blue dot. This dot appears to be pulsing when the iPhone's location services are fixing your position. The blue circle surrounding the pin is indicative of the error in the GPS system; you are most likely somewhere in the area defined by the circle.

The map can be displayed in several ways: just as a map, as a satellite photo of the area, as a hybrid of the two (a satellite photo with overlaid street and location names), or as a list. The last item is useful when performing a search with many resulting addresses.

In the Map and Hybrid modes, you may see traffic updates on major streets and highways. Note that the traffic feature is not available for certain countries and does not work with minor country roads; it works best in metropolitan areas. The traffic is indicated by colored lines on the streets. Green indicates that traffic is at normal speeds, yellow indicates a slowdown, and red indicates a major traffic jam.

To change the type of map display, tap the icon that's in the lower-right corner of the screen; it looks like a piece of paper that is curling up. You'll see buttons for all the map types, as well as buttons used to drop pins in locations or hide traffic on the maps.

■ *Red pushpins*: The red pushpins indicate locations found by the application after a search. For example, Figure 11–2 shows pizza restaurants found near zip code 80126. Tap a pushpin to view a location summary, and then tap the blue > icon for more details and options. These options include directions to and from that location, bookmarking the location and assigning the location to contacts.

Figure 11–2. *The red pins indicate locations found in a search. Tapping one of them displays the name or address of the location, and tapping the > icon displays information about the place including a phone number, web page, and street address.*

- *Directions*: To get detailed directions to or from a location, you can tap a red pin and then tap the > icon to view information. At the bottom of the Info screen are two buttons, one that for Directions To Here and the other for Directions From Here. If we wanted directions to the pizza restaurant noted earlier, we could tap Directions To Here and then use our current location (automatically entered) as the start location. Tapping the Route button generates the fastest route to the location (Figure 11–3, left) and displays the distance to the end point as well as the estimated time with traffic.

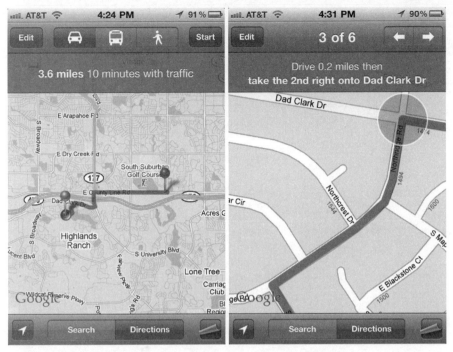

Figure 11–3. *Driving instructions from one point to another are displayed on an overview map with the total distance and estimated time listed at top (left). If you need turn-by-turn directions, they're available as well, complete with a detailed map showing each turn you need to make (right).*

If you need turn-by-turn directions, tap the Start button at the top of the screen to begin your journey. You'll see a detailed map of each segment of the trip, with a highlight for each turn you need to make (Figure 11–3, right). If you'd like to see the directions in a stepwise list, tap the "curl" at the bottom right of the screen.

What if you're not driving? The little pedestrian icon shown at the top of the map displays your best walking route and estimated time when tapped. If you're taking public transit, then Google Maps is going to be a treat.

The public transit button is the one that looks like a city bus, in between the driving and pedestrian buttons. When you tap the icon while trying to find directions, you'll see a map that displays your walk to a nearby bus stop, a bus ride to a location near or at your destination, and then walking instructions to get to your final destination (Figure 11–4, left). You can set custom departure or arrival times by tapping the clock icon to ensure that you will arrive at your destination with time to spare.

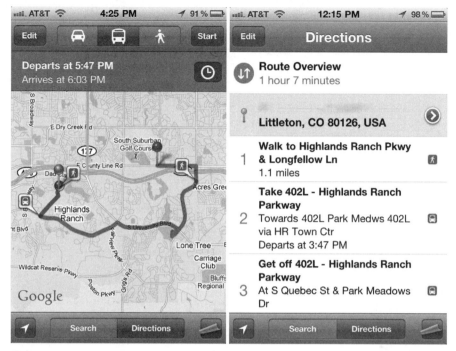

Figure 11–4. *If you're reliant on public transportation to get around town, you'll find the Google Maps public transit button to be a great help. No more needing to carry bus or train schedules with you. The overview map on the left shows the walking and riding portions of your trip, while the list view on the right shows the bus numbers and departure times.*

Tapping the curling page icon and then the List button displays the buses or trains that you'll be taking, along with the walking instructions (Figure 11–4 right).

The public transit directions option is extremely useful in metropolitan areas. Remember, smaller municipalities may not have their transit systems tied into the all-seeing, all-knowing Google databases, so your community might not have these capabilities.

Maps Tips

Here are some tips for using Google Maps on your iPhone:

- When a person or business you want to map is in your contacts list, save yourself some time. Don't type in the entire address. Just enter a few letters of the name, and select the contact.

- Tap individual items on the directions list to jump to that part of your route.

- The Recents screen (in Bookmarks) shows recent locations, searches, and directions.

NOTE: Unfortunately, you can't bookmark routes. That's a pity because it would be nice to be able to quickly pull up traffic conditions on your favorite routes.

- URLs that link to Google Maps automatically open in the Maps application, whether they are tapped in Safari, Mail, or other apps.

- Want to create your own pins to mark special places, such as where you parked your car? While viewing a map, tap the curling page icon, and then tap Drop Pin. A pin with a purple head and the name Dropped Pin appears on the map. You can drag the pin to your exact location and even assign the pin (and associated address) to a contact.

Weather

At the time of publication, the iPhone Weather application allows you to view the current temperature and six-day forecast for each of your favorite cities. Weather uses forecast data from Yahoo! and the Weather Channel to provide up-to-the-minute data on your iPhone. To launch Weather, tap the blue icon with the sun on your Home screen.

NOTE: It's always sunny and nice on the Weather icon, where the temperature is always a comfortable 73°F.

Although you currently have to add your own location to the Weather app in order to see your weather forecast, we expect the app to eventually sense your current location and add a forecast automatically.

Weather Screen

Figure 11–5 shows a typical Weather screen. From here, you can flick left and right to scroll between your cities. The dots at the bottom of the screen show that there are other cities that you've added to the Weather app. The bright dot shows which city you're viewing. The dim dots show the other cities you've added to the Weather app.

Figure 11–5. *The iPhone Weather application provides current conditions and six-day forecasts for your favorite cities (left). Tap the information i icon to add, remove, or reorder cities on the list (right).*

When you're ready to specify your cities, tap the small *i* at the bottom right of any Weather screen. This flips from the forecast to the city management screen. From this screen, you can customize your cities:

- *Add a city*: Tap the + button, enter the city name, tap Search, and then tap the city you want to add. You cannot find every city. Only those supported by Yahoo! and the Weather Channel are available.

- *Remove a city*: Tap the red – button next to any city name, and then tap Delete.

- *Reorder cities*: Use the grab controls to the right of each name to drag your cities into a new order.

- Switch between Fahrenheit and Celsius: Tap °F or °C.

Tap Done to return to the forecast screen.

Weather Tips

Here are some tips for using the Weather application:

- You can add a *lot* of cities. The Weather app is perfect for weather fans or frequent business travelers.

- Tap the Y! icon to visit Yahoo! Weather in Safari.

- You don't need to keep the default Cupertino forecast. Although the iPhone offers Cupertino as its default forecast, feel free to add your own city and remove Cupertino from the list. Apple will never know.

- There are other ways to get current and forecasted weather conditions on your iPhone. Not only are there many third-party apps available, but you can also use Safari to follow the weather. Enter "weather <zipcode>" or "weather <city, state, country>" in the search field in Safari, and you'll get an up-to-date forecast and links to more detailed information on a number of weather web sites.

Stocks

The Stocks icon looks like a blue stock price chart. Tap it to go to the application that monitors your favorite stocks using 20-minute delayed data from Yahoo!

Stocks Screen

The Stocks screen, shown in Figure 11–6, consists of a list of stocks above a list of statistical information about the selected stock. Current prices appear to the right of each stock symbol, with the changes listed in green (positive) or red (negative). From this screen, you can view and customize stock information:

- *View a stock*: Tap any stock to load its information. Tap the daily change figure once to view the current market capitalization of the stock and then again to view the percent daily price change. At the bottom of the screen, the Stock app displays historical information initially. Flick this information to the left to see a historical price chart and then again to see current financial news about the stock.

- *Choose the history length on the price chart*: When you're viewing the stock price chart, you can choose the length of time over which you want to view a stock's history. Pick from one day (1d), one week (1w), one month (1m), three months (3m), six months (6m), one year (1y), and two years (2y).

  Customize: You can add or remove stocks from your list by tapping the *i* icon at the bottom right of your screen. This opens the customization screen.

- To add a stock, tap the + button and either search for a company name or enter the stock symbol directly.

- To remove a stock, tap the red – button, and then tap Delete.

- Reorder stocks by using the drag controls to the right of each stock name.

- Tap the %, Price, and Mkt Cap buttons to see that information displayed when you return to the main Stock screen.

- Tap Done to return to the main Stocks screen.

Figure 11–6. *Yahoo! powers the iPhone Stocks application using 20-minute-delayed data.*

Stock Tips

Here are some tips for using the Stocks application:

- Tap Yahoo! Finance at the bottom of the customization screen to jump directly to the Yahoo! Finance web site. You can also tap Y! at the bottom left of the main Stocks screen to get to this web site.

- Stock quotes are delayed according to the rules of the stock exchange. This provides an advantage to on-floor traders and allows vendors to charge for premium real-time quotes.

Notes

The iPhone Notes application allows you to jot down quick notes on the go. This application isn't meant to be a full-powered word processor. It just provides a simple way to create notes and bring them with you. Those notes don't have to just stay on your iPhone, either; the app syncs to your e-mail application so that they're visible on your other devices, including your computer and iPad. To launch Notes, tap the yellow notepad-styled icon on your Home screen.

Notes Screen

Figure 11–7 shows the Notes screen. From this screen, you can add and manage notes:

- *Create new notes*: Tap the + button to add a new note.

- *Enter and edit text*: Tapping in the text area summons the keyboard. Type your note, make any changes, and then tap Done to dismiss the keyboard.

- *Delete a note*: Tap the garbage can, and then tap Delete Note.

- *Navigate between notes*: Use the left and right arrows to move between notes, or tap Notes and select the note you want to view from the list.

- *E-mail notes*: Tap the envelope, enter an address, and tap Send.

> **NOTE:** Notes can be synchronized with your e-mail client. On the iTunes Info tab, there is a check box under Other for Syncing Notes. When enabled, it synchronizes to a mailbox named Reminders in Mail and Outlook.

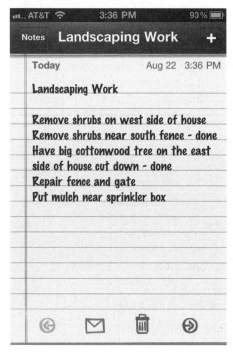

Figure 11–7. *Use the Notes screen to write quick notes. You can e-mail your notes to others and sync them to your computer.*

Notes Tips

Here are some tips on using the Notes application:

■ Use the iPhone's cut, copy and paste function to create a list of frequently used addresses you may want to use in Safari. The web addresses turn into tappable links in the Notes app.

■ You can search for words in your Notes by using the iPhone's built-in search function. From your main Home screen, flick right and enter your search term into the search field at the top of the screen. If the word is anywhere on your iPhone, including in Notes, the search function displays it.

NOTE: For some odd reason, the default font used in Notes is the dreadful (in our opinion) Market Felt. The only way to change the font in a note is to open the note in your e-mail client, change the font for the note on your computer, and then sync your iPhone and computer.

Calculator

Depending on your needs, the iPhone's built-in calculator can either be a basic four-function calculator with memory or be a rather sophisticated scientific calculator. The icon on your Home screen looks like four calculator buttons: the symbols for plus, minus, multiply, and equals. Tap it to open the application, as shown in Figure 11–8.

Figure 11–8. *The iPhone Calculator application in portrait orientation. Here, the calculator is just a simple four-function calculator with memory functions.*

The basic Calculator application, which you'll see when the phone is being held in portrait orientation, allows you to add, subtract, multiply, and divide. When you tap an operation button, a white circle appears around the button to let you know which operation will be carried out.

Use the memory buttons to add to the stored number (M+) or subtract (M–). Tap MR/MC once to replace the number in memory. Tap MR/MC twice to clear the number from memory.

> **TIP:** Do you frequently go out to lunch or dinner with friends and need to split the bill? Try one of the many bill-splitter and tip calculators in the App Store. A number of the apps are free and very useful in settling disputes.

If you're a student or engineer, you may need more than just a standard four-function calculator. Don't run to the office supply store to buy a scientific calculator; instead, just tip your iPhone into landscape orientation while you're in the Calculator app.

As shown in Figure 11–9, the iPhone Calculator app magically transforms into a full-featured scientific calculator when it's in landscape mode. It has a number of logarithmic, trigonometric, and exponent capabilities. The trig functions automatically turn into inverse trigonometric functions (for example, arcsin, arctanh), and the natural log (ln) and e^x functions become log_2 and 2^x when you tap the second button on the first line of buttons on the calculator.

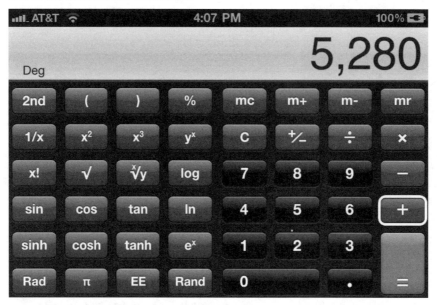

Figure 11–9. *Flip your iPhone into landscape mode while you're in the Calculator app, and suddenly the iPhone becomes a full-featured scientific calculator.*

If neither of these calculators performs the calculations that are prevalent in your industry, do a search in the App Store for one that will do the job. There are programmable, Reverse Polish Notation (RPN), "printing," and financial calculators available, most for a very nominal price.

Clock

The iPhone Clock app is more flexible than you might first imagine. It offers a world clock, an alarm, a stopwatch, and a timer—all of which you may find handy. To launch the application, tap the clock icon. You'll see icons for each utility along the bottom of the screen.

> **NOTE:** All Clock utilities continue in the background, even if you're not in the Clock application itself. You can start an alarm, a timer, or the stopwatch and go off to other iPhone applications. The utility will keep ticking away as you work on other things.

World Clock

Use the iPhone World Clock utility to keep track of time zones around the world. This utility is smart enough to take into account daylight saving time and other quirks, such as New Delhi being 30 minutes off the standard.

As Figure 11–10 shows, white clock faces indicate daytime, and black clock faces indicate night. Tap + to add new cities. Tap Edit to delete and reorder them.

Figure 11–10. *The iPhone World Clock utility monitors time around the world.*

Alarm

The Alarm utility allows you to tell your iPhone to alert you at a specified time. Use alarms to wake up in the morning or remember business meetings. You can set many alarms if you'd like, such as one to wake you up, one to remind you to catch your morning commute, another to alert you to lunchtime, and so on.

Create alarms by tapping + on the Alarm screen. This opens the Add Alarm screen, as shown in Figure 11–11. From this screen, you can set your alarm:

- *Set a time*: Spin the wheels to specify the time for the alarm to sound. Drag your finger up and down, and the wheel spins with you. Flick your finger, and the wheel continues spinning, even after your finger leaves the screen. If you like, you can also tap a number rather than spin to it.

- *Make an alarm repeat*: Alarms are day-specific. You must choose days of the week for repeating events. For a daily alarm, select every day from Monday through Sunday.

- *Select a sound*: Choose any ringtone for your sound. You can select a custom ringtone if you've added new ones to your iPhone ringtones library.

- *Allow snooze*: The Snooze button, as you might expect, allows you to delay an alarm and repeat it ten minutes later. To enable this, set the Snooze option to on. To disable snooze, set it to off.

- *Label an alarm*: Give your alarm a custom label by tapping its name and entering text with the keyboard.

- *Save an alarm*: Tap Save to store your new alarm, or tap Cancel to exit the Add Alarm screen without saving.

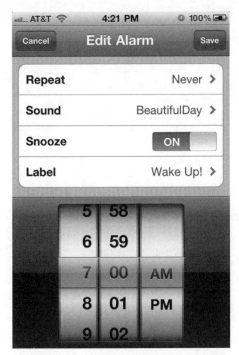

Figure 11–11. *Create custom alarms that play sounds at a given time.*

The main Alarm screen lists all the alarms you've added to your iPhone. Use the on/off toggles to activate or deactivate these alarms. To remove an alarm, tap Edit, tap the red – button, and then tap Delete. This permanently removes the alarm from your iPhone.

Timer

The iPhone Timer utility lets you play a sound after a set period of time. Unlike alarms, timers are not tied to a particular time of day. Use alarms for appointments; use timers for cooking eggs or grilling steaks.

On the Timer screen, set the amount of time you want to pass (3 minutes, 10 minutes, 1 hour, and so on), and then tap Start. After the timer counts down, the iPhone vibrates and plays a sound you've selected from your ringtones.

Stopwatch

The iPhone Stopwatch utility allows you to time events. It's great for timing your favorite NASCAR or Indy Car racers, how long it takes your children to revert to being bad, or timing how quickly you can make a bed.

On the Stopwatch screen, tap Start to begin the timer and Tap Lap to mark the latest lap time. Tap Stop to pause. Tapping Reset returns the timer to 00:00.0.

YouTube

Watch your favorite short online videos with the iPhone YouTube application. This app works very much like the standard web site, but since the iPhone does not support Flash video, YouTube and Apple made an agreement to provide access to MP4 versions of many videos. To launch the application, tap the YouTube icon, which looks like a retro-styled TV set.

Finding YouTube Videos

To find videos, tap any of these buttons:

- *Featured*: These include videos reviewed and recommended by YouTube staff.

- *Most Viewed*: The most popular videos of the day, week, or all time.

- *Bookmarks*: A collection of videos you've selected and bookmarked. To add a bookmark, tap the blue > button next to any video, and then tap Bookmark. Tap Share to send the link by e-mail instead.

- *Search*: Enter a keyword or two, and then tap Search to look through YouTube's entire collection.

- *More*: Choose from three more viewing choices or customize the display:

    - Most Recent shows YouTube's newest items.

    - Top Rated shows YouTube's collection of videos that have garnered the most viewer support.

    - History lists recently viewed items.

    - My Videos displays a list of videos that you have uploaded to YouTube.

    - If you subscribe to the videos produced and distributed by another YouTube fan, the Subscriptions button provides a way to see the latest videos from the subscriptions.

    - When you create a YouTube playlist, tap the Playlists button to display and then play your playlists.

    - Edit lets you choose which items appear on your shortcuts bar and which items appear on the More screen. Drag the categories you view the most down to the bar, and then tap Done.

TIP: Use the Clear button at the top-right corner of the History screen to erase your YouTube viewing history. People don't have to know you've been watching that skateboarding dog.

Watching YouTube Videos

Tap any video listing to begin playback. YouTube videos play back exclusively in landscape orientation, as shown in Figure 11–12. Tap the screen to toggle viewing the controls on and off:

- *Done*: Tap Done to end playback and return to the YouTube video listings.

- *Scrubber bar*: Adjust the playhead to set the playback time.

- *Aspect control*: Tap the Aspect button (diagonal arrows) to toggle between full-screen and original video aspect settings. When filling the screen, parts of the video may be cropped in order to display the largest pictures possible.

> **TIP:** As an alternative to tapping the Aspect button, you can also double-tap a video as it plays. The results are the same.

- *Bookmark*: Tap the Bookmark button to add the current video to your bookmarks. It highlights briefly and then dims. The video continues playing without interruption.

- *Reverse*: Tap Reverse once to return to the start of the video, or tap and hold it to move backward in the video.

- *Play/Pause*: Tap Play/Pause to stop and resume playback.

- *Forward*: Tap Forward to skip to the next video in the current category, or tap and hold it to move forward in the video.

- *Envelope*: Tap the envelope icon to send an e-mail message with a URL that links to this video.

- *Volume control*: The volume control appears at the bottom of the screen and allows you to adjust playback volume. You can also use physical buttons built into your iPhone to control volume.

Figure 11–12. *The YouTube video playback controls*

YouTube Tips

Here are some tips for using the YouTube application:

- You'll do better watching videos over WiFi than on a cellular connection, because the videos download much faster. This helps keep the video from hesitating and pausing as much during playback.

- Tap the blue > buttons to view the information screen for each video.

- Scroll down on the info screen to find related videos that you may want to view.

- You cannot swipe to delete bookmarks. To remove items, tap Edit, tap the red – button, and then tap Delete.

Voice Memos

Have you ever needed to take notes or remind yourself of something, but the circumstances kept you from pulling out your iPhone and taking a short note? Making a voice memo might be the fast, trouble-free way to make a memo with a minimum of fuss.

The Voice Memos app, which has an icon that displays a microphone, is an audio recorder for your iPhone. Tapping the app displays a beautifully rendered microphone (Figure 11–13). At the bottom of the display are two buttons (a record button on the left side and a list button on the right) and a sound level meter. That's all it takes to capture voice memos, listen to them, and share them.

Figure 11–13. *When a recording is underway, the top of the Voice Memos app screen pulses in a red color.*

To start a voice memo session, tap the red record button. You'll want to make sure that the recording levels on the sound level meter don't get too high, because oversaturation of the sound can result in a distorted recording. The top of the screen pulses in a reddish glow and displays the duration of the recording so far. To stop recording, tap the record button again. The red display at the top of the screen notes that the recording is paused, so if you have more to say or record, tap the record button again to continue.

When your recording is complete, tap the list button to display a list of every recording that has been made so far (Figure 11–14). The recording that was just completed begins to play back, which is helpful for making sure that you did indeed capture the minutes for the meeting you were just in.

Figure 11–14. *The list of voice memos is where you can listen to your memos, share them through e-mail or an MMS message, delete them, or do some initial editing.*

A quick tap on the > button on the left side of a recording in the list displays an Info screen where you can do provide a label for a recording, trim it, or share it (Figure 11–15).

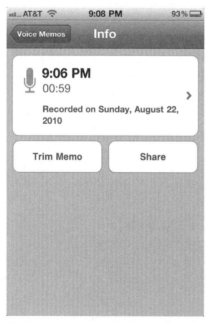

Figure 11–15. *The Info screen is your portal to adding a label to a recording, trimming it, or sharing it with others.*

To add a label to the recording to replace the default name (the time the recording was started), tap the > icon on the right side of the recording information. A list of labels is displayed, ranging from Podcast to Ideas. You can even add your own custom label by tapping Custom, and then typing in the words you need for your label.

Sometimes you may want to trim the voice memo to get rid of extraneous noise at the beginning or end of the recording. To do this, tap the Trim Memo button. If you recall the trimming function in our discussion about capturing video in Chapter 9, then you'll be immediately familiar with the method used in trimming the audio recording. A yellow trim border appears around a bar that designates the total length of your recording (Figure 11–16).

Figure 11–16. *To trim your voice memo, drag the yellow trim handles and then play the memo to verify that you've trimmed it properly. When your trimming is done, tap the Trim Voice Memo button to apply the changes and shorten your audio recording.*

The Info screen also features a Share button, which is identical in function to the previous Share button; it provides a way for you to send the voice memo via e-mail or MMS.

Voice Memo Tips

Here are some tips for using the Voice Memo app:

- The microphone for your iPhone is on the bottom of the device near the Dock Connector. When recording a lecture, you'll have slightly better recording results when the microphone is pointed at the person who is speaking. The iPhone 4 has a second, small noise-canceling microphone that is located at the top of the device next to the headset jack. This mic "listens" to background noises, such as cooling fans or traffic, and then subtracts those noises from the signal that is being recorded. The result is a much quieter recording without as much ambient background noise.

- You can use the iPhone headset with the Voice Memo app. This works well if you need to record a memo while driving (not recommended, because you'll still need to manipulate the app controls) or if you're recording in a noisy environment. With the Voice Memo app running, squeeze the headset switch once to begin recording, and then squeeze it again to end recording and save the memo.

- Voice Memos can be synced to your Music Library in iTunes on your computer. To enable this capability, connect your iPhone to your computer, launch iTunes, select your iPhone under the Devices title in the left sidebar, and then click the Music tab. Make sure that "Include voice memos" is checked to enable voice memo syncing.

- If you sync Voice Memos to iTunes, you can also share those recordings with other devices that are synced. Have an iPad? Your iPhone Voice Memos can be synced to it so you can follow up by writing a document in Pages for iPad.

Calendar

The iPhone Calendar application allows you to keep track of your appointments while on the go. With it, you can view your existing events and add new ones. Launch Calendar by tapping the white and red icon that looks like a page from an old-fashioned, tear-off calendar (see Figure 11–17). The icon always shows the current date and day.

Figure 11–17. *The Calendar icon initially appears on the top row of your iPhone home screen and shows the current day and date.*

Switching Calendar Views

The Calendar application offers three basic views: List, Day, and Month. Each of these helps you locate and review your appointments.

List View

The List view does exactly what the name suggests. It displays your calendar events as a scrolling list. The list is ordered by day and time, as shown in Figure 11–18. The easy-to- follow formatting groups all events on a single day together. All events are listed, providing a powerful overview of all upcoming happenings.

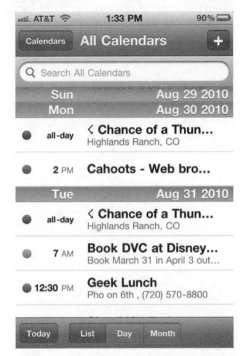

Figure 11–18. *Use the List view to see your appointments as an easily readable scrolling list.*

Here are a couple of points about the List view:

- Tap any event to view it in more detail.

- As you scroll, the currently displayed date "sticks" at the top of the screen, even as you scroll through it. It's a very cool but subtle effect.

Day View

Calendar's Day view shows your day's events in day-planner–style format (see Figure 11–19). Each event occupies a certain amount of space on the layout and is marked with the event and location.

Figure 11–19. *Display a day at a time with the Day view.*

Here are some things you need to know about Day view:

- Tap the previous and next arrows to scroll through your calendar a day at a time.

- Events vary in color depending on what calendar they're associated with. In Figure 11–19, the first meeting is for a Home calendar, while the other two are associated with a Work calendar.

- The day starts and ends at 12 a.m. So if you schedule your New Year's Eve party from 11 p.m. on December 31 until 2 a.m. on January 1, the Calendar application will split it into two Day views, even though it's a single event.

- Tap an event to open its detail view.

Month View

The month-at-a-time view highlights all days with appointments (see Figure 11–20). A small dot appears below all days containing appointments. Tap any marked day to view a scrolling list of events at the bottom of the screen. As with the other views, tap those events to view their details.

Figure 11–20. *The Month view marks a dot under all dates that contain events.*

The Today Button

Clicking the Today button in any view automatically jumps back to the display for the current day but preserves the view you are using. In other words, you'll see the current month for Month view, or you can recenter the list in List view.

Adding Events

Your iPhone allows you to add calendar events on the go. This lets you adjust and update your schedule when you are away from your computer.

Adding an event is a two-part process. First, you create a new name for your event. Then you specify the event details, including its date and time. To get started, tap the +

button at the top right of the screen. The Title & Location screen opens, as shown in Figure 11–21.

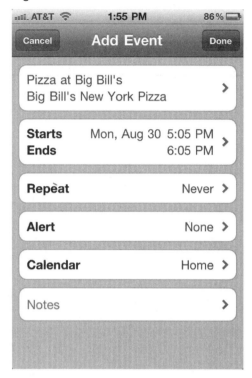

Figure 11–21. *Add new events directly on your iPhone.*

Start by entering a title and location for the event. Tap in either field, and use the keyboard to enter a name and (optionally) a place. To finish naming your event, tap Done, or tap Cancel to return to the new event screen.

Once you have named your event, you can update the event name and/or location and specify when the event starts and ends, whether it repeats, and when to play an alert to notify you about the event. You can also add a note about the event. Customize any or all of these options, as described in the following sections, and then tap Done to finish adding the event. Tap Cancel if you want to return to the List, Day, or Month view without adding the event.

Updating an Event Name or Location

Tap the name and location line (just below the Add Event title) to open an editor that allows you to update the event's name and location text. After making your changes, tap Save to save your changes, or tap Cancel to return to the Add Event screen without applying those changes.

Setting the Event Start and End Times

Tap the Starts/Ends field to open the screen that allows you to set these times. You enter the time by way of a scroll control (Figure 11–22). This control contains date, hour, minute, and a.m./p.m. wheels. You set the start and end time by scrolling your way to the proper combination.

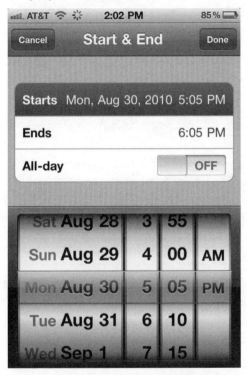

Figure 11–22. *Use the scroll control to enter the date, hour, minute and (if your default settings are set up for a.m./p.m. and not the 24-hour clock) a.m./p.m.*

Tap either Starts or Ends to switch between the two times (when the event begins and when it ends), and make your adjustments as needed.

The basic scroller is great for relatively near-term appointments. It is not so great when you're scrolling six months into the future for your next tooth cleaning or your child's commencement schedule. It can take an awful lot of scrolling to get to the date you want. For quicker access to future dates or for all-day events (such as when you go on vacation or will be out of town on a business trip), set the All-day indicator from off to on. The scroll wheel updates, replacing the date/hour/minute wheels with month/day/year wheels. You can schedule appointments this way, all the way up to December 31, 2067.

Tap Done to confirm your settings, or tap Cancel to return to the Add Event screen without changing the start and end times.

Setting a Repeating Event

When your event repeats, you can select from a standard list that defines how often: Every Day, Every Week, Every Two Weeks, Every Month, or Every Year. To make this happen, tap the Repeat field on the Add Event screen, select a repetition interval, and tap Done. To return to the Add Event screen without adding a repeated event, tap Cancel. To disable repeats, tap None and then tap Done.

Adding Alerts

Add event alerts to notify you when an event is coming due. For example, you may want a one-hour notice for those dental appointments and a one-day notice for your anniversary. The iPhone provides a nice selection of options. These include 5, 15, and 30 minutes before the event; 1 or 2 hours before the event; 1 or 2 days before the event; and on the date of the event itself.

Tap the Alert field to set an event alert. After selecting an event alert time, tap Done. To cancel without setting the alert time, tap Cancel. To remove event alerts, tap None and then Done.

Once you've saved your first alert, the iPhone offers you the option to add a second one. This allows you to remind yourself both a day before an event and a few minutes before you need to leave. This is a particularly useful feature for people who need extra reminders.

When alerts trigger, a visual reminder appears on your screen, with a rather quiet sound effect. Figure 11–23 shows a reminder in action. Tap View Event to jump into the Calendar app and view your event, or tap Close to dismiss the on-screen reminder.

> **NOTE:** Unfortunately, there are no "snooze" options for calendar events.

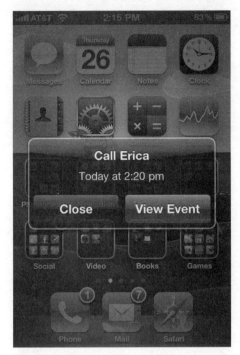

Figure 11–23. *A calendar event appears on the screen as an alert.*

Adding Notes

You can also add a free-form note to your event. Tap the Notes field at the bottom of Add Event screen, and use the Notes screen with its built-in keyboard to set the details for your event, such as phone numbers or names. As with all the other customization options, tap Done to save the note, or tap Cancel to return to the Add Event screen without saving it.

Editing and Removing Events

Tap any event in any view (List, Day, or Month) to edit it. This opens an event detail view. On this screen, you'll see an Edit button at the top-right corner. Tap it to open the Edit screen. This screen is a near twin to the Add Event screen (Figure 11–21) and offers all the same customization options found there.

To remove any event, select it, go to its detail view, and tap Edit. The Edit screen opens. Scroll to the very bottom of the screen and locate the red Delete Event bar. Tap it. The iPhone prompts you to confirm. Tap the red Delete Event bar a second time to remove the event, or tap Cancel to cancel deleting the event.

Synchronizing Calendars with Your Computer

Once you set up iTunes, you can synchronize your iPhone to your Microsoft Outlook calendars (Windows) or iCal and Microsoft Entourage calendars (Macintosh). Here's how you make this happen.

In iTunes, choose your iPhone in the source list and open the rightmost Info tab. Scroll down to find the Calendars section (see Figure 11–24), and use the settings there to specify how your touch synchronizes with your computer-based calendars.

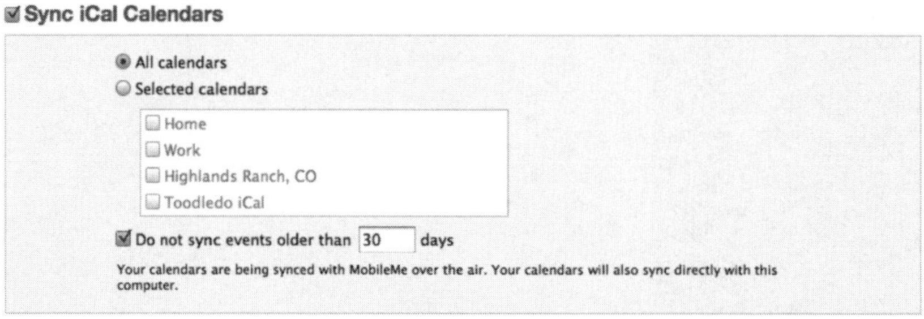

Figure 11–24. *Choose how to synchronize your iPhone calendars to your computer by using the Info tab in iTunes.*

Check the top check box to enable calendar synchronization. Then choose whether to synchronize all calendars or just those calendars you specify. You can also set a statute of limitations on how far back you want to synchronize events. The default settings do not sync events older than a month.

Note that you can also synchronize your calendars with other devices over the air using Apple's MobileMe service (see the next section). If you are using MobileMe, we recommend unchecking the Sync iCal Calendars button. Just let MobileMe take care of the syncing.

If, at any time, you want to completely update the calendars on your iPhone, scroll down to the bottom of the Info screen and locate the Advanced options. Check the box that indicates you want to replace information on this iPhone for calendars. After setting this option, the next time you sync (and only during that next sync), iTunes completely replaces the calendar on your iPhone with the information from your computer. Use this option when you set up your iPhone with a new home computer after it was previously synchronized to another host.

Syncing with MobileMe

Subscribers to Apple's MobileMe service can synchronize their iPhone calendars with their work or home computer calendars through the service. This can be extremely useful if you have many devices, such as a computer, an iPhone, and an iPad, for example. Making a change on any of the devices results in that change being updated on all devices, almost instantaneously.

After setting up an iPhone with MobileMe mail (see Chapter 5), Settings ä Mail, Contacts, Calendars ä MobileMe displays a list of items that you can sync over the MobileMe service (Figure 11–25). Turning any of the switches on ensures that information from your iPhone updates and is updated by the MobileMe service. Making a change to a calendar entry or an address book contact results in that change being synced "to the cloud" and then to every other device you have connected to MobileMe. It's a great way to keep all your devices in sync.

Figure 11–25. *Syncing of your iPhone calendar with the rest of your devices is as simple as turning the Calendars switch to on in the MobileMe settings.*

Summary

As you saw in this chapter, even the "minor" applications add a lot of functionality to your day-to-day iPhone use. They are surprisingly useful and carefully chosen to enhance the way you use your device. Here are a few points to carry away from this chapter:

- Build your Google Maps vocabulary. Instead of thinking about locations as street addresses, start thinking about people, businesses, and trips. Google Maps makes it easy for you to view route information with the least possible amount of work.

- The Stocks and Weather applications provide great ways to keep up with real-time information using classic Apple design.

- The YouTube app gives you access to hundreds of thousands of fun videos. For the best viewing experience, make sure you're using a Wi-Fi Internet connection when you launch the YouTube app.

- For capturing information on the go, the Voice Memos app is a quick way to record and share lectures, thoughts, and other sound bites.

- Perhaps it's time to finally get rid of that old scientific calculator that you bought in college. The iPhone Calculator app provides you with both a simple four-function calculator and a powerful scientific calculator, which you can swap with the flick of a wrist.

- The iPhone Calendar app can keep you informed of your current and future appointments wherever you may be.

Index

J

K

L

Y

 Z

 W

You Need the Companion eBook

Your purchase of this book entitles you to buy the companion PDF-version eBook for only $10. Take the weightless companion with you anywhere.

We believe this Apress title will prove so indispensable that you'll want to carry it with you everywhere, which is why we are offering the companion eBook (in PDF format) for $10 to customers who purchase this book now. Convenient and fully searchable, the PDF version of any content-rich, page-heavy Apress book makes a valuable addition to your programming library. You can easily find and copy code—or perform examples by quickly toggling between instructions and the application. Even simultaneously tackling a donut, diet soda, and complex code becomes simplified with hands-free eBooks!

Once you purchase your book, getting the $10 companion eBook is simple:

❶ Visit **www.apress.com/promo/tendollars/**.

❷ Complete a basic registration form to receive a randomly generated question about this title.

❸ Answer the question correctly in 60 seconds, and you will receive a promotional code to redeem for the $10.00 eBook.

eBookshop

233 Spring Street, New York, NY 10013

Offer valid through 3/11.